Feasting
on the
Spoils

Feasting
on the
Spoils

The Life and Times of
Randy "Duke" Cunningham,
History's Most Corrupt
Congressman

SETH HETTENA

St. Martin's Press
New York

www.stmartins.com

Design by Kathryn Parise

LIBRARY OF CONGRESS CATALOGING-IN-PUBLICATION DATA

Hettena, Seth.
    Feasting on the spoils : the life and times of Randy "Duke" Cunningham, history's most corrupt congressman / Seth Hettena. — 1st ed.
        p. cm.
    ISBN-13: 978-0-312-36829-6
    ISBN-10: 0-312-36829-1
    1. Cunningham, Randy, 1941– 2. Legislators—United States—Biography. 3. United States. Congress. House—Biography. 4. Political corruption—United States. 5. United States—Politics and government—1989– 6. Fighter pilots—United States—Biography. 7. United States. Navy—Officers—Biography. I. Title.

E840.8.C86H48 2007
364.1'323092—dc22
[B]

2007011840

First Edition: July 2007

10   9   8   7   6   5   4   3   2   1

Contents

I have accepted a seat in the House of Representatives, and thereby have consented to my own ruin, to your ruin, and to the ruin of our children. I give you this warning that you may prepare your mind for your fate.

—JOHN ADAMS

Feasting
on the
Spoils

Prologue

On July 1, 2005, Lamont Siller, a thirty-one-year-old special agent with the Federal Bureau of Investigation, awoke at four o'clock in the morning in his San Diego home. As instructed the previous day, Siller dressed in a white shirt and dark business suit and drove out of the city to a rendezvous point in the wealthy northern suburbs. He stopped only once, to pick up a coffee at a 7-Eleven, and parked at his destination, a lot behind the Original Pancake House. As the sun broke on the horizon, Siller checked the clock. It was 5:45 a.m. — he was fifteen minutes early — but five other vehicles were already waiting in the parking lot.

By 6 a.m., nearly twenty men and women had gathered in the lot behind the restaurant. Everyone, even the women, wore suits and white shirts. The group included FBI agents like Siller and others from the Internal Revenue Service and the Defense Criminal Investigative Service and one member of the San Diego police department. They were waiting for a signal from Washington, D.C., where an even larger group of federal agents had gathered. The carefully scripted plan called for the execution of four search warrants simultaneously on both coasts. During most searches, agents wear "raid" jackets stamped FBI in large yellow letters, but the day's instructions called for a lower profile.

While they waited, the agents passed time reviewing the warrant signed by a federal judge a day earlier. It gave them permission to search a mansion in Rancho Santa Fe, a secluded enclave that is home to more than a thousand of America's wealthiest families. Siller and the rest of the team had been told that this search would likely face a challenge in court and there could be no mistakes. "This is an important, highly sensitive investigation," the FBI's operation plan stated. "All activity related to the search will be scrutinized in the future."

Siller was sitting in a car with other agents at 7:15 a.m. when Adam Lee, the team leader, walked up and leaned into the vehicle. "Let's go," he said. All four teams were now in place. Siller and about six others drove into Rancho Santa Fe. Since it had been popularized after World War I with the help of Hollywood stars Bing Crosby and Mary Pickford, Rancho Santa Fe has always attracted the rich and those who aspire to live among them. Residents have included billionaire Bill Gates, golfer Phil Mickelson, and San Diego Padres owner John Moores, but the Ranch, as it's called by residents, has also attracted a cast of charlatans and rogues. The family of British businessman and Iran-contra figure Ian Spiro was found shot to death in their Rancho Santa Fe home in 1992; Spiro himself was later found dead of cyanide poisoning. Five years later, thirty-nine members of the Heaven's Gate cult took part in the largest mass suicide in U.S. history in a home in Rancho Santa Fe.

By design, few homes are visible from the road, and 7094 Via del Charro was no exception. A gate barred entrance to the long driveway that snaked up to the house hidden at the top of a small hill, so the agents parked across the street and walked up to the residence. Someone knocked on the door. "FBI. We have a search warrant." The seven-thousand-square-foot, Spanish-style mansion was striking, but it had not been well kept. Siller noticed snails on the outside stucco wall and spiderwebs no one had bothered to brush away. It seemed to him as though the residents could not afford to maintain it properly.

The $2.55 million home belonged to Randy "Duke" Cunningham, a Vietnam War hero serving his eighth term in Congress. The warrant the agents carried with them sought documents related to the purchase of the house and the sale of Cunningham's previous home in December 2003. Cunningham had sold his former home in the coastal community of Del Mar to a company owned by Mitchell Wade, a defense contractor and friend of the congressman's. Wade paid $1.675 million, a price that even in San Diego County's red-hot housing market was far above market value, and Wade sold the home at a $700,000 loss a year later. *The San Diego Union-Tribune* published a front-page story about the transaction, and a reporter had contacted Cunningham for comment. The congressman seemed unconcerned by a sale that was, at best, rife with conflicts of interest. "My whole life has been aboveboard and so this doesn't worry me," he said.

No one answered the door at Cunningham's mansion, so the agents summoned a locksmith. After reviewing the search warrant, the locksmith tried to pick the front-door lock and failed. He moved to a door on the southeast side of the home but failed again. Finally, he drilled a lock on a third door, and an alarm sounded as the agents entered the home. With the siren blaring, Siller and two other agents made a quick search to make sure no one was hiding inside. The alarm blasted away for twenty minutes before agents were able, through the security company, to reach Cunningham's wife, Nancy, who provided the code to turn it off.

Siller was surprised at conditions inside the house. It did not fit his image of what the home of a congressman should look like. Lamps, trash bags, boxes, and rolled-up rugs cluttered the floor, and many walls were bare. An acoustic guitar lay, strings down, at the base of the stairs. An inordinate number of armoires were in the home, many of them completely empty. Other French-provincial antiques were scattered about. A few rooms, such as the dining room and a small breakfast area, were tastefully decorated, but the rest made it seem as though the Cunninghams had never fully moved in. Personal financial documents and papers lay strewn about the kitchen countertops.

In one room, agents photographed a letter lying on a desk that had been written to Cunningham by a local defense contractor and Republican fundraiser named Brent Wilkes, a long-time friend of the congressman's. The letter, sent on the stationery of Wilkes's lobbying firm, Group W Advisors, referenced a trip Cunningham had taken with Wilkes to Kona on Hawaii's Big Island in August 2003. Cunningham had stayed as Wilkes's guest in a gorgeous $6,600-a-night suite at the Hapuna Beach Prince Hotel, located on a stretch of sand consistently been named one of the country's best beaches. Enclosed with the letter was a video of an all-day dive trip that Wilkes had organized on a chartered boat in the waters off the Big Island, a diver's paradise. According to prosecutors, during the trip, Wilkes and Cunningham had shared more than meals, drinks, and a suite. Both men had escorted prostitutes up to their rooms in the Hapuna suite on two consecutive nights.

Siller's job was to keep a detailed log of everything that transpired, an important task given the scrutiny investigators believed the search would be subject to. At 8:49 a.m., he noted in his handwritten log, Nancy Cunningham arrived at the residence. Although the FBI didn't know it, Nancy had not been living at the Rancho Santa Fe mansion. She appeared deeply concerned and somber. She said little but kept watch over the agents as they moved through the house, photographing each room, examining every desk drawer and every sheet of paper with gloved hands.

During the search, Nancy's cell phone rang. It was her husband calling. "Don't come home," she told him. "They're raiding our house. . . . I don't want you anywhere near here."

In addition to keeping his log, Siller was also given the job of staying with the congressman's wife. He noted that she appeared to be jotting down what agents were saying in a small notebook. At one point, she asked to use a house phone to call her husband's attorney in Washington, K. Lee Blalack II. Blalack spoke by phone with one of the FBI agents and instructed him and everyone else on the search team not to speak to Nancy. Meanwhile, Blalack's Los Angeles–based partner, Mark Holscher, raced down to Rancho Santa Fe. Appearing harried, Holscher reached the home around 11:30 a.m., after calling for directions. Once Holscher arrived, Siller noticed that Nancy seemed to relax a bit. Holscher and the congressman's wife kept exiting the house to have conversations in the yard, out of earshot of the agents.

One of the agents asked Nancy if there was a safe in the house. Yes, she told them, there was one in the garage. The agents couldn't locate a safe in the garage, but they did find one upstairs. Nancy tried several times to spin the tumbler and open the safe, without success. The agents decided they were going to drill the lock. Holscher was not pleased and forbade the agents to do so. The search team checked with supervisors in San Diego, who gave them the go-ahead. Finally, Nancy gave the combination to an IRS agent, who was able to open it.

Sometime after 1 p.m., Siller heard the sound of a helicopter circling the house. Five hours after agents first entered, word of the search had leaked out. Reporters began calling the FBI spokeswoman in San Diego for comment. Agents backed their sports utility vehicles into the garage to stay out of camera range as they loaded the ten boxes of materials, mostly financial and real estate documents, they had gathered.

Shortly before 2:30 p.m., the search team gathered in the garage. They had done their final walk-through and agreed that their job was finished. As quickly as they had come, the agents left the property and drove off.

While Siller and the San Diego agents had been waiting in the Original Pancake House parking lot, a pair of FBI agents, a man and woman, approached the clubhouse at the Capital Yacht Club in Washington, D.C. Located across the Potomac from the Jefferson Memorial, the club consists of four docks that jut into the waterway. Members, who include senior government officials, attorneys, lobbyists, and retirees, value their privacy, and on each dock a locked gate keeps the public out. A handful of members of Congress belonged to the club, including Randy Cunningham, who lived aboard a boat called the *Duke-Stir.*

Scott Schramm, a cable company executive with close-cropped hair and a thin mustache, served as the club's rear commodore, which made him responsible for security. He was on his boat that morning when the office manager called. A few people from the FBI had arrived, and they wanted to get on Cunningham's yacht. Although not an attorney, Schramm inquired whether the agents had a warrant with them. They did not. "No way," Schramm said. "You have them sit down. Offer them a cup of coffee. I'll get there when I get there. They are not entering this marina."

Schramm made his way to the clubhouse, where he found a pair of agents and asked them about a warrant. There was a warrant signed by a federal judge, they told Schramm, but the agent who had it had not yet arrived. Finally, the agent with the warrant reached the waterfront and showed the paperwork to Schramm. Everything appeared to be in order and Schramm told the agents to proceed. The FBI agent spoke into his radio, and ten agents popped out of vans and descended on the dock.

An FBI agent asked Schramm if he knew anything about the *Duke-Stir*. Schramm was intimately familiar with the boat. He had owned and lived aboard the forty-two-foot, gasoline-powered Carver yacht for nearly a year before Cunningham had expressed an interest in it. He showed the agents to the *Duke-Stir* and was surprised at the boat's condition. When he had lived on the boat, Schramm had kept it pristine, but now it was a mess. As in Cunningham's home, piles of papers and junk were scattered all over the cabin. In the salon, Schramm noticed boxes of wine and stacks of receipts, both of which interested the federal agents. Schramm did not venture into the stateroom and left after a few minutes. The agents spent a few hours aboard the boat and collected enough papers and other items to fill several cardboard boxes.

Cunningham had been living on the *Duke-Stir* since the fall of 2002. Before then, he had been living on a bigger boat, the *Kelly C,* and had wanted a smaller one, while Schramm had wanted to move up to a bigger boat. A mechanic who worked on both boats told Schramm that the congressman was interested in Schramm's boat, and Cunningham had offered Schramm $140,000 for it. Later in the day, the congressman had arrived with Mitchell Wade, who signed the checks for the boat. Schramm knew something wasn't right. That night, Schramm told his partner about the sale. "Somewhere, somehow, someday, somebody's going to go to jail for this," he said.

Randy "Duke" Cunningham, ace fighter pilot, Top Gun instructor, and an eight-term U.S. representative who'd never lost an election, was the most corrupt congressman in U.S. history. In addition to the mansion and the yacht, Cunningham accepted bribes large and small that included a Rolls-Royce and hundreds of thousands of dollars' worth of antiques. Defense contractors flew him aboard private chartered jets, picked up the tab at expensive restaurants, and even paid for his daughter's graduation party. By the prosecution's estimation, Cunningham had collected $2.4 million in bribes in five years, a series of acts on a scale that's unequaled in the long, sordid history of congressional corruption. No criminal case involving a member of Congress had ever dealt with so much money.

In November 2005, Cunningham shocked the nation by pleading guilty to charges of fraud and tax evasion. "The truth is I broke the law, concealed my conduct, and disgraced my high office," Cunningham said tearfully outside the San Diego courthouse. "I know that I will forfeit my freedom, my reputation, my worldly possessions, and most importantly, the trust of my friends and family." Less than six months later, a federal judge sentenced him to more than eight years in prison, the longest sentence handed down to a member of Congress in the past forty years.

Once Cunningham fell, they all started to fall. Tom DeLay, the House majority leader, resigned under indictment in Texas for violating state election law to raise money for his political action committee. Lobbyist Jack Abramoff pleaded guilty to defrauding American Indian tribes and corrupting a member of congress, Bob Ney, who himself later pleaded guilty. Mark Foley, chairman of the House Caucus on Missing and Exploited Children, resigned in the face of allegations that he had sent sexually explicit messages to former House pages. Democrats, too, had their share of scandals. The FBI raided the congressional office of William Jefferson, the first such raid in U.S. history, and found $90,000 in cash tucked in a freezer at the congressman's home.

These scandals arose not in a vacuum, but against the backdrop of a spending orgy that was authorized and funded with the oversight of what will surely go down in history as one of the most wasteful Congresses ever. This was a Congress famous for authorizing hundreds of millions of dollars for two "bridges to nowhere" in Alaska: one connects to an island inhabited by fifty people; the other, to a patch of scarcely habitable marshland. Such earmarks, tucked away in massive appropriations bills, were not merely a distraction; the quest for earmarks became so all-consuming that Congress neglected other duties.

This carnival of corruption led by Cunningham and his cohorts was a decisive factor in the Democrats retaking control of the House and Senate in 2006 for the first time in more than a decade. Equally important, the Cunningham scandal emboldened the Justice Department. Its offshoots included an investigation into Jerry Lewis, the chairman of the House Appropriations Committee, one of the most powerful chairmanships in all of Congress. It pulled in Washington lobbyists, military contractors, senior Defense Department officials, and the upper ranks of the Central Intelligence Agency. Investigators visited the Watergate, one of Washington's most infamous landmarks, and reporters were soon chasing allegations that one of Cunningham's close friends had provided the congressman with prostitutes. The FBI's public corruption program became "a sleeping giant that we've awoken," in the words of the agent in charge of it.

As long as there has been a Congress, lobbyists and businessmen have plied its members with gifts, meals, and services. Samuel Ward, the "King of the Lobby," charmed lawmakers with lavish meals. "The way to a man's 'Aye' is through his stomach," he famously remarked. In the 1830s, a powerful financier gave Senator Daniel Webster, the famed orator and future U.S. secretary of state, $32,000 in what would today be considered bribes. "The lasting contribution of Daniel Webster to American politics was his demonstration to the financiers and manufacturers spawned by the Industrial Revolution of the value of an able friend in the Senate," one historian noted. "The lesson was so thoroughly digested that the acquisition of lawmakers has been one of the primary objectives of big business ever since."

Cunningham was no mere congressman lining his pockets. Along with the damage to his own once-stellar reputation was the damage Cunningham did to the nation that placed its trust in him. Amazingly for a pilot who had risked his life numerous times for his country, Cunningham wreaked havoc on the nation's national-security apparatus, over which he wielded authority. He corrupted a brand-new intelligence agency, created after the September 11, 2001, attacks with the laudable goal of ferreting out terrorists and foreign spies. He used his authority to enrich two unscrupulous businessmen, browbeating, bullying, and threatening lowly government bureaucrats whose jobs were to ensure that contracts were fairly administered. He pumped millions into programs that the military did not request, did not want, and sometimes did not need. "Cunningham's motivation was to ensure that his co-conspirators gorged themselves at the national trough, regardless of the national interest," prosecutors wrote.

Given Cunningham's background, that he may well remain the symbol of the rampant corruption in the 109th Congress was all the more puzzling. Cunningham was a Navy ace, a hero in an unpopular war, and his wartime achievement stands untarnished. He performed brilliantly in the cockpit, downing five enemy planes in less than six months. That someone of his stature could fall so low suggested that something deeply troubling was at work in Washington. "Duke is a symbol of how far off the mark this Congress has drifted," said Scott Lilly, a former staff director of the House Appropriations Committee.

Even as a weeping Cunningham was led off to prison, the mysteries surrounding his stunning fall seemed only to deepen. While story after story chronicled the means of Cunningham's bribery, few probed the deeper questions that lay at the heart of the scandal. How did one of the Vietnam War's most highly decorated pilots become the most corrupt congressman in U.S. history? What led a man who showed such strength and resolve in battle to show such moral weakness later in life? Had he become a prisoner of greed or was he manipulated by others far more cunning than he? What happened to Randy Cunningham?

1

---•◆•---

The Duke

Ronald McKeown was in a mood to celebrate. The handsome, square-jawed Navy lieutenant commander had just been picked for his first command, and it was the one he had been dreaming about. The message the thirty-four-year-old had picked up in the end of May in 1972 in the pilots' ready room on the aircraft carrier *Midway* was the answer to his prayers. He was headed to San Diego to take command of the newly commissioned U.S. Navy Fighter Weapons School, better known by its code name, Top Gun. For a fighter pilot like McKeown, it meant training pilots for dogfighting, the thrill of air-to-air jet combat at five hundred miles per hour.

McKeown could have been ordered up by central casting to play the part of a fighter pilot. A former Navy running back, he brimmed with confidence and bristled with intensity and a fierce competitive drive. His boxing skills and pugnacious attitude earned him the nickname Mugs. McKeown grew up in the west Texas town of Ysleta, where he became a football star. Princeton, Harvard, and Dartmouth had all sent letters of acceptance, but the Naval Academy offered something the Ivy League schools didn't: the chance to play in the Army-Navy game, which, in the days before the advent of the Super Bowl, was the biggest football game in the world. In 1960, McKeown's third year at the academy, Navy was ranked third in the country and played in the Orange Bowl, and McKeown's teammate Joe Bellino won the Heisman Trophy.

During that magical 1960 season, Navy played the University of Washington on the road. The team practiced at a naval air station in Seattle on a field next to a landing area, where three F-8 Cougars landed and rolled to a halt. The pilots got out, locked up their planes, and three women in convertibles drove up. Watching the scene, McKeown thought to himself there was a lot to be said for naval aviation. Football brought out McKeown's ultracompetitive nature, his hatred of losing, which fit the classic fighter-pilot profile. McKeown found that he loved to fly and loved dogfighting more. Even though his father wasn't a hunter and there were no guns in his household growing up, McKeown discovered that he excelled at air-to-air gunnery. He would hit the target 17 percent of the time, when 8 percent was considered excellent.

Dogfighting had become something of a lost art after the Korean War. In Vietnam, Navy pilots fared poorly against the Soviet MiGs flown by the North Vietnamese. The Navy had lost one plane for every two Soviet-made MiGs they shot down over North Vietnam, the worst ratio in the history of American naval aviation. Top Gun began informally in 1969 in a trailer at Miramar with the goal of turning these trends around. The results had been impressive, and Navy pilots soon dominated the skies over Vietnam. The majority of Navy kills were made by pilots who had gone through Top Gun. Success bred success, and the Navy had established Top Gun as a formal command. McKeown was determined to make sure the school didn't disappear when the conflict in Vietnam did.

Before he even got to San Diego, McKeown had heard through the Navy grapevine that one of the instructors under his command was Lt. Randy Cunningham, the first ace of the Vietnam War and the Navy's most celebrated pilot. Tall and physically imposing, Cunningham had a broad face, a flat nose, a Caesar haircut with a pair of long sideburns, and eyes that squinted when he smiled. If any in the Navy didn't know Cunningham and what he had done in Vietnam, they had probably been underwater for months on a nuclear submarine.

On May 10, 1972, flying with Bill Driscoll in a two-man F-4 Phantom, Cunningham had shot down three enemy planes in the biggest air battle of the Vietnam War. On his way back to his carrier, the USS *Constellation,* Cunningham's plane was shot, but he somehow kept his burning aircraft rolling toward the coast until he and Driscoll were able to reach safe waters and avoid capture by the North Vietnamese. Cunningham's three kills that day brought his total for the war to five, which, under a tradition that dated back to World War I, conferred on him the exalted status of fighter ace and put him in the pantheon of fighter-pilot heroes.

Until he became an ace, the thirty-year-old pilot from Shelbina, Missouri, had a so-so Navy career. He applied for augmentation to leave the reserves and join the ranks of regular, career officers on three separate occasions in 1971 and 1972, the last time ten days after his first MiG kill. He was turned down each time. "Lt. Cunningham was not a fast starter as a junior officer; however, his performance and overall potential to the Navy has continued to steadily improve," read one letter of recommendation. "Since his decision to request augmentation into the regular Navy there has been a very noticeable increase in overall performance as well as enthusiasm for Navy life." In Cunningham's copy of his military records he handwrote in the margin of this letter, "Sound like Navy trash me." But all was forgiven the moment he became the Navy's ace. Realizing that losing Cunningham would be a public relations disaster, the Navy made a rare at-sea appointment to the regular Navy and decided to send him home to capitalize on his publicity.

The Navy plucked Cunningham and Driscoll out of Vietnam and sent them on a five-month publicity tour of the United States in the hopes of building support for an unpopular war. The two aviators visited New York, where they stayed in a suite at the Plaza Hotel, took in a Broadway show, and dined at the "21" Club, one of the city's most famous restaurants. They arrived in Washington, D.C., on May 18 for four weeks of closely scheduled public appearances, press conferences, and meetings with senior military and congressional leaders. The tour took them to Norfolk, Charleston, St. Louis, San Diego, Pensacola, Denver, Boston, and Jacksonville, and by the end of the tour, Cunningham and Driscoll made more than five hundred speeches. Adoring audiences heaped praise on them. "During those five months I received thousands of cards and letters lauding our efforts and accomplishments," Cunningham wrote in his 1984 memoir, *Fox Two*. "I found but one adverse note. There were no ticker tape parades, no large crowds gathered to honor us as they did the POWs, but I did appreciate the small civilian and military groups full of questions and appreciation." During a visit to his hometown of Shelbina, it seemed to Cunningham that all 2,000 residents turned out to cheer the local hero as he paraded through town in the back of an open convertible.

Cunningham's new status sparked a good deal of jealousy in the ultracompetitive community of fighter pilots. After Cunningham's triple kill, McKeown had sent a message over to the *Constellation*: "Send Duke home. Give us a chance." Many pilots felt that given the same opportunities Cunningham had had, they could have accomplished the same thing and also become an ace. The simple truth, however, is that no one else in the Navy did. Air-to-air combat was a lot scarier than many macho pilots wanted to admit. Cunningham was gifted in the cockpit. As a natural hunter he showed almost no fear, and he trained and practiced with the dedication of an Olympic athlete. There may have been better pilots than Cunningham, but few were more aggressive or better prepared.

While Cunningham was off touring the country in the fall of 1972, three Top Gun instructors who knew him well from Vietnam approached McKeown as he got settled in his office in Hangar Two at Naval Air Station Miramar in San Diego. The pilots told McKeown to make sure he kept an eye on Cunningham, warning him that Cunningham had an oversize ego and tended to exaggerate. Some in the squadron believed that Cunningham had been shot down by a MiG pilot, not a surface-to-air missile as he claimed. "Well, I'm used to that," McKeown replied. "I've been around fighter pilots my whole life."

McKeown already knew Cunningham from their first meeting years earlier. At the time, McKeown was briefing fighter squadrons in San Diego on the latest tactics for the Sparrow missile system. When he had finished, Cunningham asked McKeown if he had enough fuel left in his plane to take a few turns in the air. "What do you mean?" McKeown asked.

"I was just wondering if you want to go up in the air and do one-on-ones for grins," Cunningham asked.

"Sure," McKeown replied coolly.

Someone in the squadron prodded Cunningham to ask McKeown if he was up to the challenge. "Yeah, you think you can hack me?" Cunningham asked.

"I don't think anybody's been born that can beat me," McKeown replied. "But go ahead."

The two men got into two good mock dogfights, and to the amusement of others in the squadron listening in on the radio, Cunningham lost both.

When Cunningham's publicity tour ended and he reported to Top Gun, it was apparent that his ego had grown even bigger than McKeown remembered. Pilots were supposed to have a healthy ego, a sense of confidence, maybe even the arrogance that there was none better. After all, a moment's indecision in the cockpit at supersonic speeds could be deadly. In the eyes of some of his fellow pilots, however, Cunningham had crossed the line of what was acceptable.

Many pilots considered it in poor taste when Cunningham took to shamelessly promoting himself as a war hero. Even though his reputation usually preceded him, Cunningham introduced himself as "Randy Cunningham, the first MiG ace." He carried signed eight-by-ten, glossy photos of himself in a briefcase and had business cards printed up that read, "Have MiG, Will Travel." Several pilots recalled the ace doing commercials for a Datsun dealership, and many pilots winced when they opened the newspaper in August 1972 to find a photo of a grinning Cunningham showing off the new license plate on his Datsun, which read MIG ACE. He might as well have had the words NAVY HERO tattooed on his forehead.

Still, for the students or "nuggets" at Top Gun, Cunningham was a living legend, the embodiment of what a pilot was supposed to be. Whatever he said, one former student recalled, was gospel. Fellow instructors, however, were not so impressed by Cunningham as a teacher. "He wasn't thinking about teaching kids, of telling them, 'The hell with who I am, let's work on you and make you the best fighter pilot you can be,'" said Gregg Southgate, a fellow instructor who had served with Cunningham in Vietnam. Cunningham's focus seemed to be Cunningham, and he continued his self-promotion even when he had to cover the costs out of his own pocket.

The public appearances, McKeown felt, were starting to affect Cunningham's performance at Top Gun; other pilots had to cover for him when he was out giving speeches. McKeown, who had shot down two MiGs himself, didn't believe that Cunningham's heroics in Vietnam excused him from his duties at Top Gun. Cunningham needed to improve in many areas. For one, his writing was atrocious. He seemed unable to write a simple declarative sentence. When McKeown filled out Cunningham's fitness report, he ranked him in the bottom third. Cunningham was upset. He believed that he deserved to be ranked number one.

McKeown felt that in some ways Cunningham's poor performance wasn't the fault of the ace. The Navy had sent him around and around on publicity tours, and Cunningham hadn't matured as an officer. "As the Navy's sole MiG ace, Lt. Cunningham has inordinate demands made upon his private life and leisure time," McKeown wrote in his review. Still, McKeown felt he couldn't in good conscience give Cunningham high marks. He had a squadron full of talented officers, and he told Cunningham so. "Duke, these other guys can fly. Not only can they fly, but they can write and they can read," McKeown said.

For their actions on May 10, Cunningham and Driscoll were nominated for the Medal of Honor, the highest military honor in the United States. Usually awarded by the president, often posthumously, the medal honors members of the military who show extraordinary gallantry and bravery. Through the award process, the recommendation was downgraded to the Navy Cross, the service's second-highest honor. Cunningham was deeply upset. As the Navy's only ace in Vietnam, he believed he deserved the Medal of Honor and told his wife,

Susan, that he couldn't understand why the Navy wouldn't give it to him. Shortly after his arrival at Top Gun, Cunningham tried to enlist McKeown's help and advice. He told McKeown he had been promised the Medal of Honor by an aide to Adm. Elmo Zumwalt, the chief of naval operations. McKeown told Cunningham that the Medal of Honor required concurrence from all the branches of the service, and the Army and the Air Force would be unlikely to sign off on it.

"Well, I'm planning on that money," Cunningham said.

What money? What was Cunningham talking about? Cunningham explained that Medal of Honor winners do not have to pay taxes. McKeown couldn't fathom what Cunningham was saying. Even assuming that what Cunningham was saying was true, his tax savings would be minimal. He wasn't a millionaire who might actually save large amounts of money by avoiding taxes. At the time, Cunningham was earning $1,500 a month as a pilot.

"Well, I'm going to hold out for the Medal of Honor," he told McKeown.

"Duke, you don't hold out for the Medal of Honor," McKeown replied. "You die for the Medal of Honor."

Like McKeown, Cunningham had grown up in a small town. Born in Los Angeles on December 8, 1941, the day after the surprise attack on Pearl Harbor, Randy spent his early years in Fresno, where his father, a fuel-truck driver, had saved up enough money to buy a service station. Randy was the older of two boys. His father, Randall, was a large, stern Oklahoma native. Cunningham's mother, Lela, was a loving, petite housewife who, as one person observed, couldn't have weighed more than eighty-five pounds soaking wet. Lela was originally from Alabama, but moved as a child with her family to Oklahoma, where she met her husband at a roller-skating rink in Shawnee. When

Oklahoma became a dust bowl in the 1930s, Lela's family moved to California and Randall hitchhiked across the country to be near her.

When Randy was in the sixth grade, his father sold the gas station and moved the family to Shelbina, Missouri, a farm town of two thousand people. Cunningham's father, Randall P., ran a five-and-dime store there that was part of a family-owned chain. Shelbina, located in the middle of the country, was and remains the kind of town where no one locks the door, where everyone knows everybody else's business, and where pastors stress morals and ethics during Sunday church services while parishioners keep silent track of who failed to show. It was a patriotic place, where local sons and daughters serve in the military with pride, a town where the Pledge of Allegiance is said at local gatherings.

The thirteen-year-old Californian found rural Missouri a tough adjustment. Randy was not happy about the move to a town he later described as "about as redneck as you can get." The move left him sullen and obstinate, smarting off around his father. Cunningham and his brother also got a rude welcome to town. The Cunningham brothers both had squinty eyes, and the local boys started calling them "Japs," an insult in a town that had not quite forgiven Japan for World War II. Louis Hawkins, who had sold the Cunninghams their two-story house, didn't tolerate prejudice and informed Sam, his eleven-year-old son, that he was going to start playing with the Cunningham boys. Sam Hawkins helped ease Randy into Shelbina. They both attended Shelbina Baptist Church and served in the same Boy Scout troop, and Sam introduced him to his circle of friends, which included Ronnie Cullers, who soon became Randy's best friend.

Tall and slender, Cunningham lettered in basketball and was a crack swimmer, but high school football was the main attraction in town on Friday nights. Cunningham played tight end for Shelbina High under the direction of a fierce coach who would scream blood and guts and slam kids around. Cunningham didn't mind the occasional tussle.

Missouri also inspired Cunningham's love of hunting, which would become a lifelong passion. He and his friends would pile into Cunningham's father's old station wagon, drive out to the Missouri countryside, and ask permission from area farmers to hunt quail and rabbits. Randy worked part-time at his father's store but preferred working outdoors for local farmers, heaving bales of hay into barn lofts for $1 an hour or a penny a bale. Cunningham could heave hundreds of bales a day in the hot sun, and he and his friends used the money at the movies, the local pool hall, and a popular spot called Teen Town, where Cunningham's father often chaperoned.

Moving to a new town made Cunningham insecure, and he overcompensated by becoming a bully in high school. He picked on people who were much smaller than him, including his friend Sam Hawkins, who was about a foot shorter. "He was always hauling off and hitting me, and he thought that was funny," Hawkins recalled. The abuse continued until Randy's senior year, when Hawkins went through a growth spurt that put him near eye level with Cunningham. The bullying wasn't limited to Hawkins; others in Shelbina were subjected to Cunningham's abuse. Hawkins speculated that the bullying was likely a product of insecurity. Cunningham felt as if he didn't fit in and wanted to be well-liked. "Everybody has their nemesis, and you were mine," Hawkins told Cunningham years later. "When I saw you on *The 700 Club* and saw you'd been saved, I was the happiest guy."

Cunningham dated an attractive cheerleader named Linda Parker during high school. "When I knew him, he was a good man," she said, but "he wasn't the love of my life." He was respectful, although on one occasion she did see Cunningham's anger directed at someone else. Cunningham was smitten with Parker. When another boy, Harley Kropf, showed interest in her, Cunningham threatened to "kick his tail" one night. In his senior year, Cunningham asked Parker's mother if he could give her a ring. Parker's mother said no, and when Cunningham went off to Northeast Missouri State Teacher's College in

Kirksville, about fifty miles away, Parker's mother said no to the relationship.

After one year at the Teacher's College, Cunningham transferred to the University of Missouri. His grades improved and he got a graduate assistant position, responsible for teaching physical education, swimming, and political science. "At the university, he was as close to being a BMOC—a big man on campus—as anybody could be for a nonathlete," said Gary Dye, a classmate and fellow physical education major, who would go on to marry Linda Parker, Cunningham's high school sweetheart. "He was really good at drawing attention to himself." In addition, Cunningham struck Dye as a bright, serious student, actively involved in his political science class. When students would gather in the common area to watch *Combat!*, a 1960s TV drama about World War II, Cunningham always had his nose in a book. "When you're eighteen, nineteen years old, and you're good enough to get a scholarship at a major university, especially in two sports, and I was also offered a pro baseball contract, too, you know I had an ego, but I was still impressed with him," Dye said.

Even though he wasn't particularly handsome, Randy's swagger was attractive to Susan Albrecht, a brunette freshman. In his senior year, the two started dating and fell deeply in love. A marriage was planned for the following year. Susan said she had second thoughts before the wedding, but the invitations had gone out and some presents had arrived and she chalked it up to bride's jitters. They were married on August 8, 1964, in St. Louis. Susan was disappointed when Randy, who had promised her a honeymoon in Lake Tahoe, took her to the Ozarks instead, where they stayed in the same hotel where Cunningham's best friend was attending a family reunion. After a few days the hotel needed the room they were in and the newlyweds moved into a bug-infested room. Randy went on to complete his master's degree in education at Missouri. Susan dropped out of school, earning money on campus jobs to support them.

A chance meeting at the university pool landed Cunningham his first job. He was working as a lifeguard one day when a man named Don Watson walked up and introduced himself. Watson ran the swim program at Hinsdale High School in suburban Chicago, and he had stopped by to take a look at Missouri's aquatic facilities after dropping his daughter off at college in Louisiana. Watson's wife had noticed Cunningham and sent her husband over to talk to him. Watson was looking for a new assistant coach. He'd taken over the Hinsdale program two years earlier and was building the school into a swimming powerhouse. Cunningham struck Watson as a "country boy," somewhat naïve, but he had a nice personality and was easy to talk to. Watson thought he could train him and felt Cunningham might be a good fit for the opening at Hinsdale, so he helped Cunningham get the job.

At Hinsdale, Cunningham coached freshmen and sophomore swimmers and was in charge of running evening practices and deciding the lineup for swim meets. An aggressive man, he would come up from behind and squeeze you on the neck. The gesture, Watson felt, was intended to remind you who was in charge. His writing and spelling were atrocious, but Watson found he could depend on Cunningham and never had any problems with him. Watson was fond of Cunningham's wife, Susan, and later helped the Cunninghams adopt their first child, Todd.

One day in 1966, during his third year at Hinsdale, Cunningham walked into Watson's office and announced he would be resigning his job to join the Navy. Watson, who had served in the Navy as an enlisted sailor, tried to talk him out of it, but Cunningham had already made up his mind. Worried about his math skills, he even got permission to sit in on an upper-level math class at the school to brush up before entering the Navy, Watson said.

What prompted Cunningham to change careers was the death of

his best friend, Ron Cullers, who had become a Marine lieutenant and was killed in July 1966 in Vietnam. Cullers and Cunningham had spent their high school years together, and Culler's house was like a second home to Cunningham. Later, Cullers was the best man at Cunningham's wedding to Susan in St. Louis. Cunningham's parents had called him to break the news that Cullers, then twenty-three, had died when his helicopter had been shot down by enemy fire in Quang Tri in South Vietnam. Cullers's death had deeply affected Cunningham, and his then wife, Susan, recalled seeing him visibly upset and crying; it was the first time he had had to deal with the loss of someone his own age. After Cullers's death, he decided to go to Vietnam "and make them pay for Ronnie's death."

Unlike Cunningham, Cullers was well-liked and highly regarded in Shelbina. When Randy later had his victory parade through town, he acknowledged that many in the crowd didn't like him because of his bullying. "There's a lot of you standing out here today that wish I'd been the one that died instead of Ronnie," Cunningham said.

Cunningham has made much of the fact that he volunteered. Susan recalled that Randy had a low draft number and decided that if he was going to serve, he wanted to do it on his own terms. He started taking flying lessons and found his calling. "It was almost like I had been born in an airplane. Or maybe like a concert pianist or prodigy who does well from the first time they touch the keys of a piano. I felt like part of my soul was in the airplane," Cunningham said without a trace of modesty.

Cunningham began basic training in Pensacola, Florida, on July 16, 1967, and finished thirty-second in a class of ninety-nine. Like all young recruits, he faced Marine drill sergeants who broke him down and rebuilt him, an experience many pilots said was captured in the 1982 film *An Officer and a Gentleman.* His commander at advanced jet-training school in Texas described him as "a mature, talented officer who performed his duties as a student naval aviator in an outstanding manner."

After his arrival in San Diego in 1968, one commander, Carl Wynn, noted some weaknesses. Cunningham had difficulty writing, Wynn wrote, he could be impulsive, and fast-changing situations could flummox him. Others wrote that he was "untiring" in the performance of his duties. By 1971, Cunningham enrolled in the Top Gun program just as it was getting started in the trailer at Miramar and impressed instructors with his passion, aggressiveness, and hunger to learn. He took his flying very, very seriously, studying the great aviators of World War I in his off-hours with an almost religious zeal. He was fond of quoting famed ace Manfred von Richthofen, the "Red Baron": "A fighter pilot patrols in the area allotted to him in any manner he sees fit. When he sees the enemy, he attacks and kills. Anything else is rubbish." Like von Richthofen, Cunningham was so dedicated to his craft, his hunger to be the best, that nothing else seemed to matter.

He was a stickler for preparation. He recognized that when pilots approached each other at combined speeds of a thousand miles per hour, opportunities for a kill were fleeting. Pilots who weren't well prepared would miss out. Cunningham didn't make those mistakes. During each training mission, the switches in Cunningham's plane would all be set to strike should opportunity present itself. "People ask me why I became an ace, and the other guys didn't," Cunningham told one interviewer. "For one thing, I was very lucky; I had the chance. But when the chance came, I was prepared. It was a combination of Navy training and my own discipline." Before every mission, he rubbed a lucky rabbit's foot and told himself, "This is the one where I get a MiG."

If it didn't involve flying or shooting down planes, however, Cunningham often wasn't interested. Instructor Jim Fox thought Cunningham made an average or below average officer. Cunningham didn't have time for the paperwork, fitness reports, and more mundane duties—von Richthofen's "rubbish" that came with the job and was crucial to advancement. Although the Navy instilled in its officers the idea that they are officers first, aviators second, Cunningham had it backward. "My idea of a Navy officer," he conceded later, "was a shit-hot pilot who shot down airplanes, and to hell with the paperwork."

He also had a hot temper and was, at times, in poor control of his emotions. During a cruise aboard the carrier USS *America,* Cunningham had walked off the ship in Hong Kong with stitches below his eye. Cunningham had been shaving and showering that morning in the room he shared with seven other junior officers when he and one of the smaller guys in the squadron got into an argument. Another officer had been sitting in his bunk, quietly listening, when he decided that he had heard enough. He leapt out of his rack and decked Cunningham square in the face. Cunningham went flying, then got to his feet, grabbed a golf club, and started chasing his assailant. Stark naked, both men tore through the corridors like a pair of hurdlers, leaping through passageways.

Cunningham did not hide his disrespect for command. In his book, *Fox Two,* written while he was still a lieutenant, Cunningham stated that he didn't want anyone who outranked him for a wingman. Many of the senior officers, he wrote, just wanted to be sure to make it back, and Cunningham wanted to hunt MiGs. "Why let rank lead, when ability can do it better?" By his own admission, he once told Al Newman, his commander, that a decision of his to use centerline fuel tanks was "fucked up," a galling display of insubordination.

On January 19, 1972, Cunningham proved himself to be more than just a big mouth. Cunningham and Driscoll had been assigned to protect a photo reconnaissance mission to an airfield in North Vietnam from attack by enemy MiGs. As their F-4 swooped over the Tha Quan Lang Airfield, the North Vietnamese launched a barrage of eighteen surface-to-air (SAM) missiles at Cunningham and his fellow pilots. "There is nothing, absolutely nothing, to describe what goes on inside a pilot's gut when he sees a SAM get airborne," he later wrote.

Evading a SAM, which flew at more than three times the speed of sound, required Cunningham to wait until the last possible moment as the missile approached, then turn as hard as possible and hope the missile couldn't follow. The wait was agonizing. Panic rose in his throat. Finally, he pulled up into a bone-crushing eight-g turn and the missile exploded harmlessly below. As other missiles roared up at them, Cunningham dove down.

Flying just above the treetops on the jungle floor, Cunningham spotted two MiG-21s. He locked onto one of the planes and squeezed off a Sidewinder missile, which missed as the pilot banked hard. But the MiG pilot had made a fatal mistake: he had turned too hard. That cost him precious airspeed, allowing Cunningham to lock in again and squeeze off a second Sidewinder that flew right up the MiG's tailpipe. The jet's tail came apart and the rest of the plane went into a violent, tumbling crash that ended in a fireball.

For the first time in eighteen months, a MiG had been sighted and destroyed by an American fighter pilot. Back aboard his carrier, the USS *Constellation*, the crew greeted him in celebration. Commanders organized a small party and someone asked, "Duke, what was it like to kill another human being?" The question stopped Cunningham cold. "The words hit me full force, as if I were being knocked to the floor. I looked at my questioner, unable to reply. I turned and headed straight to my room feeling as if the whole world had blown up. Always thinking of myself as a hard-core professional, I had believed that such a question would never faze me."

A sickening feeling dug at his stomach as he thought about watching the twisted machine carry another human to a horrible death. He made "excuses" for himself—"it was in the line of duty"—but he feared relating his feelings to anyone, even his friends. Cunningham turned to the ship's chaplain, telling him he had a "personal problem" he wished to discuss in confidence. "My mind was in turmoil as many questions poured out, questions that had to be answered, questions I had never let myself think about," Cunningham wrote in *Fox Two*.

The next day, his commanding officer, Al Newman, summoned Cunningham and confronted him with what he'd told the chaplain: "Randy, how do you feel about combat flying now?" Furious at the chaplain's betrayal, Cunningham could nevertheless understand Newman's concern. Would Cunningham hesitate the next time? Cunningham assured his commander he would kill again, but he didn't relish the thought. "Before I left, I had the basic problem worked through. I knew I would be able to do the same thing again, but I didn't have to like it—the act of killing someone was never a pleasant experience for me. The after-effects remain with me to this day," he wrote.

Newman sent Driscoll and Cunningham for a few days of R&R in the Philippines, and Cunningham received a Silver Star for his first kill. Still, it would have been impossible to miss the implication of his experience with the chaplain: revealing one's feelings was a sign of weakness.

Cunningham had worked too hard and loved his job too much to give it up. Besides that, he was beginning to enjoy the attention that came with being a "MiG killer." Sometime after his first shootdown in 1972, he decided to change his call sign, which for years had been Yank, to Duke, the same nickname as his hero, the actor John Wayne. The nickname Yank, with its superpatriotic connotations, had been chosen for Cunningham and it seemed more fitting, but Duke was in keeping with Cunningham's newly emerging perception of himself as a larger-than-life hero. Cunningham and Driscoll returned to the skies, and on May 8, 1972, Cunningham scored his second kill of the war, sending a MiG-17 that crossed his path into a mountain.

May 10, 1972, the day that changed Cunningham's life forever, began as any other. He awoke in his bunk on the *Constellation* and made his way up to the flight deck before breakfast. Dawn was breaking over the Gulf of Tonkin, where other carriers were massing for an assault deep into North Vietnam, which had launched a major invasion of the south. The sun rose behind the low, wispy clouds hugging the Gulf of Tonkin. The crew was testing the ship's catapults, which roared and hissed steam.

Sketched out in the *Constellation*'s operations room was the day's mission. Cunningham was taking part in the second strike of the day against the Hai Duong Rail Yard, a marshaling area for supplies that lay halfway between the coast and Hanoi. The squadron could almost certainly expect to do battle. The North Vietnamese were sending every available aircraft to the vicinity of the Hai Duong Rail Yards, and U.S. intelligence could hear the radio traffic buzzing with activity. Cunningham began to grow anxious as he waited for his mission to begin. He walked back up to the flight deck to get some air. Another pilot, even more nervous, was vomiting over the side. Cunningham calmed himself by recalling a quote from George Bernard Shaw's play *Major Barbara*: "If a man cannot look evil in the face without illusion, he will never know what it really is or combat it effectively."

Sure enough, a host of MiGs came raining down on them when Cunningham's thirty-two-plane strike force reached the target. Cunningham had never seen so many enemy planes in one place before. There were as many as twenty MiGs, two of which swooped down to attack Cunningham. Unlike Cunningham's F-4 Phantom, armed only with missiles, the MiGs had cannons on their noses, and both planes were blasting away. The muzzle flash jetted out the length of a football field. Cunningham turned hard into the path of the lead attack plane. The MiG couldn't follow and overshot him. Cunningham got behind the MiG and squeezed off a Sidewinder missile that blew his attacker to pieces.

Cunningham pulled up and spotted eight MiGs circling in what's known as a defensive wheel. In the middle of the wheel were three U.S. Navy Phantoms. One, flown by Jim Fox and Dwight Timm, came roaring out of the circle, barely missing Cunningham, with three

MiGs in pursuit. Cunningham got in behind them and waited until he had a clear shot at one of the MiGs chasing Fox. Cunningham fired, scoring his second kill of the day.

Fox's plane headed back for the coast and Cunningham decided to follow. On the way, Cunningham spotted a MiG-17 below them headed right for him. As the MiG opened fire, Cunningham pulled straight up into the sky and was surprised to see the enemy pilot following below him. At the top of the climb, the MiG fired again. Not willing to admit that he was being beaten, Cunningham told Driscoll, "That SOB is really lucky."

It was more than just luck, however. Whatever Cunningham did, his adversary matched him maneuver for maneuver, and Cunningham barely escaped becoming a casualty himself. The two planes again raced skyward in the pure vertical, but this time Cunningham pulled the throttle to idle and hit the speed brakes. The MiG shot out ahead. Now Cunningham had the advantage and the enemy in his sights. The MiG pilot tried to flee by aiming his plane right at the ground. Cunningham followed and squeezed off another Sidewinder missile for his third kill of the day, his fifth of the war. The Navy had its first ace of Vietnam. "That's it, baby," Cunningham said. "I got five . . . that's all I want. We're getting out of here!"

A few miles out, something shook Cunningham's Phantom and a nauseating feeling crept into his stomach. He checked his instruments. Everything was normal. Cunningham fired his afterburners, pushing his plane close to the speed of sound, and hurrying back to the *Constellation*, waiting in the Gulf of Tonkin. Less than a minute later, his plane yawed violently to the left. His control gauges showed he had almost no hydraulic pressure, and with it, he had lost almost all control of his plane. His control stick was useless; it felt limp. Driscoll glanced behind and spotted fire on the left wing.

Cunningham leveled off and glanced below. From the air, the wall-to-wall houses of North Vietnam reminded him of Los Angeles. If he

ejected here, he would almost certainly be taken prisoner to face tor-
ture and death. If he could hang on for a few minutes and reach the
water about twenty miles away, they had a good chance of being rescued. Cunningham and Driscoll decided to stay in the plane as long as
they could. The two had decided never to use the word *eject* until it
was time to get out of the plane.

The plane still had power in its rudders, and when the plane's nose
rose again, Cunningham forced it down with his right rudder. When
the plane leveled out, he cut power to his engines and hit the brakes to
prevent the Phantom from going into a dive. For twenty miles, Cunningham kept the plane moving to the coast. Fire crept up the fuselage
and smoke began to pour into the cockpit. An explosion ripped
through the plane, but they were still over land so they hung on. The
radio filled with the screams of Navy pilots urging them to eject as
they watched the airplane burn.

As they crossed the beach, another violent explosion shook the aircraft. This time, when the nose rose up, Cunningham couldn't force it
back down and the plane went into a spin. Cunningham hadn't gotten
the word *eject* out of his mouth when Driscoll pulled the ejection handle. Cunningham heard Driscoll's seat fire, and after a split second
that seemed to last an eternity, the rocket motor below Cunningham's
seat fired and spat him into the sky at twelve thousand feet.

Massive g-forces crushed him in his seat as he rose several hundred
feet in the air. His damaged fighter jet tumbled beneath him toward
North Vietnam. Then, the rocket beneath his seat burned out and his
seat fell away from him. Noise faded to the sound of the wind. Cunningham began to plummet, headfirst. He had never parachuted before. He was beginning to wonder if something was wrong when his
orange and white parachute blew open with a sharp jolt that sent a
wave of pain through his back. The lush delta of North Vietnam's Red
River Valley lay below. Was he headed for land? Cunningham saw
two enemy patrol boats cruising up the Red River toward his position.

A few hundred feet away, Driscoll drifted down in his own chute. Driscoll watched their F-4 fall back to earth. Burning badly, it fluttered in the sky like a falling leaf, then exploded. Later, reporters asked Driscoll what was going through his mind as he drifted down in his parachute. He told them, "My thoughts were perhaps I had made an incorrect decision in leaving the Army Reserve in Boston."

The Red River rose up beneath Cunningham and he plopped face-first into the warm, muddy water. He noticed something bobbing in the water next to him. It was a corpse, dead several days, of a North Vietnamese man. Driscoll spotted schools of sea snakes. Haiphong Harbor was three miles away. Big Mother 62 and Big Mother 65, two huge U.S. Marine Sea King helicopters, were on their way to the rescue.

Once aboard, Cunningham passed a note up to the cockpit asking them to contact the USS *Constellation* and verify his three kills. "It dawned on us that we had a celebrity aboard," the pilot of Big Mother 65 later recalled.

A crowd gathered on the deck of the USS *Constellation* as a Marine helicopter ferried him back aboard. It seemed to Cunningham as if the entire crew of five thousand were waiting to greet him. He made his way through the crowd. Gregg Southgate, a fellow F-4 pilot, pulled Cunningham aside. Southgate had realized that Cunningham's triple kill was one of the biggest events of the war. Lots of people, Southgate thought, would be interested in Cunningham's story. There were opportunities for a book, TV appearances, possibly even a movie. "Randy, if you think about this real hard, there's a real possibility of making some money off of this," Southgate said. If Cunningham wanted to leave the Navy, Southgate would be his agent. Cunningham just laughed.

The Navy arranged a special ceremony for Cunningham in the fall of 1972. Navy Secretary John Warner was visiting Miramar to commission two new squadrons that would be flying the brand-new

F-14 Tomcat, and during the ceremony, Warner would present Cunningham and Driscoll with their Navy Crosses. The day before the ceremony, McKeown was in the Top Gun ready room talking with other instructors when Cunningham and Driscoll walked in and asked to speak with him. In front of other officers, Cunningham stated that he and Driscoll had decided not to accept the Navy Cross at the ceremony.

McKeown smiled and said, "I'm sorry, Duke. I could have sworn you said you're not going to accept the Navy Cross."

McKeown told Cunningham and Driscoll to follow him into his office, and he left the door open so the other instructors could hear the message he was about to deliver loud and clear.

McKeown told the two men they didn't need to sit down. "I'm going to give you about twenty seconds' worth of lecture, and then I'm going to throw your asses out of my office. Starting in about twenty seconds from now, you guys are going to get out of here and you're going to go get your hair cut. You're going to go get your blues pressed and make sure your gold braid is nice and shiny and your shoes are shined. Tomorrow, you're going to be resplendent in your blues while a grateful nation heaps its praise on two of its heroes. Anything less than that and I guarantee I'll rip your tits off. Now get the hell out of my office."

The next day, Cunningham and Driscoll received their awards, as ordered.

To McKeown, Cunningham seemed like an odd duck. Cunningham didn't go for the alcohol-fueled camaraderie with other pilots. He preferred to be off by himself hunting or riding dirt bikes with his friends. When he did show up at the Officers' Club, Cunningham sipped Courvoisier stingers, a blend of cognac and crème de menthe. Cunningham seemed to think it made him seem sophisticated; McKeown told him to order something else. He was taking good Courvoisier and obliterating the taste of it by adding sweet mint juice in it. "Everyone thinks you're an idiot," he said.

The more McKeown got to know him, the stranger Cunningham seemed. McKeown saw in Cunningham enormous insecurity, which was best exemplified in his tendency to embroider his own legend. Cunningham told audiences that during his last of three engagements on the day he became an ace, he had faced Vietnam's top fighter pilot, the legendary Colonel Tomb or Toon. McKeown and other pilots didn't believe a word of it; Colonel Tomb was a wartime myth, a view confirmed later by aviation historians who searched in vain for any record of Tomb. Asked how he knew of Colonel Tomb, Cunningham replied that the answer was classified, and it remained a secret long after the war had ended.

The truth didn't get in the way of Cunningham's telling of the story, which became a practiced part of his stock speech. His fanciful recounting found its way into his book, *Fox Two*, where he referred to his North Vietnamese adversary by the pejorative *Gomer.* "As I looked back over my ejection seat I got the surprise of my life: there was the MiG, canopy to canopy with me, barely 300 feet away! I could see a Gomer leather helmet, Gomer goggles, Gomer scarf . . . and his intent Gomer expression. I began to feel numb. My stomach grabbed at me in knots. There was no fear in this guy's eyes as we zoomed some 8,000 feet straight up." Audiences loved to hear about his duel to the death with Colonel Tomb, the thrilling, but heavily exaggerated, climax to his heroic tale.

Later, McKeown learned that Cunningham claimed to have shot down MiGs during classified missions with the Israeli Air Force in the Bekáa Valley of Lebanon, a story that Cunningham continued to tell years later to other members of Congress. True, Cunningham had worked with Israeli pilots and had visited Israel, but the notion that he flew with them on combat missions was pure fantasy. To McKeown,

Cunningham's exaggerations were the hallmark of an enormously insecure man. Cunningham was the ace, the elite among the elite, and what he had done many pilots would consider the crowning moment of their aviation career. But if the story could be tweaked just a bit, Cunningham couldn't help himself. The joke among pilots became that Cunningham was like the man with the nine-inch penis who brags that his dick is fourteen inches long.

Top Gun's new executive officer, Jack Ensch, arrived at the school in January 1974 after a harrowing experience in Vietnam. Ensch, who was in the backseat when McKeown shot down two MiGs, had later been shot down himself when his plane was hit by a surface-to-air missile in August 1972. During ejection, Ensch's left hand was badly mangled and both elbows were dislocated, leaving his forearms pushed up halfway up the inside of each upper arm. Ensch landed in a rice paddy and ended up in a twelve-by-twelve room at the Hanoi Hilton, the infamous prison in North Vietnam. For the next three days, he was interrogated around the clock. He refused to answer questions and was essentially told that he would receive no medical attention unless he talked. He grew delirious as he watched his arms lose circulation and felt his life slipping away. Finally, he decided to answer a few questions, which seemed to satisfy his captors. He was taken from his cell, blindfolded, and strapped to a table. A "doctor" amputated his thumb without anesthesia, then sat him in a chair, put a foot on his chest, and yanked his arms back into position. He was released in March 1973. His Navy buddies gave him a new nickname, Fingers.

A week or so after his arrival at Top Gun, Ensch had his first encounter with Cunningham, who came into his office and asked for his help. McKeown was making another of his trips back to Washington to brief Congress on Top Gun and its needs. Cunningham hadn't been invited along, but he told Ensch he needed to go.

"I've got to get back there and check on my Medal of Honor. I was supposed to get a Medal of Honor," Cunningham said. "All I got is the Navy Cross."

"Randy, what do you mean?" Ensch said.

"Well, it's not fair that I only have a Navy Cross and other people have Navy Crosses, too, and they don't have five MiGs."

Ensch bit his tongue. How stupid could Cunningham be? Ensch was one of the "other people" who had been awarded a Navy Cross, and he wore it with pride. Ensch tried a diplomatic approach, explaining to Cunningham that he had set the standard for a Navy Cross. Because of Cunningham's triple kill, shooting down more than one MiG in a single engagement became a prerequisite for a Navy Cross.

Later, Ensch repeated this conversation to McKeown, who replied that he definitely wasn't going to take Cunningham to Washington with him again. McKeown had already brought him once, and Cunningham had proved to be an embarrassment. He had brought along a suitcase filled with photos of himself signed "Randy Cunningham, first MiG ace" and passed them to secretaries at the Pentagon and passengers on the plane.

A short while later, Jack Ready took over as head of Top Gun after McKeown left to take a job at the Pentagon. Like McKeown, Ready also didn't rank Cunningham number one in the squadron, which only enraged Cunningham even more. One weekend, Cunningham used a key given to all instructors to enter Ready's offices. He read through the fitness reports of his fellow officers and compared himself. He realized he was ranked at the bottom of the pack. When Ready returned to work, Cunningham confronted him. He asked Ready why he hadn't been ranked number one, then cited the names of others who had been ranked higher than him.

"How do you know that?" Ready asked.

"Well, I came in here and looked at your records," Cunningham said.

Ready was livid. He and Ensch discussed bringing Cunningham before a court-martial or an administrative hearing known as a captain's mast, which would effectively have quashed any hope for career advancement. A court-martial conviction would have ended Cunningham's career. Ready took his request for punishment forward to his superiors, but the chain of command decided not to bring down the career of the Navy's Vietnam ace. In the end, Ready sat Cunningham down in his office and gave him a verbal reprimand. "He was a MiG ace at the time," Ready said. "He had a lot of respect from people who didn't know him deeply, and I didn't want to make a big issue of that."

Becoming an ace had saved Cunningham's career once before, and now it saved him again. There would be no record in his personnel file to let future commanders know that he had entered his commander's office without permission and examined other pilots' private performance assessments. The Navy was apparently willing to apply a different standard for its ace.

In some ways, Cunningham was a product of the Navy's special treatment of him. The Navy essentially condoned Cunningham's bad behavior, and this only fueled his sense of invulnerability, that he could do no wrong. He was becoming a man who felt, not incorrectly, that the rules did not apply to him.

When journalist Gregory L. Vistica revealed this episode in 1995, Cunningham flew into a rage and instructed his staff to get Ensch on the phone. Cunningham angrily told him that the incident had never happened.

"Randy," Ensch replied calmly, "you and I both know it happened."

"Well, it's not true," Cunningham insisted.

2

———◆◆◆———

Frozen in Amber

While civilian audiences welcomed Cunningham as a war hero, his wife, Susan, began to see a darker side of his personality. Unable to conceive a child on their own, Susan and Randy had adopted a son, Todd, who turned three the year his father became a celebrated pilot. They began the adoption of a second child in the fall of 1971, an infant daughter named Kristin, who was placed in their home in September. A beautiful girl with sandy blond hair, Kristin had a hint of olive in her skin, which Susan liked because her skin, too, had a touch of olive in it. Kristin didn't seem to like Randy; he left for overseas duty shortly after she arrived, and when he returned, she often cried when he entered the room, and that could bring out Randy's temper.

Randy would show dangerous flashes of anger at home in front of his wife and children, which Susan thought might be possible signs of post-traumatic stress disorder. Once, when Kristin was crying, Susan recalled, Randy had taken her upstairs and "thrown, and I mean thrown," her in the crib, which only made her scream louder. Another time, Kristin's hands and forearms got scalded with hot water when Randy took her into the shower with him, and when he washed her with a cloth, the skin came off. Kristin had a gamma globulin deficiency, and the medicine she was taking made her sensitive to light and heat. Susan rushed Kristin to the hospital for treatment. Although Susan didn't feel that Randy had meant Kristin any harm, the episode didn't endear him to his daughter.

Todd, too, had borne his father's wrath. Cunningham had taken a belt to the boy when he crossed the street without having an adult with him. "He whipped and whipped and whipped," Susan recalled. Randy had even started to use force against her once while she was ironing. She wheeled around, holding up the hot iron, and Randy backed off. At night, Randy slept with a loaded, black .357 magnum revolver under his pillow to make him feel safer, although it wasn't clear what he was afraid of. The gun, Susan couldn't help but notice, was pointed at her.

Mary Sherman, who lived across the street from the Cunninghams, befriended Susan, and the two women would have tea while Todd played with Sherman's two children. Unlike Susan, who Sherman found to be a sweet Midwesterner, Randy seemed to be controlling, temperamental, and severe, and Sherman did her best to avoid him. One day, when Susan was leaving Sherman's home after tea, Randy pulled up in his car and started yelling at Susan, demanding to know where she had been. "If you're not going to work, you better goddamn well stay in the house where I can reach you." On another occasion, Sherman was at the Cunninghams visiting with Susan in the living room while Randy ate in a dinette next to the kitchen. "Suzy," he bellowed, "get in here and get me a glass of water!" Susan, who never showed emotion in these incidents, calmly got up and fetched him a glass of water.

Soon after Cunningham returned home a Vietnam hero, the marriage fell apart. On December 7, 1972, the day before his thirty-first birthday, Randy handed Susan a note. In it, he explained that he had almost flown his plane into a mountain because he had been out the night before with another woman. Randy wanted out of their marriage; he had proposed to the other woman. Susan had long suspected Randy was not being faithful. There were rumors he was playing around while on overseas duty, and when he was at home, his behavior aroused suspicions. He would tell Susan he was going out to play basketball, then wind up at the Miramar Officers' Club, where local women often flocked to meet pilots.

Other wives of officers in the squadron, Susan learned to her embarrassment, knew about the woman in Randy's life. Named Pam, she was the wife of a professional football player for the Los Angeles Rams, who lived in an adjoining subdivision. One day, while Susan and Randy were in the midst of separating, Cunningham had attended a party at Pam's house. Shortly after he returned home, the doorbell rang. Susan, who was upstairs, heard a commotion, then overheard Randy on the phone explaining what had happened. Pam's football player husband had come over to Cunningham's house and "cold-cocked him" on the front porch.

Randy turned the tables on Susan in his book, *Fox Two*, in which he accused Susan of cheating on him and made his faltering marriage seem another obstacle he had to overcome on his road to glory. Shortly before he became an ace, he wrote that he had received a Dear John letter from Susan, telling him she wanted out of the marriage. (Susan said she did write Randy a letter, but it was to let him know that she felt they needed to work on the marriage.)

The letter weighed heavily on him the day he became an ace. As he ejected from the plane and drifted down in his parachute, Cunningham wrote, his thoughts shifted from thoughts of capture by the North Vietnamese to his wife's letter. "I seriously questioned if I would have what it takes to go through the camps if I were captured. We had been told the two major sustaining forces in captivity would be a strong faith in God and a loving wife. I was deficient in both areas. Thinking about my wife, I cried like a baby for a moment or so. My life was falling apart in great emotional upheaval. Again, I vowed to change my life for the better if I got out of this." Cunningham was rescued and sent home to an emotional reunion with his family, but he claimed that he found out Susan had been seeing another man who lived a block away from their home. (Mary Sherman, who introduced the man to Susan, said the two met after she divorced Randy.) "It was more than I could take, so we filed for divorce. This was going on while I was supposedly the happy ace touring the country." His insides, he wrote, were "being torn apart."

Susan was outraged when she heard about Randy's book. After enduring his years of skirt-chasing, he had now rewritten history to blame *her*. She briefly thought about suing him, but she was at the time taking a Bible class that urged forgiveness, and she ultimately decided not to. But Randy's accusation bothered her for years. "It wasn't me who was out fooling around. It was him," she said.

Susan filed for divorce in January 1973, citing irreconcilable differences. In some ways, it was a relief. For years, she had endured Randy's insults as he mocked her appearance, telling her he would give her money for clothes if she lost weight. He also belittled her intelligence, lording over her the fact that he had finished college, while she had not yet gotten her degree. The first hearing in the case was February 15. On the way to court, Susan had to return Kristin to the adoption authority because Randy had never signed the papers to complete the adoption. It tore at Susan's heart to give up the daughter she had fed, clothed, and cared for over the past eighteen months; it left an emotional wound that would never fully heal. Randy, Susan said, didn't seem to care, and in his book and the stories he told again and again, he never acknowledged the daughter he had once had and lost.

While the divorce was being finalized that year, Randy met Nancy Jones, an attractive, twenty-one-year-old, blond kindergarten teacher at the Officers' Club at Miramar. Nancy was also emerging from a divorce, and when Randy proposed, she gladly accepted. The week before he married Nancy in February of 1974, Randy asked Susan to get back together with him. "No, of course not," she told him.

One month after the wedding, Randy asked the court to lower the amount of money he had to pay in child support to his ex-wife. A judge denied the request. Susan found Nancy to be particularly mean-spirited, and feeling that she had almost no support in San Diego, Susan decided to move with Todd to St. Louis. One of her lasting memories of Nancy was when Susan picked up Todd from a visit with his father and his new wife to take him to Missouri, Nancy stuck her thumbs in her ears and blew raspberries at her.

In Nancy, Randy had found someone who complemented his own exaggerated sense of himself. Gregg Southgate, a fellow instructor who knew Cunningham well, felt that Nancy wanted an awful lot for Randy, who was, at essence, a man of simple tastes, who liked the outdoors, hunting and fishing and riding his dirt bike with friends around San Diego. Southgate didn't know Nancy well, but she gave off a bad vibe. Mary Sherman, who lived across the street, found her to be a "silly-ass woman." After Nancy moved in with Randy to the home he once shared with Susan, she became the talk of the neighborhood. The twenty-one-year-old was seen emerging from her home wearing a bikini, picture hat, and high heels to water the front yard.

Shortly after he and Nancy were wed, Randy came into some money. By April, Randy had received an advance for his book, *Fox Two*, from Zondervan, a Christian media and publishing company in

Michigan. On April 15, Randy and his friend Dan McKinnon jointly purchased a forty-five-acre ranch in east San Diego County adjoining an Indian reservation. Cunningham's ranch was a beautiful property with a small, rustic home built into a hillside, a pond, and a small stream that flowed after rains. It was not far from a much larger ranch that McKinnon owned. The son of a former congressman and a devout Christian, McKinnon was trying to help Randy make some smart investments. Records show that Cunningham and McKinnon paid $24,000 for the property, but two years later, Nancy listed the property's value in court papers at more than four times that amount. In 1988, Cunningham sold the property for $275,000.

Randy's anger did not disappear with his new wife. He continued to sleep with a gun under his pillow, and his temper could flare dangerously out of control. In October 1976, two years into their marriage, Nancy filed for divorce. Now twenty-four, she sought and received a restraining order against Randy. In a declaration filed with the court, she stated Randy "has indicated to me, on prior occasions that he would clean the house out"—leave Nancy with nothing—"if I ever filed for a dissolution. Further, he has threatened me with physical violence if I ever filed for a divorce. He is a very aggressive, spontaneously assaultive person and I fear for my immediate physical safety and well-being." She also related how he slept with a knife and a gun under his pillow. A judge issued a restraining order on October 29 preventing Randy from entering the home. Shortly after she filed the papers, Nancy and Randy were reconciled. "He put on that poor sad-dog face of his," Nancy told writer Kitty Kelley in *The New Republic*. Three months later the divorce case was dismissed, and the following year the couple had their first child, April.

In 1978, the Navy sent Cunningham to the Pentagon, a sterling opportunity for career advancement that gave him a taste of life in Washington. Cunningham was assigned to an office that compiled the naval aviation budget and briefed lawmakers. The office was known in the Navy as a "flag maker," since few who passed through didn't go on to command a ship or make admiral. Cunningham was a congressional liaison, a job that involved briefing members of Congress on the Navy's aviation budget. Harold Bernsen, a Navy captain who would go on to make admiral, worked in the office along with Cunningham. "That is the first occasion where he was exposed to the Congress and the Congress was exposed to him," Bernsen said. "I suspect that's precisely the time when he determined that might be his future career."

Had he applied himself to his job with the same passion he showed in the cockpit, Cunningham might have risen through the ranks to wear an admiral's stripes or command an operational fleet squadron on a carrier, but, as before, Cunningham's focus was himself. Most Pentagon employees kept photos of their families or loved ones on their desk. Cunningham's photos were all of himself, and they faced outward, toward the visitor. Neighbors living next to the home Cunningham rented in Virginia were puzzled by the aviator who went around passing out glossy photos of himself.

His boss, Ramsay Lawson, was unimpressed; Cunningham applied himself only when he had to and was nothing more than a big blowhard. Lawson felt Nancy Cunningham was the equally self-important wife of the Vietnam ace. Cunningham's colleagues soon found themselves wondering about him. How had he wound up in an office packed with some of the Navy's brightest? They swiftly wrote him off and started having fun at his expense. Cunningham's desk was tucked behind a wall and couldn't be seen from the doorway to the office. One of his coworkers would walk in and ask, "Where's the prince?"

"It's Duke, God damn it," Cunningham would growl from his desk. "It's Duke."

A few years after his stint at the Pentagon ended, he was posted to an out-of-the-way Navy station in the Philippines. While there, he was sent to Korea as a Navy liaison and spoke to Korean pilots about his experience in Vietnam. His fame as an ace still got him invited to speak to military pilots in Thailand, Canada, and the U.S. Air Force. "Commander Cunningham is an invaluable Navy asset that should be utilized to the fullest," a commander wrote in 1982. Although he held the rank of commander, the Navy had doubts about Cunningham's fitness for command of an operational squadron. In a clear measure of Cunningham's failings, he had applied for command and been turned down.

Ron McKeown, Cunningham's former commander at Top Gun, heard what was happening and felt it reflected badly on the Navy. McKeown called up several admirals he knew and told them the Navy couldn't treat Cunningham this way. He was no fan of Cunningham's, but he respected what the man had done in the air. "I mean, he's an asshole, but he's an ace, and the Navy doesn't look good," McKeown told them. Why not give Cunningham a squadron to command for a year and let him retire? He didn't deserve it, but at least the Navy would show that it could be gracious. McKeown's message got through. The Navy plucked Cunningham from obscurity and sent him back to Miramar for his first command.

McKeown never told Cunningham what he had done, and Cunningham continued to blame McKeown for ruining his career by giving him poor ratings in his fitness reports. Years later, after he retired from the military, Cunningham approached McKeown in a big crowd at the annual Tailhook Convention and asked to speak with him. Jack Ensch, who was standing nearby, thought Cunningham was going to take a swing. Instead, Cunningham stuck out his hand and apologized. He had learned what McKeown had done. It was the one time, McKeown said, that Cunningham had shown a bit of class.

On June 6, 1985, a Navy band was playing patriotic music as the invited guests took their seats in the hangar of Fighter Squadron 126 at Miramar Naval Air Station. Hanging from the rafters, an enormous American flag formed the backdrop to the day's festivities. Dressed in their crisp, white uniforms, members of the squadron stood ready to welcome Randy Cunningham into his first command.

Following Navy tradition, Nick Criss, the outgoing commander, presented the troops to Cunningham. Criss and Cunningham walked alongside the nearly three hundred members of the squadron, who were lined up on a U-shaped platform that ringed the guests. Criss had some qualms about handing command over to Cunningham, who had failed to do much of anything during the eighteen months he had served as Criss's executive officer. Cunningham wasn't the worst executive officer Criss had ever seen, not by a long shot. But a bad executive officer was one thing; a bad commanding officer could be disastrous.

For the first time in Cunningham's nearly two-decade-long Navy career, there would be no one there to clean up his mess if he got into trouble. If the squadron had a serious problem, Criss feared that Cunningham wouldn't be around to handle it. Criss had gone so far as to voice his concerns to the chief of staff for Adm. Thomas J. Cassidy, who oversaw the squadron. Cassidy's chief of staff told Criss that the Navy wanted Cunningham in command of VF-126 to capitalize on his public relations value. Once again, the Navy was willing to lower its standards when it came to its ace.

As Criss and Cunningham walked past the troops, Criss scanned the guests, glancing at his family, friends, and fellow officers, almost all of whom were in uniform. In the last row of seats, Criss spotted two young men wearing shiny, black leather jackets with ties and aviator sunglasses, who stood out from the well-dressed crowd.

He turned to Cunningham. "Are those friends of yours?"

"No," Cunningham replied. "I thought they were with you."

When the ceremony ended, the two young men introduced themselves. They were actors starring in a movie that was being filmed that summer at Miramar, and the Navy had sent the pair to the change-of-command ceremony to get a feel for the base. One of the two, short, with dark hair, flashed a big white smile. He seemed surprised to find himself starring in a movie about fighter pilots. Criss felt as if he were talking to his son. The name Tom Cruise meant nothing to him. Neither did the name of Cruise's costar, Anthony Edwards.

Cruise and Edwards followed along to the official change-of-command reception at the Miramar Officers' Club and spent more than an hour chatting with Criss and Cunningham. Cunningham gave the two actors free signed copies of his book, *Fox Two*. It had taken more than ten years, but the book had finally been published the previous year by an aviation museum in Arizona. Cunningham must have been impressed with the pair. It was a rare day when a visitor left with a copy of *Fox Two* without paying for it.

Cunningham had seemed uninterested in his largely bureaucratic job, as had been the case throughout his career, when he reported for duty as Fighter Squadron 126's executive officer in January of 1984. Cunningham had almost immediately requested permission to make three cross-country trips to give his talk about his exploits in Vietnam to the Air Force. The Navy, Criss said, had gotten tired of hearing Cunningham's story, but it was still new to the Air Force. Criss told Cunningham he was needed around the squadron to do his job, and Cunningham reluctantly agreed to stay.

Cunningham struck Criss as a bad blend of qualities: impulsive and not very bright. Criss had been aware of Cunningham throughout his career. After graduating from Princeton in 1967, Criss had been sent to Miramar and flown over Vietnam at the same time as Cunningham, but their paths never crossed. Like everyone else in the Navy, Criss had been awed by what Cunningham had done in combat, but he had also heard that Cunningham was riding his fifteen minutes of fame a bit too long.

Typically, Criss, as commanding officer of the squadron, got to have a say in who would be his executive officer, the number two position in the unit and his successor as commander. Cunningham had, however, been chosen for him personally by Navy Secretary John Lehman, who said he had selected Cunningham for his abilities as a natural fighter pilot and an ace. A good executive officer, Criss believed, should take care of all the mundane administrative tasks and leave the commanding officer free to worry about bigger things. It was clearly the wrong job for Cunningham, who showed his distaste for paperwork by not doing any of it.

His office was an administrative black hole, and any important paperwork that found its way in there never emerged. Still, Cunningham was liked by the pilots in the squadron. He knew enough to let people do their jobs and not get in their way most of the time, and his officers, in return, looked out for him. Recognizing that Cunningham had a "tendency to drift," the officers had an informal "Duke Patrol" to keep track of where he was and what he was up to. Later, as commander, Cunningham had an excellent executive officer, who handled all the important administrative work and left Cunningham free to do as he pleased.

For Cunningham, as before, that meant flying and advancing his own image. While Tom Cruise was on the base filming *Top Gun*, Cunningham had his maintenance crews back up an A-4 Skyhawk in front of the squadron's hangar. The enormous flag from the change-of-command ceremony was hung in the background, and Cruise and Cunningham, both dressed in flight suits, clambered up on the wing and posed for photos. But, despite his claims to the contrary, Cunningham had little to do with the movie.

Other officers suspected that their new commander had to report to his real boss, Nancy, who kept her husband on a tight leash. Nancy was unpopular with many of the squadron officers and their wives; she came across as cold and aloof, with a bearing that made others feel she was looking down on them. "She was the ice woman, man," said T. J. Davis, a former pilot in the squadron.

Nancy had a fondness for jewelry. At a welcoming party the night Cunningham took command, she arrived with two enormous pieces of gold jewelry around her neck. Many pilots gave their loved ones "sweetheart wings," a half-inch gold replica of the wings the aviators wore. Nancy's wings were enormous, about three times the size of the wings a pilot wore. She also had on a gold replica of the badge that commanders such as her husband wore. An actual badge is about the size of a quarter; Nancy's was the size of an Olympic gold medal. Nancy always seemed to be wearing huge amounts of jewelry. She might have on a half dozen bracelets, eight or nine necklaces. "She invented bling," Davis said. The junior officers in the squadron took to calling her Mrs. T, after the Mohawk-wearing actor Mr. T, who was famous for the piles of gold jewelry he wore around his neck.

At Fighter Squadron VF-126, Cunningham was beginning to show signs of greed in his private life. One day, Cunningham called the squadron's safety officer, Bob Clement, and asked him to accompany him to Long Beach, where the Federal Aviation Administration was hosting an annual meeting for civilian pilots. More than one thousand people were expected to attend, and Cunningham was the guest speaker. Cunningham was much in demand for lectures following the publication of *Fox Two*. Clement, a blue-eyed pilot with a warm smile, was happy to join Cunningham, the man he had once idolized. As a young officer flying the F-14 at Miramar in the mid-1970s, he had seen the Navy's ace, but had been too afraid to talk to him. Cunningham was larger-than-life, the Navy superstar, the hero, the MiG killer, the best Navy pilot there was.

Before he headed into the Long Beach auditorium, Cunningham

popped open the trunk of his car. The trunk held boxes of *Fox Two* and canvas Bank of America money bags, weighed down with cash and coins. Clement helped him unload the bags and the books at a small table by the stage.

Halfway through his talk, Cunningham took a break for an intermission. He instructed Clement to ask people in line for a book to spell their names. Clement was to write the name down on a note in the front of the book so Cunningham could spell it correctly. Each book cost $20.

"You collect the money," Cunningham told him. "No checks, cash only."

"What if somebody has a check?"

"You tell them to cash it with somebody else in line, a friend, otherwise they don't get a book because I'm not taking checks."

Clement helped sell a few hundred books, collecting the money and stuffing it into the canvas bank bags. Cunningham took to the stage again, and when he was finished, Clement helped sell another couple hundred books. By the end of the night, he guessed he had sold at least six hundred copies.

The next morning, Clement reported to the squadron at eight o'clock. As soon as he set foot in the door, the duty officer told him that Cunningham wanted to see him. Clement walked into Cunningham's office thinking his commanding officer wanted to thank him for his help or ask him what he thought of the talk.

"I'm fifty dollars short," Cunningham told Clement.

"Fifty dollars short?" Clement asked. The amount didn't even make sense since it would mean that Cunningham was missing the equivalent of two and a half books.

"Yeah, I'm fifty dollars short. Either a book's missing or we didn't get the money someplace, but I'm fifty dollars short."

Clement was flabbergasted. The canvas money bags were full of coins and cash. Was Cunningham sure how much money he had going into the lecture? Yes, Cunningham said, he knew exactly how much he had. He had stayed up the night before counting his money.

Was it possible, Cunningham asked, that Clement might have some money stuffed in a pocket of the uniform he had been wearing the previous evening? Clement didn't think so, but he told Cunningham he would check when he got home that evening.

"No, I want you to go home *now* and check," Cunningham said.

Clement turned around, drove to his home in the northern suburbs of San Diego, and checked his Navy uniform. He found no money and drove back to the squadron to report the news to Cunningham. "Well," Cunningham repeated, "I'm fifty dollars short." Clement wasn't sure what he was supposed to do. It almost seemed as if Cunningham expected him to write a check. Clement never did, but several times over the next few weeks, Cunningham came up to him and asked if he had ever found that $50.

Half of all the royalties Cunningham collected on the book were supposed to go to his coauthor, Jeffrey Ethell, an aviation historian who had helped smooth out the rough spots in the narrative. Initially, Cunningham kept up his end of the bargain. By 1991, however, Ethell had angrily confided to another aviation writer, Bob Dorr, that Cunningham had stopped paying him royalties. Six years later, Ethell died in a P-38 plane crash.

The glow that young pilots such as Clement had once seen around Cunningham was beginning to fade. Cunningham was a likable guy, but he wasn't much of a leader, and he could show a stunning lack of knowledge in the cockpit. One time, Cunningham was flying an A-4 Skyhawk with a photographer in his backseat to snap photos of a squadron's return to Miramar from an overseas deployment. As family members had gathered on the airfield below to welcome the squadron home with signs, balloons, and flowers, the usual fanfare for a military homecoming, Cunningham rolled his plane over for a better view. Suddenly, he radioed, "Mayday, Mayday," and said his plane was chugging and stalling. He safely landed the plane, then figured out what had happened. Cunningham had either forgotten or failed to realize that, unlike newer planes, the older A-4 wasn't designed to fly upside down. By rolling the plane over, Cunningham had run the plane out of fuel.

Some of the squadron's top-notch pilots found they could beat Cunningham in the air simply by arousing his anger. T. J. Davis found Cunningham incredibly competitive, almost frighteningly so. As they got ready to fly, Davis would jokingly tell Cunningham he was going to kick his butt. Veins would pop out on Cunningham's forehead, his face would get red, and his breathing would become heavy. Pilots soon learned to push Cunningham's buttons to get him so mad that he would be overly aggressive in the air and bleed out all his airspeed, zooming around trying to beat everyone. "There was nothing better than beating the Duke," Davis said. Clement noticed that when Cunningham lost, he disappeared: "When there was anything that was an embarrassment to Duke, you couldn't find Duke."

Anger made Cunningham weak. Some of the pilots in the squadron liked to play a dice game called Klondike. The game could get serious quickly and become incredibly expensive; car keys had been handed over. One time, when the squadron was in Yuma, Arizona, Davis was playing Klondike with Cunningham and six other men. After a few plays, everyone dropped out except for Davis and Cunningham. Cunningham lost. "Double or nothing," he said. He lost again, and the pot grew once more. After several games of double or nothing, the pot had grown to $600. Veins were popping out on Cunningham's forehead, and Davis found himself silently rooting for his commanding officer.

"Oh, God," he thought as Cunningham rolled the dice again. "Please, please win. Please win." Finally, Cunningham did. Davis was relieved. The money didn't matter to him. He wanted to avoid his commander's wrath. Davis never played Klondike again.

For a man who shared a nickname with tough-guy actor John Wayne, Cunningham could also be remarkably thin-skinned. Fighter Squadron VF-126, like many other squadrons, kept a notebook, a "hit log" to record instances of buffoonery or stupidity by its members for posterity. No one was immune. Two former Vietnam prisoners of war had run the squadron, and they had come in for their share of ribbing in the squadron's hit log. After taking command, Cunningham had attempted to write something funny in the log, but his English was so tortured it made almost no sense. In the log's next entry, someone in the squadron wrote, "Just a classic case of the rare disease Dukelexia." Cunningham lit up when he saw that. He demanded to know who had written it, and when no one came forward, he took the log into his office. "It's the end of the hit log," Cunningham told the squadron. "I destroyed it and it will not return."

Cunningham was something of a loner. Fraternizing among fighter pilots, often over cocktails at the Miramar Officers' Club, was almost part of the job. The pilot who didn't socialize with his commanding officer could pay the price in his fitness reports, but the men in Cunningham's squadron rarely saw their squadron leader outside of work. He didn't socialize at the Officers' Club, where he and Nancy had met; instead he preferred to go off by himself on hunting trips in a customized van. He disapproved of the drinking and rowdiness that was a huge part of fighter pilot culture. Case in point was the 1985 Tailhook convention. Each year, Navy aviators gathered in Las Vegas for a meeting sponsored by the Tailhook Association, named for the hook beneath Navy aircraft that caught the arresting wire during carrier landings. Navy squadrons hosted "hospitality suites" at the Las Vegas Hilton that served up alcohol, huge quantities of alcohol.

The 1985 convention became known as the Year of the Kamikaze for the mixed drinks that the Top Gun hospitality suite dished out by the gallon. Those who swallowed fifteen over the three-day convention earned a headband similar to the one Japanese kamikaze pilots wore during World War II. Being fighter pilots, they competed to be the first to win the headband, with some downing all fifteen kamikazes on the first night of the convention. The Top Gun suite ran out of alcohol. It was madness. Pilots wandered out of control through the third floor of the Hilton, and Las Vegas strippers joined the party. One of the female officers in Cunningham's squadron said someone had reached out and grabbed her ass as she walked down the hallway. Cunningham wrote to the board, urging them to get the convention under control:

> As a member of the board as a professional aviator I feel that several issues should be reviewed and corrected by the association prior to Hook 86. I viewed with disdain the conduct or better put the misconduct of several officers and a lack of command attention which resulted in damage and imprudent action.
>
> A. The encouragement of drinking contests, the concept of having to drink 15 drinks to win a headband and other related activities produced walking zombies that were viewed by the general public and detracted from the Association/USN integrity.
> B. Damage to the Hilton should not be tolerated and restitution should be made by the command in charge of the suite.
> C. Dancing girls performing lurid sexual acts on Naval aviators in public would make prime conversation for the media . . .

I am proud to state that the VF-126 Bandits were there in force and not one won a headband.

The Tailhook board failed to heed Cunningham's prescient letter. The outrageously lewd behavior at the 1991 Tailhook Convention was a disaster for the Navy. More than 80 women and 7 men were assaulted, and 117 officers were implicated in acts of indecent assault, indecent exposure, and other charges. The careers of 14 admirals and almost 300 naval aviators were ruined by Tailhook.

While he was lecturing the military about drunken pilots, Cunningham was ignoring a problem much closer to home. His son, Todd, was now a sixteen-year-old who had gotten into trouble with drugs while living with his mother in St. Louis. Todd was placed in a drug treatment center in San Diego in 1986, where he would be close to his father, but Randy refused to pay. "You wanted full custody, you pay for it," he told his ex-wife. When Susan traveled out to San Diego to meet with Todd and the therapists working with him, she discovered that Randy had never bothered to show up to visit his son.

In his final year of command, the squadron was training in Fallon, Nevada, more than hour's drive from Reno, when Cunningham decided to take his pilots on a tour of the infamous Mustang Ranch, Nevada's first and largest licensed brothel. Cunningham acted like a Boy Scout leader, taking his troop on a mission of discovery, and T. J. Davis found the whole experience surreal. What was Cunningham thinking? Why was he taking his men on a tour of a brothel? At the gate, bodyguards with two .357 magnums strapped to their legs stood guard. As Cunningham and his men walked into the whorehouse, the prostitutes who weren't entertaining customers lined up and smiled at them. Cunningham introduced his men to the owner, Dave Burgess, a childhood friend of Nancy's.

The brothel visit was especially strange, given Cunningham's new-found faith. Davis, a boisterous patron of the Miramar Officers' Club, had once gotten a strange lecture with religious overtones from Cunningham. "Is your life on track?" his commanding officer asked. "Are you doing the right thing?" His only response was "Yes, sir," but in the back of his head, Davis recalled thinking, "Man, this is weird."

In *Fox Two,* Cunningham had described how his friend Dan McKinnon had introduced him to Hal Lindsey, an evangelist who forecast the coming of Armageddon. Cunningham met Lindsey in 1972 on a motorcycle weekend with McKinnon. Together with McKinnon, Lindsey and his wife, Jan, helped bring a lost pilot to God:

> I asked the Lord to come into my life and take over. I had run things so far and it was a total mess. There was certainly no doubt about the sin question—I had done enough of that. The forgiveness was complete as He washed inside me. Sure, the problems didn't go away, but the Spirit of God had entered me to run the show. And being a new Christian wasn't easy, either. Dan, Hal, and Jan never left me alone to flounder around. They always encouraged me to face things with the Lordship of Christ in mind, rather than selfish ambition. That was tough for an ego-centered guy like me. But it had been tough for another guy Dan introduced to me— Johnny Cash. Wow, had *he* been through some rough times before he finally made peace with God and himself. . . . These three couples had much to do with my keeping that promise to God. As a result, my life has meaning again; much more than it had before.

Not everyone in the squadron thought Cunningham a buffoon. Charles Nesby, a lieutenant commander in VF-126, found his commanding officer to be an exceedingly fair man. Nesby, the son of one of the Tuskegee airmen of World War II, was the lone African-American in Cunningham's squadron and, for that matter, at Miramar for many years. At the time, Nesby said, an unspoken rule dictated that no matter how well he performed in his duties, as an African-American he could never rate higher than number two. Cunningham didn't let that bother him. In 1987, he rated Nesby the top officer in the squadron.

Doing well in that job allowed Nesby to screen for command of an air wing, and he retired with the rank of captain. Later, he told Cunningham how much he appreciated what he had done for him. According to Nesby, who remains a loyal friend, Cunningham put more minorities in the service academies than the Hispanic and African-American caucuses combined. Cunningham sponsored Nesby for his job as director for minority affairs at the Veterans Affairs from 2001 through 2005.

Randy Cunningham's Navy career came to an end in April of 1987. In addition to the Navy Cross, Cunningham had been awarded over his career two Silver Stars, a Purple Heart, fifteen Air Medals, three Navy Commendation Medals, and a Presidential Unit Citation, to name but a few. His retirement was noted in Congress, where Congressman Duncan Hunter from San Diego paid tribute to the career of "the original Top Gun." Before Cunningham said farewell, Gregg Southgate stopped by to wish his old friend well. He had been with Cunningham on the USS *America* when Cunningham had gotten socked in the face, and he was there on the USS *Constellation* to congratulate Cunningham the day he became an ace. Southgate had served with Cunningham at Miramar as a fellow instructor at Top Gun, but Cunningham was no longer the person he once knew.

It wasn't that Cunningham wasn't a nice person—he was, and Southgate felt that Cunningham would have done anything for him, but, at the same time, Cunningham was in a different world. Cunningham had gotten so full of himself that he'd lost sight of what and who he was. The war was over and other pilots like Southgate had moved on to new challenges, but Cunningham's world continued to revolve around May 10, 1972, the moment of his greatest triumph. Becoming an ace had come to define him. The events of that day had opened doors, but Southgate saw that Cunningham seemed unable to move on, and instead of letting go, Cunningham held on tighter and tighter to that moment. He now seemed stuck in time, like an insect in amber. "Randy never got out of that moment, quite frankly," Southgate said. "That was his undoing."

Although the Navy clearly bent the rules for its ace and fueled his oversize sense of self-worth, there were limits, even if some of his comrades felt he got away with too much. The Navy recognized that Cunningham was not fit to wear an admiral's stripes. He retired as a commander, which many took as a sign that his personal flaws had gotten in the way of a career that should have been on a glide path to the Navy's uppermost ranks. "There was always somebody there to check his six, to cover for him, to keep him inside the lifelines," said Jack Ensch, Cunningham's former executive officer at Top Gun.

3

Voters Deal an Ace

Highly decorated military veterans often find work in San Diego's large defense community, but Cunningham returned instead to the academic life he left behind twenty years earlier. He was hired as dean of the flight school at National University in San Diego, which enrolled many veterans. A colleague recalled that Cunningham spent most of his time out of the office, giving speeches, as he had done in the Navy. Former Navy comrades spotted him at air shows hawking his book. He seemed to be a man searching for something to do.

On July 5, 1987, churchgoers filled the seats at the West Coast Church in Mission Viejo for a ceremony that mixed songs and prayers with patriotic celebration. Several members of the congregation wore their uniforms to show their pride in their service. After an American flag rose beneath an arch of red, white, and blue balloons, Randy Cunningham, the guest speaker, addressed the congregation.

The runaway success of the movie *Top Gun* had reignited interest in naval aviation and Cunningham's exploits during Vietnam. His well-honed tale had changed with his recognition that a fifteen-year-old war story held less interest for the audience than Tom Cruise and the blockbuster film that was still fresh on their minds. The congregants at West Coast Church did not go away disappointed as the Cunningham inflated his legend once more.

Cunningham said he had a role in the research for the movie, although he almost backed out since he didn't want to do anything to jeopardize his job as commander. He told churchgoers that a scene in the movie where Cruise flies upside down over a Soviet plane was based on one of his maneuvers over the Sea of Japan. He declared the movie a success because it showed the professionalism involved. "Most movies show officers as buffoons," Cunningham said.

That same year, Cunningham starred in a documentary, *Top Gun: The Story Behind the Story.* Appearing glassy-eyed, Cunningham stood in front of a parked plane as he narrated his well-honed tale of his dogfight over Vietnam, using his hands to tell the story. The photo of Cruise and Cunningham posing together found its way into the film.

When National University gutted its aviation program, Cunningham switched jobs in early 1988 to become a marketing consultant for the university. In July, he was out of the office yet again, flying beside an eleven-year-old Californian who was attempting to become the youngest pilot to cross the Atlantic. Chris Mooney, the son of a commercial airline pilot, had, at age ten, become the youngest aviator to fly across the United States, a feat that was upstaged a few months later by a nine-year-old boy. When Chris decided to repeat Charles Lindbergh's 1927 transatlantic flight, the boy and his mother recruited Cunningham after meeting him at an air show. "A lot of people think this is a lark, but this a very serious thing that Chris is doing, and the potential for hazard is always there," Cunningham said.

Cunningham limited Chris's flying time to eight hours at a stretch as the forty-six-year-old ace and his eleven-year-old charge hop-scotched their way to Paris. Their arrival at Le Bourget airfield was delayed one day when the single-engine Mooney 252 experienced engine trouble and bad weather with low visibility near Greenland. Cunningham said he was forced to take over the controls to fly the plane fifty miles back to Greenland. Cunningham had trouble finding the airfield on Greenland's southeast coast. "I didn't think I was going to live," he said. They landed safely in Paris the following day.

A few months later, Cunningham resigned from National University. Out of work, he fell back on his most precious asset, his fame from Vietnam. He gave three or four speeches a week and commanded tens of thousands of dollars in speaking fees through the Washington Speakers Bureau. Cunningham started a home business, Top Gun Enterprises, out of a $435,000 home he purchased in 1987 with his wife in the wealthy seaside community of Del Mar. He sold aviation knickknacks, including copies of his speeches and tapes, lithographs of himself, a Top Gun baseball cap, and the $595 Randy "Duke" Cunningham Ace Kalinga Style Buck Knife. The business did well; he later valued it at between $250,000 and $500,000. But it wasn't enough for Cunningham. He began to give serious thought to a career in politics.

For years, Congressman Duncan Hunter of San Diego had been trying to persuade Cunningham to run for office. Tall, dark, and gruff, Hunter was an outsider, a product of Southern California's ranch country who looked as if he had ridden into Washington from the backcountry and slept in his suit to get there. Hunter's father, a Southern California real estate developer, had made an unsuccessful bid for Congress, but the lessons he learned helped his thirty-one-year-old son unseat a long-serving Democratic incumbent in 1980. Instead of siding with the GOP moderates in the House, Hunter aligned himself with the brash revolutionary Newt Gingrich, who famously declared that the only way to seize control of the House of Representatives was to wreck it. Hunter was an early member of Gingrich's Conservative Opportunity Society, a group of conservative Republicans that laid the groundwork for the 1994 GOP takeover of the House. Hunter also nursed powerful ambitions that would much later lead him to take the bold step of running for president.

Hunter and Cunningham got along well. They loved to fish and hunt, and they were cut from the same ideological cloth. Both men were deeply patriotic with an abiding love of the military, and both Hunter and Cunningham had absorbed the values of the rural communities in which they were raised. Hunter, a native of Riverside, California, had earned a Bronze Star in Vietnam, where he served with the 173rd Airborne and 75th Army Rangers, and in Congress he served on the House Armed Services Committee. Unlike Cunningham, however, Hunter was humble about his own military service. He rarely spoke about it to friends and insisted time and again that he "just showed up."

By reputation, congressmen are terrible judges of candidates, but Hunter knew he had something in Cunningham. Taking Cunningham under his wing, he introduced him to the campaign trail in 1988 at an appearance in Florida for Republican Connie Mack, who was running for the Senate. He brought Cunningham to Washington in 1989 for the inauguration of George H. W. Bush, where he told Dee Dee Castro, a campaign aide, "I want to get this guy to run for Congress."

Cunningham has said he wrestled with his decision whether to run. According to a former aide, Nancy was concerned, too, knowing how her husband could easily be swayed, a tendency that could land him in trouble in Congress. She worried about the lack of privacy for her young daughters, now eight and eleven. Cunningham, however, seemed as though he could hardly wait. In 1988, his name was leaked to the local press as a potential challenger to Representative Jim Bates, and the following year he said he was looking for a house in Bates's district. "I was told today, 'Don't say you're going to run for Congress, Duke,' so I won't," he said. As if he lacked for encouragement, former president Ronald Reagan called and personally asked him to run.

At the age of forty-eight, Randy Cunningham became a politician. He announced his candidacy for California's Forty-fourth Congressional District—the first office he ever ran for—in February of 1990. Hunter, who had won election in the same district a decade earlier, served as his campaign chairman. Cunningham was against drugs, for education and protecting Social Security, but the centerpiece of his platform was his support for a strong military. Even as the Berlin Wall lay in ruins, Cunningham remained suspicious of the Soviet Union. "It certainly doesn't make sense to immediately throw thousands of persons in defense-related jobs out of work and make our country militarily weak without being sure of the final outcome of the revolution taking place over there," he said as he announced his candidacy. "The way of the future is liberty, not communism or continued aggression. Our government must take the necessary steps to hasten the demise of communism and dictatorships in this hemisphere."

Cunningham wore the mantle of the war hero during the campaign and spoke emotionally about taking another human life. His brochures included the photo he had taken with Tom Cruise, and he passed off his embellishments and exaggerations as truth, claiming in his first official announcement that "his experiences were the subject of much of the movie *Top Gun*." He also spoke of his "Christian family values," and Cunningham attended Billy Graham rallies and professed to be born-again. "Maybe I'm made of mom and apple pie, but that's really how I am," Cunningham told *The San Diego Union-Tribune*. Outside of the Navy, few doubted that.

His main opponent in the June Republican primary was Joe Ghougassian, an Egyptian-born Armenian who had run the Peace Corps in North Yemen and served as U.S. ambassador to Qatar. While in Qatar, Ghougassian said he had been recruited to run for Congress and began to test the waters after returning home. He solicited support from local leaders, including Hunter, who invited him to an annual barbecue at his home in Alpine, in the mountains east of San Diego. When Ghougassian told him of his plans to run for Congress, Hunter asked if he knew Randy Cunningham, who was also running.

Ghougassian had not heard that Cunningham was going to be a candidate. He arranged a meeting with Cunningham, who was blunt. "Yeah, I'm going to run and I want you out of the race, because I'm going to take you down," Cunningham told him. Falling back on his diplomatic experience, Ghougassian chose his words carefully and told Cunningham that he had a head start raising money and many people were committed to his campaign. Cunningham wasn't swayed, and later he called Ghougassian at home. "I want you out of this race. You're not going to make it. I am simply going to knock you out. You don't know who you're dealing with," Cunningham said. Ghougassian took it as a threat.

One of Ghougassian's staffers, Salvador Viesca, wrote Tom Cruise to let him know that Cunningham was using his photo in his brochures. Cruise's lawyer told Cunningham to stop. According to Cunningham, the lawyer also told him Cruise no longer shared his values, which Cunningham attributed to Cruise's performance as Ron Kovic in *Born on the Fourth of July*, the story of a disabled Vietnam veteran who became an antiwar activist. Cunningham explained Cruise's response by saying that he felt Cruise might have gotten a bit too wrapped up in playing the part of Kovic.

Even more revealing, a check of voting records showed that Cunningham had not registered to vote between 1966 and 1988. At a gathering of the conservative, pro-business Lincoln Club, Ghougassian revealed Cunningham's voting record. Taken by surprise, Cunningham went on the defensive and tried, lamely, to rebut the charge by claiming that as a pilot he was out of the country "basically as a captive of the U.S. Navy." Embarrassed and furious, Cunningham again called Ghougassian at home.

"Now it is war," Cunningham told him. "You should not have done that, Joseph, because now I'm going to be all over you."

Ghougassian, too, had his problems. Ghougassian was losing the support of his lone paid staffer, Salvador Viesca, who was growing more and more fond of Cunningham. Viesca found Ghougassian to be pompous, arrogant, and self-serving. For example, Ghougassian never revealed his position on abortion to Viesca until the day before a pro-life rally when Ghougassian announced he opposed abortion. Ghougassian attended the rally and tried, without success, to address the crowd.

Cunningham, who opposed abortion in most cases, was a scheduled speaker at the rally and approached Viesca and asked whether Ghougassian was going to address the crowd. Viesca explained that his boss had not let people know what his position was in time. Cunningham then asked Viesca if he wanted Ghougassian to speak, and Viesca said yes, it was the right thing to do. "Consider it done," Cunningham said, and went off to talk to the rally organizers. When he returned, he said Ghougassian had been added to the list of speakers.

"Duke, I really appreciate it," Viesca said.

"Salvador, it's the right thing to do."

Ghougassian had seen Viesca speaking with Cunningham. "I don't want you fraternizing with the enemy," Ghougassian said.

"The enemy just got you to be a speaker," Viesca told him.

Cunningham showed that he could also be a vicious campaigner.

Although he had a strong lead and appeared headed for a primary victory, Cunningham wanted to bury Ghougassian for embarrassing him during the campaign. "I'll make sure he never makes it for dogcatcher," he told a campaign staffer. A few weeks before the primary, voters received a mailer that asked:

Which candidate for Congress is bankrolled by Arab oil interests?

Joe Ghougassian, candidate for U.S. Congress, was born and raised in the Middle East and has been out of the country for the last 8 years in Arab countries. He only returned about 9 months ago to run for Congress and has been influenced by Arab Oil interests.

The proof is in his campaign contributions. Joe Ghougassian has received thousands of dollars in campaign contributions from Arab Oil interests.

Remember the long lines at gas stations following the Arab oil embargo of 1973? We don't need a congressman bought and paid for by those interests, do we?

With its drawings of Saudi king Fahd, Libyan leader Col. Muammar el-Qaddafi, and an oil barrel dripping money, the brochure dashed any lingering hope for a Ghougassian victory. Six Arab-American contributors and a political action committee were listed, but the hit piece didn't mention that they gave only $1,750, little more than 1 percent of the more than $147,000 Ghougassian raised in the campaign. "It's garbage. It's racism, pure and simple," Ghougassian said. Cunningham tried to show he was no Arab-hater. "It's not bad to be an Arab," he said.

California governor George Deukmejian, a fellow Armenian, wrote Cunningham directly to express his disappointment. "I find your efforts to smear his long and excellent record of service to this nation uncalled for and beneath a person of your caliber," the governor wrote. Ed Rollins, the chairman of the National Republican Congressional Committee, said he was "appalled" by Cunningham's mailer. In a letter to Ghougassian, Rollins wrote, "Campaign smears that attack someone because of their racial, ethnic or religious background are outrageous, unacceptable and have no place in the party of Lincoln."

Crude as it was, the brochure was effective in painting Ghougassian as an Arab, not an ambassador. When phone-bank volunteers called seeking voter support for Ghougassian, they were told, "We're not going to vote for an Arab." The night of the June 5 primary, Cunningham told Ghougassian, "Joe, I want you to know you have been the toughest fighter in my life." Cunningham easily won the primary with 45 percent of the vote in a four-man race.

Brimming with confidence after his primary victory, Cunningham turned his attention to Democrat Jim Bates, a four-year incumbent. The odds were stacked against Cunningham. District boundaries had been drawn to favor Bates, and he held the advantage when it came to raising money, the oxygen of politics. In a rare moment of candor, Congressman John G. Rowland, a Connecticut Republican, told the Associated Press in 1990, "Let's face it. You have to be a bozo to lose this job."

Jim Bates, however, was a bozo. He humiliated his female campaign staffers, who fled his office in tears and finally complained to the House Ethics Committee. In the first case of its kind in Congress, an investigation in 1989 found Bates had sexually harassed two female staff members. One former staffer said Bates had straddled her leg between his and started moving up and down. He put his hand on the knee of another former staffer and grabbed her buttocks while giving her a hug. A third staffer, who unlike the others was not identified, related that Bates had asked if she would, "you know," if they were on a desert island. Bates had issued a statement apologizing for any "kidding and flirting which may have been misconstrued" and said he had sought professional guidance and counseling. In October, the Ethics Committee issued a formal letter of reproval—the mildest form of disciplinary action—and directed him to issue a written apology to two female staffers.

By his own admission, Bates was unaware of the changing climate of gender politics in Washington. Two events that would make sexual harassment a household word, the Navy's Tailhook scandal and the Anita Hill–Clarence Thomas Supreme Court confirmation hearings, were right around the corner, but Bates didn't have a clue. "I never felt somebody up. I never said, 'Sleep with me or lose your job.' I didn't even know what sexual harassment was, but I was kind of a womanizer," Bates said. As the investigation dragged on for two years, women were coming forward and claiming that Bates had come on to them. "It was probably true, you know. I'd come on to any girl," he told me.

Cunningham promised to restore integrity to the office. His simple but effective campaign slogan was "A Congressman We Can Be Proud Of," a message that reminded voters of Bates's problems. "This guy is a sexual pervert who's guilty as sin," Cunningham told the *Los Angeles Times*. "These women were violated. I don't need to bring that up because, by now, everybody knows what a jerk this guy is. He's a disgrace, unfit for public office." Cunningham dismissed Bates as "just another MiG, and an unethical one," and said he would "shoot down" his opponent during a debate, "knock him right out of the sky."

On the campaign trail, Cunningham continued to weave new threads into his legend. He claimed that as a swimming coach in Hinsdale High School, he had trained Olympic gold and silver medalists, something that had previously appeared in his official Navy biography. It was another of Cunningham's exaggerations. He had appropriated the achievements of Hinsdale's head coach, Don Watson, who had coached Olympic medalists. During the campaign, Watson didn't dispute what Cunningham was saying, but it wasn't true. "He didn't have anything to do with these Olympic swimmers," Watson told me.

While on the attack against Bates, Cunningham quietly hid any blemishes from his own past. On June 15, ten days after his primary victory, he joined his wife in filing a motion to seal the records from their aborted divorce in 1976. The Cunninghams told the court they feared that reporters or representatives of Bates's campaign could publish the contents of the divorce file, which could prove to be an embarrassment to the Cunninghams and their young children. Judge Daniel J. Tobin agreed to seal the file. Nancy was also concerned about appearances in other ways during the campaign. Cunningham's campaign staff noticed that when photos were taken of the family, Nancy always seemed to exclude Todd, Randy's adopted son from his first marriage.

Believing that he could handle anyone the GOP threw at him, Bates ran a lackadaisical campaign and made a series of critical mistakes. He had emptied his campaign accounts to win a tough Democratic primary and even overdrew his House bank account to buy TV time. His primary against former governor Jerry Brown's legal affairs secretary, Byron Georgiou, cost Bates a third of his voters — "the feministas," as he called them — and they never came back. Instead of campaigning, Bates spent most of his time in Washington, where Congress was dithering over the budget. Back in San Diego, two consultants with different ideas about the campaign were running Bates's reelection effort, a surefire recipe for trouble. "Everything went wrong in that campaign," according to Bates.

Too late, Bates realized he had badly underestimated Cunningham. In October, Ed Rollins, the chairman of the National Republican Congressional Committee, who had been "appalled" by Cunningham's anti-Arab mailer, called Bates out of the blue and told him that an internal Republican poll showed the race was extremely close, closer than Bates had realized. Bates had viewed the Navy ace as not too bright, and a poor match for the Democratic district. But Cunningham had a formidable ally in Congressman Hunter, who knew the district well and went to work on Cunningham's behalf, raising money and drawing on his extensive contacts. In contrast to Bates, Cunningham ran a smart campaign, targeting "Reagan Democrats" and evangelical Christians.

One of Hunter's ideas was to use area pastors to campaign for Cunningham. Hunter understood the power of evangelicals, since pastors and church members had helped him get elected to Congress a decade earlier by passing out two hundred thousand pieces of Hunter literature in the final two weeks of the campaign. In a letter to ministers inviting them to a September 4 meeting with Cunningham, Hunter wrote, "Duke Cunningham is a man with the highest character and integrity. I have personally known Duke for many years, and I know that he maintains the same high standard of conduct that we do. Once you ask him about his views on the relevant issues of today, I'm sure you'll feel as I do that Duke is a solid reflection of the strong morals and values of your family, your ministry and your local community." If Cunningham was going to win, Hunter wrote, it was crucial for pastors and their key laypeople to be organized and involved.

At the rally in the San Diego suburb of Bonita, Hunter, who had returned from a trip to Idaho that day in Cunningham's van, introduced his friend by comparing him to the Navy lieutenant played by William Holden in the 1954 film *The Bridges at Toko-Ri.* Cunningham took the microphone and professed his faith. "I've been traveling to the different churches and giving testimony," he said. "When they talk to you about wearing Jesus Christ on your sleeve, tell them there's only one way to do that, and that's over your whole body." He then launched into the story of Vietnam and how he'd found God.

Pastor Hal Lindsey talked of Satan's influence in America, the end of days, the danger of accepting homosexuality, and the importance of sending men like Randy Cunningham to Washington, "who once he gets there will not forget the principles that brought him there." Cunningham stands for all that made America great, Lindsey said, and the only way a God-fearing man like him could get into Congress against an incumbent was by a "miraculous effort" of Christian people. "That's the only organization Duke's really got," he said. Another pastor told Cunningham and the crowd that if the evangelical community was going to get out and "break their backs" for him like the Israelite forces marshaled by Gideon, "then we expect him to vote according to God's word and according to God's plan."

The San Diego Union-Tribune threw its considerable weight to Cunningham and dismissed Bates as a "fumbling legislator" mired in the "ethical swamp" on Capitol Hill. In an editorial titled "Voters Can Play an Ace," the newspaper noted, "The differences between the character of these two candidates could not be more stark. Throughout his campaign, Duke Cunningham has promised to be a congressman the people of the 44th District can be proud of. And with the help of enough voters who believe their ballots can in fact make a difference, Cunningham will get the chance."

The vote was extremely close. The final tally showed Cunningham with 1,665 more votes than Bates out of more than 200,000 votes cast. The evangelicals had likely made the difference in the election, which would be the closest of Cunningham's political career. Cunningham, like his mentor Congressman Hunter, consistently earned 100 percent ratings from the Christian Coalition throughout his career.

The Randy Cunningham who arrived in Washington in January 1991 was a congressman who believed he could make a difference. As he had promised in his campaign, he refused to accept a $28,500 pay raise that the House had voted for itself the year before. Instead, Cunningham directed the additional money to a checking account he'd set up in his district. He established a $150,000 annual fund that went to scholarships for low-income students, a health clinic and new church, and Barrio Station, a popular San Diego community center serving the city's poor neighborhoods. His staff included Hispanics, blacks, and other minorities reflecting the makeup of his district. And, in his early years in Congress, Cunningham disdained the crowd of lobbyists and congressmen who gathered at the Capital Grille, a steakhouse for seeing and being seen, preferring to spend nearly every weekend back in his district.

In his second week on the job, Cunningham had the kind of attention that other congressmen took decades to attract. He had arrived in time for a historic debate over whether to give President Bush the power to drive Saddam Hussein's troops out of Kuwait. His first remarks to the House on January 11 drew praise: "For those of us that have fought for life, and those that face death in Saudi Arabia, life has a special flavor that you, the protected, will never know." TV's *Today* show and CNN solicited his insights, as did *The Washington Post*'s top political reporters, David Broder and Haynes Johnson.

"For me, being a freshman in a minority party is just one more challenge," Cunningham told Barry Horstman in a glowing profile in the *Los Angeles Times*. "When I talked about getting some of my swimmers in the Olympics, people said it would never happen, but I ended up coaching a couple of gold medalists. Then they said I wouldn't be able to shoot down a MiG, but I did. They said crossing the Atlantic with an eleven-year-old pilot couldn't be done, but it was. And last year, they said there was no way a first-time candidate could beat an entrenched incumbent."

Cunningham paused and then smiled broadly as he surveyed his congressional office.

"Well, I'm here," he said. "And, when I leave this place in ten or twenty years, I think I'll have left my mark."

His first few weeks in Congress were not without missteps. Cunningham's office announced on January 18 that fifty or more "hardcore terrorists" were operating in the United States, including the San Diego area. The FBI took exception with Cunningham's statements, issuing a denial and warning against unduly alarming the public. When pressed for more details, Cunningham said he based his statements on intelligence sources he could not divulge, but no one in the area's congressional delegation could confirm it. For Arab-Americans, it only confirmed their suspicion that Cunningham had something against them. In another blunder, Cunningham introduced an amendment to a foreign aid bill at the wrong time and was forced to withdraw it. Instead of ensuring the House would approve sanctions against Jordan for supporting Iraq before the Gulf War, Cunningham ended up weakening the sanctions. Even so, his press secretary put out a release trumpeting the amendment's passage.

As he settled into his new life in Washington, Cunningham was a political novice and looked to others for guidance. Congressman Hunter continued to mentor him, and the two were such a pair that Democrats dubbed them Duke and Dunk. Cunningham joined the House Armed Services Committee, where Hunter also had a seat. He and Hunter voted the same way forty-three out of forty-four times during Cunningham's first four months in office. Frank Collins, who had been working as Hunter's district director, became Cunningham's chief of staff.

The two men were close, almost like brothers. They often appeared together at political fund-raisers. They hosted an annual pancake breakfast in Washington, where they would auction off the aprons they wore to raise money for their campaigns. For the first few years of Cunningham's political career, he voted in lockstep with his mentor, and when the two men publicly disagreed over an issue in 1991, it was news in San Diego.

In public, Hunter always showed his admiration for Cunningham, but in private he was not always so deferential. On one occasion in Hunter's office, when Cunningham spoke during a discussion on pending legislation, Hunter made it clear that Cunningham didn't know what he was talking about and should keep his mouth shut. "Duncan treated Randy Cunningham in such an incredibly condescending way that I was overwhelmingly uncomfortable," a former House staffer recalled. "He just treated him like he was the redheaded stepchild." Cunningham bowed his head and said nothing, and the former House staffer left feeling sorry for him.

Cunningham was just getting used to his new surroundings when the political map of California was redrawn. A panel of retired judges had been appointed to redraw districts when Republican governor Pete Wilson and the Democratic legislature failed to reach agreement on how best to reflect the population changes revealed in the 1990 census. When the maps were unveiled December 2, much of Cunningham's old Forty-fourth District had been folded in a new district designed to include as many minorities as possible. For a white Republican man, that spelled trouble. It was only a matter of time before he lost his seat, and Cunningham began to plot an extremely ambitious political gambit.

For Cunningham, a much more attractive possibility lay in a new district to the north. The Fiftieth District was overwhelmingly white and wealthy. This was Republican country, and whoever snapped up the district would enjoy a long career in Congress. It was perfect for Cunningham. The district also included Del Mar, where Cunningham still had his former residence, and Escondido, where his children attended school and his wife was a principal. There was one problem: much of the area had been represented in Congress for the past twelve years by Republican Bill Lowery.

Rarely do two incumbents from the same party face each other in a primary, since someone was sure to lose his seat in such a game of political chicken. Behind the scenes, however, Duncan Hunter was pushing Cunningham to run against Lowery. "In the machinations," reporter Mark Z. Barabak observed, "Cunningham's political guru, Republican Rep. Duncan Hunter of El Cajon, played Jeff Gillooly to Cunningham's Tonya Harding." Hunter had to move districts as well, decamping from his old home in the wealthy enclave of Coronado to a rural district to the east that stretched across the desert all the way to the Arizona border.

Hunter and Lowery did not like each other. They had both ridden Ronald Reagan's coattails into office in 1980, but they had such different personalities that they were almost destined to clash. Backslapping and gregarious, Lowery, at forty-four, was the slick political insider, while Hunter remained an outsider in the boisterous Gingrich camp. Hunter eschewed the party's old guard, led by House minority leader Robert Michel, but Lowery cultivated them. Lowery's loyalty had won him a seat on the Appropriations Committee, the supremely powerful body that dispensed the government's money. There was, it seemed, a touch of envy in Hunter's dislike of Lowery.

Lowery thought Cunningham lacked the gravitas to be a congressman and thought the ex-fighter pilot didn't stand a chance against Bates. When he heard Hunter was introducing Cunningham to key contacts in Washington, Lowery remarked, "Can you believe this ass-hole is walking Cunningham around?" Cunningham claimed that Lowery "actually fought against me" by telling other members of Congress that their support would be better directed to another candidate, who ultimately lost.

In December 1991, shortly after the new census maps were unveiled, Cunningham announced he would run against Lowery. With no time to waste before the Republican primary in June, which was shaping up to be the key test in the campaign, Cunningham immediately launched a highly aggressive campaign that made party leaders cringe. "It was like Lowery was flying a MiG and he was flying an F-86 and he was trying to shoot us down," said Joe Dolphin, Lowery's campaign manager. "Every time he would get around Lowery, he would start firing the machine gun and the rockets." While Lowery touted his experience during a televised debate, Cunningham attacked his rival as a "good old boy who will tell you one thing and do another" and had "no more than a high school degree." When the cameras were off, Lowery handed his opponent newspaper clips that Cunningham had said did not exist. Cunningham leaned toward Lowery and told him he was full of shit.

Once again, Cunningham had chosen his opponent well. Lowery was like a jack-in-the-box stuffed with scandals waiting to pop open at any moment. Lowery's campaign picked up the bill when the congressman spent sixty-six nights from 1984 to 1986 in a luxurious San Diego condominium owned by a defense contractor who later went to prison for defrauding the federal government. Lowery's ties to defunct savings and loan operators had nearly cost him his seat in 1988. Don Dixon, who looted his Texas savings and loan operation to pay for lavish homes, a Rolls-Royce, and call girls, had thrown a fundraiser for Lowery and funneled thousands into his campaign account. Lowery had barely won reelection in 1988 against a La Jolla psychiatrist who penned verse about his opponent: "Lowery took the loot, give him the boot!"

Unlike most politicians, Lowery enjoyed fund-raising and wouldn't hesitate to ask for money anywhere at any time. According to a long-time friend, he once asked a man urinating in the stall next to him for a contribution. Then, there were the women. Lowery didn't just have a zipper problem; he didn't have a zipper. An attractive San Diego campaign consultant once had a dalliance in college with Lowery, who wouldn't let it go. He picked her up in Washington at the airport in a new Lincoln Town Car with a bottle of champagne chilling in an ice bucket in the front seat. Another time he asked her on the phone, "Wanna order a pizza and fuck?" During a game of charades at a baby shower, he shocked his friends by pouring ketchup on his shirt and writhing on the ground to simulate childbirth. Even his friends called him Congressman Dirtbag.

Despite the enormous amount of baggage he carried, the Lowery campaign believed it could have survived with the likes of George Gorton, the consultant to Governor Wilson, on the team, but the House banking scandal dealt the congressman a knockout blow. The affair involved more than 350 members of the House who were over-drawing their House bank accounts without penalty. Some carried overdrafts for months, amounting to interest-free loans, while others took what amounted to unauthorized advances on their paychecks. Although no public money was involved and no formal House rules were broken, the scandal left the clear impression that lawmakers were abusing their privileges, and the public was outraged. Lowery had three hundred overdrawn checks worth $103,698 over three years. At an emotional news conference, Lowery and his wife, Katie, apologized profusely, prompting Hunter to remark, "The in thing now is to appear weeping before the press to draw on public sympathy."

Both Hunter and Cunningham had their own problems with the

House bank. Cunningham, who had insisted he was innocent in the scandal, expressed surprise when he learned that he had overdrawn his account by $1,000 to buy a new Ford Explorer from a car dealer in Pennsylvania. A check written on an account with insufficient funds at most banks would result in a bounced-check fee, but the House bank covered the fees or held overdrawn checks until members deposited enough money.

Cunningham produced a letter from the Ford dealer, which took responsibility for depositing the congressman's check right away instead of holding it for a week as he had asked. "I have worked hard to be accountable to the voters, to shoot straight on the tough issues and to behave in an honorable manner suited to the office I hold," Cunningham wrote in a letter to *The San Diego Union-Tribune* in October 1991.

Hunter refused to apologize for his problems with the House bank, which were even more troubling. He had overdrawn his account routinely since first taking office and admitted writing 407 overdrafts worth more than $129,000 over three years. A local scholarship fund to which he had contributed $12,000 since 1985 "paid" for the perk of free overdrafts and brought him into "moral balance" on the matter, he argued. Hunter set up a card table in March 1992 outside the courthouse in El Cajon, east of San Diego, to speak to his constituents, but after a few days he decided to put the matter to rest by returning half of his take-home pay to the U.S. Treasury. Hunter sued his Democratic opponent, Janet Gastil, for libel when she ran TV ads showing Hunter's face inside a bouncing ball, while an announcer accused him of kiting checks.

Unlike Cunningham and Hunter, however, Lowery's political career would not survive the scandal. The tracking polls now showed Cunningham ahead and gaining momentum. Clair Burgener, a patrician former San Diego congressman, met privately with Lowery in

Washington and told him that it would be best for the party if Lowery didn't continue in the race. Bowing to the inevitable, Lowery admitted he no longer had "the instinct for the jugular" and withdrew from the race on April 14. Cunningham's victory was a lock. The right-wing editorial board of the *Union-Tribune* endorsed him once again, as it would throughout the rest of his political career.

Back in Washington, a new enemy flew into Cunningham's sights in the fall of 1992. He told *The Washington Post*'s "Reliable Source" column that the entire leadership of the Democrat-controlled House should be "lined up and shot," a comment that, if nothing else, doomed his chances of passing any meaningful legislation. If the House leadership was bad, Bill Clinton drove Cunningham into hysterics. "Clinton was a Jane Fonda–Tim Hayden–Ramsey Clark draft evader and antiwar protester. I was shot down over Vietnam, Mr. Speaker, and I cannot imagine having a commander in chief that was a coward and an antiwar protester," Cunningham said on the House floor in September.

The following month, Cunningham and Hunter joined two other Republican congressmen, Sam Johnson, a former POW from Texas, and the ringleader, Robert Dornan, a redheaded, gravelly voiced conservative firebrand from Orange County, California, to attack the Democratic presidential nominee on the House floor. In a freewheeling, late-night, "special order" speech, Cunningham posed the "unanswered questions" about Clinton's 1969 visit to the Soviet Union while he was a Rhodes Scholar at Oxford. "Who did you meet with in Moscow?" Cunningham asked in a speech to an empty House chamber carried live on C-SPAN. "Are you willing, as a man, to admit that they might have been KGB agents who manipulated the whole peace movement in their country at least?"

Accusing a future president of being a KGB dupe angered many in

Cunningham's district. Some Republicans were disenchanted with Cunningham's "foolishness" with the KGB. "Cunningham boasts he has 'cut my own rudder' in politics, but critics prefer another nautical metaphor for the 50-year-old Republican: a loose cannon rolling around the deck of a ship," Gerry Braun wrote in *The San Diego Union-Tribune*. As anachronistic as his comments sounded to some, others nodded in silent approval. San Diego was a place where communist conspiracy theories had an unusually long shelf life. Members of the San Diego Padres, including pitcher Eric Show, were openly affiliated with the anticommunist John Birch Society. Some in San Diego still cling to the belief that adding fluoride to drinking water is a communist plot to ruin America. San Diego remains the largest metropolitan area in the United States that does not fluoridate its water.

Like Cunningham, President Bush was interested in Clinton's Moscow trip, and the president and his chief of staff, James Baker, met the four congressmen in the Oval Office on October 6, a month before the presidential election. "This is an issue that will kill Clinton when people realize what a traitor he is to this country," Cunningham told the president, according to an account the congressman provided to the *Los Angeles Times*. "In some countries, if something like this came out, he would be tried as a traitor. Tokyo Rose had nothing over Clinton." Baker laughed and later said the president must "remain aboveboard." The following day, however, Bush went on Larry King's CNN talk show and called on Clinton to "level with the American people." Bush's remarks were widely criticized and he promptly backtracked, saying he had not suggested anything unpatriotic, but the damage had been done.

Clinton skillfully used the incident during the first presidential debate in St. Louis on October 11 to make Bush's use of the Moscow trip seem like an act of McCarthyism. "You even brought some right-wing congressmen into the White House to plot how to attack me for going to Russia," Clinton said of Cunningham, Hunter, and company. "But when Joe McCarthy went around this country attacking people's patriotism, he was wrong. He was wrong. And a senator from Connecticut stood up to him named Prescott Bush. Your father was right to stand up to Joe McCarthy, you were wrong to attack my patriotism. I was opposed to the war but I loved my country, and we need a president who will bring this country together, not divide it."

Combat framed Cunningham's entire political life. "I urge you to help me in my battle for Christian values," read a June 1992 campaign ad. Democrats were just another MiG to be shot down, not colleagues who might be able to help him do some good. Bashing the next president got him attention, but at the cost of political capital that might benefit the people who had voted him into office.

Cunningham had marginalized himself as an ineffective legislator. How effective could he possibly be under a president for whom he had nothing but contempt and a Democratic leadership he thought merited the death penalty? Small wonder that none of the sixteen bills or resolutions Cunningham authored in his first two terms made it out of committee. As long as the Democrats were in power, Cunningham would be little more than a brash backbencher.

Feeling powerless, Cunningham resorted to bullying and bravado. During a debate on an appropriations bill in 1994, Cunningham exchanged some sharp words with Dave Obey, the powerful Democratic chairman of the House Appropriations Committee. "I do not like to be threatened, and if the individual wants to threaten, we can handle that real good," Cunningham told him. "If the gentleman wants to do something, he can just come right over here."

A frequent target of Cunningham's abuse was Democrat Bob Filner, who had taken over the San Diego district Cunningham had abandoned when he headed north to run against Bill Lowery. Filner, who had spent several months in a Southern jail as a Freedom Rider during the civil rights movement, was one of the House's more left-leaning members. Cunningham openly despised Filner. He called him a communist to his face and described him as a backstabber in an interview. Filner seemed afraid of Cunningham. "He attacked me once and he's on the verge of attacking me all the time," Filner confided once to a San Diego reporter. "He's crazy. There's always the incipient violence there. Everybody feels it, not just me."

4

The Brawl in the Hall

Four decades of Democratic control of the U.S. House of Representatives had come to a swift end in the midterm elections a month earlier, and a staggering fifty-four House seats swung from Democratic to Republican, including the district held by Tom Foley, who became the first Speaker of the House to go down in defeat since the Civil War era. Other powerful Democratic committee chairmen lost their seats as well, including former Ways and Means chairman Dan Rostenkowski, who had been indicted earlier in the year in the House post office scandal. Not one GOP incumbent lost.

Republicans could scarcely refrain from gloating. "Oh, what a beautiful morning," conservative William F. Buckley wrote at the end of 1994. The GOP had capitalized on a widely held perception that the House under Democratic leadership was corrupt. Conservatives, too, took their revenge on President Clinton and his wife, who had led an aborted effort to reform national health care. The new House speaker, Newt Gingrich, pledged to restore the bonds of trust between America and its elected representatives with a "Contract for America" that pledged to bring an end to a government that had become too big, too intrusive, and too easy with the people's money. One of the top priorities was to have an independent auditing firm scrutinize Congress for waste, fraud, or abuse. "I am committed to hunting down every appropriation that we can find that is discretionary spending, that is some politician taking care of himself," Gingrich declared.

Following the Republican takeover, Cunningham had gone after one of the highly coveted seats on the Appropriations Committee, perhaps the most powerful committee in the House. While other lawmakers subpoena witnesses, issue reports, and attack the party in power, the appropriators quietly meet behind closed doors to decide how money is spent. Everyone comes to see the appropriators with their hands out, every lawmaker seeking a new post office or a wider freeway in his or her district, every contractor who does business with the government, any country that relies on U.S. foreign aid. The committee's dominion over Congress is such that the chairmen of its subcommittees are known as the "thirteen cardinals."

Getting on the committee required the blessing of the California Republican delegation, which met behind closed doors in the Cannon House Office Building. Both Cunningham and Frank Riggs, a Northern California Republican, took turns explaining to the delegation why they each deserved the seat on Appropriations. When they were finished, the members wrote down their votes on pieces of paper and tossed them in a basket. When the votes were counted, Riggs had beaten out Cunningham by one vote. Cunningham was furious and stormed out of the room. "I'm going to resign," he said.

Ron Packard, a courtly, avuncular Republican from northern San Diego County, followed Cunningham out and tried to talk him down. He told Cunningham that resigning would be the most foolish thing he could do. Cunningham stomped off and headed to his office, where he scrawled a letter of resignation and returned with it to the meeting, waving it around. Finally, Packard and some other legislators were able to change his mind. In December 1994, Cunningham grudgingly accepted a post as chairman of the House Economic and Educational Opportunities subcommittee on early childhood, youth, and families. Cunningham remained on the House National Security Committee (since renamed the House Armed Services Committee), where Congressman Hunter became chairman of a subcommittee on military procurement.

Around the same time, the newly elected Republican whip, Tom DeLay, picked Cunningham to serve as one of his assistant whips. As assistant whip, Cunningham was charged with contacting other Republicans and learning their positions on key pieces of legislation. The Republican leadership quickly found that Cunningham was not much of an asset. DeLay, who came to be known as The Hammer for his tightly run whip operation, expected his assistants to quickly produce an accurate tally, and Cunningham wasn't particularly good at the job. The vote cards Cunningham handed in were full of undecideds, which meant that he wasn't having much of a conversation with members, if he was having one at all. The job eventually went to somebody else.

Long before he became the subject of a federal investigation, the House leadership generally viewed Cunningham as a strange character, highly unstable and someone to avoid. One of DeLay's jobs was to keep Republican House members on track, and he would take Cunningham aside for private talks. "Cunningham was not somebody you would have looked to, to be a problem-solver, somebody you wanted to depend on, and because of the volatility you would have wanted to give him a wide berth," a former DeLay chief of staff said. The former

Randy Cunningham, age 10, and his brother, Robert, appear in a 1951 Christmas photo taken shortly before the boys moved to Shelbina, Missouri, where their father ran a five-and-dime store. *(Courtesy National Archives)*

Randy Cunningham races a motorcycle in 1970 during time off from duty at Naval Air Station Miramar in San Diego. He remained a man of simple tastes who preferread hunting, fishing, and riding bikes to carousing with his navy comrades. *(Courtesy National Archives)*

Lt. Randy Cunningham poses for his official navy photograph, taken in 1971. At the time, he had a so-so career as a reservist and had been denied augmentation into the regular navy. *(Courtesy National Archives)*

Lt. Randy Cunningham and his backseater, Lt. (j. g.) Bill Driscoll, climb aboard their F-4J Phantom on May 10, 1972, the day that they became the first flying aces of Vietnam. *(Courtesy National Archives)*

Cunningham and Driscoll take a break on the aircraft carrier USS *Constellation* after shooting down three aircraft and ejecting from their burning aircraft over North Vietnam on May 10, 1972. *(Courtesy National Archives)*

Cunningham crouches by his Datsun
240Z with a license plate lettered "MIG
ACE." Some fellow navy pilots were
offended by what they saw as Cunningham's relentless efforts to promote himself and his utter lack of humility.
(Courtesy National Archives)

Cunningham relaxes at his ranch,
located east of San Diego, in 1975.
(Courtesy National Archives)

Cunningham and Driscoll receive their Navy Crosses, the service's second-highest honor, from Navy Secretary John Warner
at Naval Air Station Miramar in San Diego. According to their
commanding officers, Cunningham and Driscoll almost didn't
attend the ceremony because they were upset that they had not
received the Medal of Honor. *(Courtesy National Archives)*

Brent Wilkes, left, and his best friend, Kyle "Dusty" Foggo, right, during a visit to the Arizona home of Edith Hartin, Wilkes' old high school girlfriend in March 1989. The two were later indicted in a conspiracy involving CIA contracts. *(Courtesy Edith Hartin)*

Cunningham debates fellow Republican Congressman Bill Lowery in 1992. Cunningham left behind the south San Diego district that first elected him to Congress two years earlier to challenge Lowery for the new 50th district seat in the wealthier northern suburbs. *(John Nelson/*San Diego Union-Tribune*/ ZUMA Press)*

While in Washington, Cunningham lived aboard the *Duke-Stir*, a $140,000 yacht purchased for him by defense contractor Mitchell Wade in 2002. (*Hans Ericsson*/San Diego Union-Tribune/*ZUMA Press*)

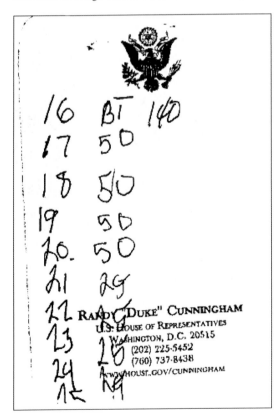

Found aboard the *Duke-Stir* and brought to the attention of federal investigators, this sheet of paper was one of the most damning pieces of evidence. According to Wade, the column of numbers on the left represented the size of the contract in millions of dollars that could be had for the bribe listed in the left column. In the first bribe, "BT" stands for the *Duke-Stir*. (*Courtesy U.S. Department of Justice*)

Nancy Cunningham appears publicly by her husband's side for the last time when he announced on July 14, 2005, that he would not run for reelection following the disclosure of his home sale to a defense contractor. Nancy was investigated by the government for possible tax violations related to her husband's bribes. While Nancy had maintained she knew nothing about her husband's bribes, she had benefited from them by living in the Rancho Santa Fe mansion. *(Courtesy K.C. Alfred/*San Diego Union-Tribune/*ZUMA Press)*

Cunningham's $2.55 million home in Rancho Santa Fe, California. A journalist's discovery that Cunningham had bought the house in 2003 after selling his previous home to Mitchell Wade for an overinflated price touched off the investigation that led to the congressman's resignation and guilty plea. *(K. C. Alfred/*San Diego Union-Tribune/*ZUMA Press)*

Cunningham cries outside of federal court in San Diego on November 28, 2005, as he announces that he has pleaded guilty to accepting more than $2.4 million in bribes from friends. *(Nadia Borowski Scott*/San Diego Union-Tribune/*ZUMA Press)*

DeLay aide and other staffers assumed he was "one of these adrenaline-junkie fighter jocks" who made it into Congress off his reputation. "He was all about living off of the legend of Duke Cunningham, fighter pilot," the DeLay staffer said. "From a leadership standpoint, it was mostly considered a management issue in terms of his instability and, broadly speaking, his ability to kind of stay in touch with reality."

"Mr. Chairman, do we have to call the gentleman 'the gentleman' if he is not one?" Representative Patricia Schroeder asked on May 11, 1995.

The question hung in the air of the House chamber after another outburst from Cunningham. What had led him to fly off the handle this time? A boring debate on an amendment to the Clean Water Act that would have eliminated an exemption for the Navy's nuclear carriers and submarines. The amendment was doomed to defeat, but that was now beside the point, considering how deep into his mouth Cunningham had just shoved his foot.

"Mr. Chairman, I am shocked," Cunningham said, pounding the lectern. "I am absolutely penetratively shocked. I do not think the gentlewoman from Colorado has even been shocked about anything in her life, especially this. Second, I look at the individuals that are offering this. Is there any shocking doubt the same people that would vote to cut defense $177 billion, the same ones that would put homos in the military, the same ones that would not fund BRAC [Base Realignment and Closure], the same ones that would not clean up?"

Schroeder asked if Cunningham would yield. He refused. Congressman Bernie Sanders, a Vermont independent and self-described socialist, rose to speak as well. "Sit down, you socialist," Cunningham thundered.

While Cunningham ranted about the "lunacy" and the "ludicrousness" of the Democrats' use of government rules and regulations to diminish national security, Sanders asked, "My ears may have been playing a trick on me, but I thought I heard the gentleman a moment ago say something quote unquote about homos in the military. Was I right in hearing that expression?"

"Absolutely," Cunningham said, "putting homosexuals in the military."

"Was the gentleman referring to the thousands and thousands of gay people who have put their lives on the line in countless wars defending their country?" Sanders asked.

After the House rejected the amendment, Barney Frank, an openly gay congressman from Massachusetts, rushed to the floor. Frank had been out of the chamber when the House voted, but he had learned what Cunningham had said and stormed in to express his contempt for such a gratuitous slur:

"Mr. Chairman, I very much regret taking the time away from members on this serious subject, but the time is over when I will let that kind of gratuitous bigotry go unchallenged, and I take the floor simply to express my contempt for the effort to introduce such unwarranted and gratuitous slurs on decent human beings on the floor of the House."

Frank, then in his fourteenth year in Congress, had seen antigay remarks fall out of favor, but they were returning with the Republican takeover of 1995. Newly elected House Majority Leader Dick Armey of Texas had called Frank "Barney Fag" during an interview with a group of radio broadcasters in January. (Armey claimed he had mispronounced Frank's name.)

For Frank, Cunningham's remark wasn't a slip of the tongue. His comments were often cruel and degrading. "He was aggressively homophobic," Frank said, "one of the last of the explicit bigots" in Congress. Other Republicans were even worse, in Frank's view. But Cunningham's antigay stance was often personally directed at him.

Frank felt the former pilot couldn't help himself around him. "He seemed far more interested in me than I in him," Frank said. On one occasion, a defense contractor recalled that when Frank walked into the Congressional Dining Room, Cunningham started whistling and jeering, "Incoming, incoming." When Frank asked to know when Democrats would be allow to air their concerns about an immigration bill at a conference hearing in 1994, Cunningham spat, "You want to talk about prostitution rings in basements? We can do that, too." (The House reprimanded Frank in 1990 after learning that a male prostitute was running a prostitution ring out of Frank's apartment when the congressman was not at home.)

Frank, however, was a skilled debater, and he could easily hold his own against Cunningham, who tried to steer the discussion back to the issue of whether gays should serve in the military. Frank was unwilling to let Cunningham off the hook and pressed him on his choice of words.

"Mr. Chairman, I come to Congress prepared to do a number of things that are difficult," Frank explained. "I like the job, and I will undertake them, but trying to prove anything to the gentleman from California goes beyond the pale of my oath, and I will not try. I will say again that we are not here talking about the merits of that issue. We are talking about the gratuitously bigoted formulation of it by which it was injected into this debate, and I find that to be beneath the dignity of the House."

By "formulation," Frank was referring only to Cunningham's choice of words "homos in the military." But in his response, Cunningham didn't seem to understand what Frank was talking about. He said he had meant to "formulate" that people who do not support the military were trying to tie its hands.

"The defense of a bigoted remark makes even less sense than I had expected," Frank said.

Cunningham replied, "It is this member's opinion that homosexuals in the military do not do service to national security of this country." He went on to insist that he said nothing bigoted.

Finally, Cunningham got the point: "Reclaiming my time, Mr. Chairman, let me say that I used the shorthand term and it should have been *homosexuals* instead of *homos*. We do misspeak sometimes."

A short while later, Cunningham's office released a statement explaining in more detail why he had used the word *homos* without apologizing for it. "In listing several items that I feel are degrading the readiness standing of the military forces, and under time pressures to complete my statement within the allotted time, I used a shorthand term for homosexuals. I should have used the term homosexual."

The following day, the Human Rights Campaign, the nation's largest gay political organization, called a news conference to condemn Cunningham's comments. Cunningham was not invited, but he showed up anyway and listened to the criticism from his fellow lawmakers. "Duke Cunningham, who's standing right here, has been racist, has been homophobic, has been outrageous, and has disrespected his colleagues," said Maxine Waters, a California Democrat. "He should seek some psychiatric help." Cunningham took the abuse and then took the microphone. "To me, using that short term was not wrong," he said, "but if it is offensive, then I apologize, and I will not use it again."

Later, his office put out another statement, explaining why he had not apologized sooner. In making his point about Democratic policies that have resulted in a "dangerous" lack of military readiness, "I did not realize that using the 'shorthand' term for homosexuals would be taken in an offensive and derogatory manner. It was not my intent to be offensive or mean-spirited in any way. Now that I realize that it has been taken that way, I apologize."

Back home, Cunningham got a public scolding. *The San Diego Union-Tribune,* which had supported Cunningham in every election, chastised him for setting such a poor example. While the reaction was on the whole negative, his comments were welcomed by some in his district and around the country. To them, Cunningham's blunt style was appealing, and his refreshing honesty won their respect. There's little doubt that Cunningham wasn't the only one in Congress who used such pejoratives; the others just did so when no one was recording their words. "Perhaps he was not politically correct," one reader wrote *The San Diego Union-Tribune,* "but he was right on the mark. I believe if the truth were known, the majority of Americans would agree with him."

Cunningham said that, regrettably, the phone calls and faxes to his office were overwhelmingly supportive. "My staff has advised me to do it again because the calls have been so positive," he told *The San Diego Union-Tribune.* Part of his problem, he acknowledged, was that he never had any friends he knew were gay.

A few weeks later, Elizabeth Birch, the new director of Human Rights Campaign, met with Cunningham in his office to discuss gay rights issues. It was one of Birch's first introductions to Congress. A former corporate attorney for Apple Computer, Birch was accompanied at the meeting by Daniel Zingale, HRC's policy director. They sat down with Cunningham and his staff for forty-five minutes. Birch and Cunningham disagreed on a variety of issues. At the end of the meeting, Birch and Zingale were packing up and preparing to leave when Cunningham asked Birch to wait. The congressman closed the door to his office and returned to his desk, where he leaned back and asked, "So how do you know?"

Although she had a sense Cunningham was referring to her sexual identity, Birch asked the congressman what he meant.

"You know, how do you know if you're that way?" Cunningham said.

Birch, the daughter of a former Royal Air Force pilot in World War II, grew up in Canada and knew from an early age that she was gay. She told Cunningham that she had developed an early awareness as a child that she was different. TV commercials and billboards designed to appeal to women didn't make sense to her and made her feel lost. As she matured and gained self-esteem, she grew into herself.

"Yeah, yeah, yeah," Cunningham replied. "You're really little and then you grow up, and then you have to get some self-esteem and you grow and grow." Finally, he revealed why he had asked such a personal question: "Because I've loved men."

"Was that in a military setting?" Birch asked in surprise.

"Yes, indeed, on the field of battle. But I've also loved men."

"You know," Birch said, "these feelings are healthy. Those feelings are good feelings. They come from a good place. It's what the world does to them. It twists them and makes them ugly."

Although they couldn't control what came out of his mouth, Cunningham's chiefs of staff did have influence over many other aspects of the congressman's life. The job of chief of staff for Cunningham came with a special set of responsibilities. In addition to running the office, the chief of staff's job was to keep Cunningham out of trouble. The congressman, as his Navy comrades knew well, tended to veer in the wrong direction and fall in with the wrong crowd. "He was like a big kid," said one former staffer. "He needed adult supervision."

Cunningham's staff would often be called out at odd hours to extinguish the political fires that broke out over the bizarre things that would fly out of the congressman's mouth, which often involved shooting things. During a debate over the assault weapons ban in 1994, Cunningham announced, "I have flown an F-14 over this Capitol with a twenty-millimeter gun that could shoot six thousand rounds a minute. I could disintegrate this hall in a half-a-second burst. Yet the gentleman from New York would tell me that I cannot carry a ten-shot .22." He also told a reporter he would have no trouble shooting Vietnam War protesters.

Bill Driscoll, who had sat behind Cunningham as the two men shot down five planes over Vietnam, could commiserate with the congressman's staff. "I know what your job is," Driscoll told a staff member one day. "Your job is what my job is. We have the shovels at the end of the parade."

Even the twenty-year-olds in Cunningham's office could see that the congressman surrounded himself with unscrupulous characters. If left to his own devices, Cunningham would and did place himself in the hands of wheeler-dealers, greedy businessmen, and even a convicted felon, who would exploit their association with the congressman to the hilt. They flattered the old pilot, indulged his hoary war stories, told him what he wanted him to hear, and filled his mind with their personal schemes. "He was a very poor judge of character, just a terrible judge of character," said Gregg Parks, a young legislative assistant in Cunningham's office. "He thought the most shady people were the greatest guys in the world." One of the chief of staff's duties was to keep these people at arm's length.

Few people exemplified this better than Thomas Kontogiannis, a Greek-born businessman with a felony record who had been introduced to Cunningham by a mutual friend shortly after he arrived in Washington. According to government sources and lawyers, Kontogiannis was a member of the Greek mob and had gotten his start in a car-theft ring. He had been convicted in 1994 in a scheme to bribe employees of the U.S. embassy in Greece and sentenced to five years' probation. Cunningham didn't seem bothered by his friend's felony record. When Kontogiannis was arrested for receiving more than $2 million in 2000 in a kickback and bribery scheme involving New York

City schools, Cunningham wrote a letter to the Queens district attorney: "It has been alleged that there may be a political agenda being waged against [a] former superintendent . . . and therefore Mr. Kontogiannis is being allegedly victimized."

Cunningham lost it again in September of 1995 as he continued to bully his way through the 104th Congress. During a meeting of the House Committee on Economic and Educational Opportunities dealing with cuts in student loans, Cunningham said the Republicans were really fighting the socialist tendencies of the Democrats, including "communist supporters" such as Labor Secretary Robert B. Reich. "He goes along with Karl Marx in many of his writings," Cunningham said of the former Rhodes scholar and Harvard professor.

"There you have it!" yelled Pat Williams, a Democrat from Montana. "If you think the far right is now running this joint, there you have it."

"Duke, I think we need to both step outside," Congressman Jim Moran told Cunningham on November 17, 1995.

For Moran, a Democrat who represented D.C.'s Virginia suburbs, Cunningham personified his mounting frustrations with the new Republican leadership. A silver-haired Irish-American who grew up in the suburbs of Boston, Moran felt the partisan tactics of the Republicans were more than just words; they were actually hurting his constituents. The federal government had ground to a halt in November when the president failed to reach an agreement with Congress over bills needed to keep the government running. By noon on November 14, about eight hundred thousand federal employees were sent home from their jobs, including many who lived in Moran's district. Only military personnel, "essential" government workers, and members of Congress remained at their jobs.

Cunningham had insulted Moran during a debate on a Republican-sponsored measure that would have prevented any money from being spent to send U.S. troops to Bosnia. The bill was largely symbolic. It faced a certain White House veto, and Democrats saw the bill as a thinly veiled attack on the president, who was orchestrating peace talks to end three years of war in the Balkans. Moran told his colleagues, "It is at least inconsistent, at worst hypocritical, to make our foreign policy based upon the party affiliation of our commander in chief." He was interrupted by Cunningham, who had become a champion of the Serbian cause. Cunningham said Moran had "turned his back" on the troops who fought in Desert Storm. Steny Hoyer, a Maryland Democrat, interjected and had Cunningham's words stricken from the record.

A few moments later, Cunningham calmed down and apologized to Moran. By this point, Moran wasn't interested in an apology. He had had it. He was fed up with Cunningham, who Moran felt had done nothing but bully and intimidate dozens of Democrats from the day he came to Congress. As he walked up to Cunningham's desk in the House chamber, Moran felt it was time to do something about it and told him they needed to step outside.

Cunningham refused to go outside, but Moran insisted that it was something they needed to do. Cunningham wasn't getting up from his seat, so Moran grabbed his shoulders to pull him up off it. The two men walked to a large glass door. Cunningham stopped.

"I'm not going to go out there," Cunningham told him.

"Oh, yes, you are," Moran said, and shoved Cunningham into a door that opened with a loud clang that resounded through the House chamber.

Outside, Cunningham and Moran faced off. Moran, an amateur boxer with meaty hands, isn't sure what happened next in the heat of the moment, but he was told later that their fists collided. Cunningham walked around for several weeks after the fight with a cast. Nursing a broken hand, he was instantly out of the fight, but his friends and fellow lawmakers rushed to his defense.

Representative Bob Dornan ran out and jumped on Moran's back. Dornan was a friend of Cunningham's, and Moran felt that B-1 Bob, as Dornan was known, was just as bad. Moran drove his elbow as hard he could into Dornan's solar plexus, and Dornan flew off Moran's back. At that point, George Miller, a California Democrat, came through the door. Moran's recollection is that Miller grabbed Dornan under the neck and picked him up off the ground. Dornan screamed at Moran, "I'm going to kick your Irish ass."

So Moran turned his attention to Dornan. Moran was just as upset with Dornan's tactics as he had been with Cunningham's. Moran had not forgotten that the two men were part of a group of four legislators who had used late-night speeches to lob rhetorical bombs at President Clinton before the Republican takeover of Congress. People like Cunningham and Dornan, Moran felt, couldn't have cared less about the government employees across the country who were out of work. "George," Moran said, "drop him. I'm not going to hit him while you're holding him." Dornan continued kicking and screaming.

Dave Obey, a bearded Wisconsin Democrat, was the next to arrive at what was fast becoming a bench-clearing brawl. "What's going on here?" Obey asked outside the House chamber. Bill Baker, a conservative California congressman, grabbed Obey's arm and told him to stay out of it. "You let go of my arm or I'll put your ass on the floor," Obey told him. According to Moran, Baker and Obey started going at it.

Capitol Hill police rushed to the scene. Moran hadn't known there were so many officers on the Capitol Hill force. With the floor crowded with police, tempers quickly died down. When things had calmed a bit, Moran started looking for Cunningham. He wanted to tell him he was sorry. He ran into Congressman Duncan Hunter, who told him Cunningham's feelings were hurt and chastised Moran for getting physical with Cunningham. Hunter finally told Moran that Cunningham was in the House cloakroom. And that's where Moran found him, in the corner, crying. "I saw the other side of Duke," Moran said. Cunningham apologized to Moran, who felt bad and wanted to shake his hand, but Cunningham's hand was broken.

After that, Cunningham and Moran became friends. Moran delivered a gracious public apology a few days later: "If this were an athletic ring, a Top Gun Navy fighter pilot the size of Duke Cunningham would certainly have made for a fair fight of it. But we are supposed to be engaged in a battle of ideas, demonstrating to the American people and other countries how we settle our differences in a nonviolent way." They had nothing in common in terms of ideology or public policy, but the two got along well. Each time he returned to Washington from California, Cunningham would bring Moran a gift box from See's Candies.

Cunningham and Moran made a trip to Vietnam in 1997. Cunningham initially refused the invitation from Douglas Peterson, the newly named U.S. ambassador to Vietnam. Peterson, a former Democratic congressman from Florida and a retired Air Force colonel, was held as a prisoner of war in North Vietnam for six years after his plane was shot down. Peterson persisted and Cunningham accepted. Cunningham felt that if Peterson could put his Vietnam experience behind him, then maybe he could as well. Bill Driscoll, his backseater from Vietnam, came along on the trip.

During the trip, the U.S. delegation were all seated at a large table and the congressmen took turns addressing their Vietnamese hosts. One by one, the congressmen spoke of the historic nature of their visit and how two former enemies could find common ground and learn from the past. When Cunningham's turn came, he said, "Well, what I'm thinking is the last time I saw you gooks was when you were shooting at me, when I was up in a plane and you were shooting at me, and then you shot me as I was coming down in a parachute." The remarks caused a bit of consternation on the part of his Vietnamese hosts at what was supposed to be a diplomatic occasion. "Duke," Moran said, "you were dropping bombs on them."

Cunningham's lack of control didn't stop him from winning a fourth term in office. Not only did he receive more than twice as many votes as his Democratic opponent, his colleagues in Congress gave him the seat on the Appropriations Committee over which he had nearly resigned two years earlier. Better still, Cunningham got a seat on the most powerful of the thirteen Appropriations subcommittees.

After two years, Frank Riggs, the California Republican who had beaten Cunningham by one vote for a spot on the committee, had had enough. Appropriations sessions were long, contentious, and all-consuming. "To be candid with you, at the end of that Congress, it was pretty clear that despite the best intentions of the Contract with America and those early, heady days, we weren't going to be able to make a significant dent in federal spending," Riggs said. Riggs called Cunningham and made the swap. It was almost unheard of for a member of Congress to give up one of the most sought committee seats, so unusual that Congressman David Dreier called Riggs to make sure he wanted off.

As a member of the Defense Appropriations subcommittee, Cunningham was no longer a mere congressman. He wielded the power of life and death over billion-dollar weapons programs and could shred a corporate balance sheet with a few words in a defense bill. In 1997, the year that Cunningham joined the committee, it doled out more than $247 billion for the Defense Department and the Central Intelligence Agency. Cunningham's home state, California, received more of this money than any other. Its $31 billion share was more than that of twenty-six other states combined.

In Cunningham's first year on the committee, he and his House and Senate colleagues larded the defense bill with $4.3 billion in earmarks, the beginning of an explosive growth in congressionally directed military spending. Buried in bills and reports of almost Talmudic complexity, earmarks are the secret favors that Congress quietly dispenses like candy to reward campaign contributors, local businesses, friends, family members, their dentist, whomever they choose. Conversely, by withholding money, the committee could halt a weapons system, imperiling jobs, military careers, and company earnings. Members of Congress are constantly tempted to hand earmarks out in exchange for golf trips to Scotland, profitable land deals, and, sometimes, cold, hard cash.

"Anybody with any brain can figure out that if they can get on the Defense subcommittee, that's where they ought to be — because that's where the money is," Congressman Charlie Wilson, a Texas Democrat, who had joined the committee in 1980, told author George Crile in *Charlie Wilson's War*. "Once I got on Defense, I went from being the skunk to the prettiest girl at the party."

While Cunningham railed on and on about the damage Clinton's cuts in the defense budgets were wreaking, he was silent about curbing the obvious waste that Defense Appropriations belched up in each year's bill. In his first year on the committee, the earmarks in the defense bill included $15 million for electric vehicles and $100,000 to preserve a Revolutionary War gunboat discovered on the bottom of Lake Champlain. A $3.5 million earmark for an observatory in New Mexico prompted Senator John McCain, a pork critic, to observe that he wasn't sure whether he should be afraid of a national security threat from another country or another solar system.

The corrupting nature of this power is the stuff of congressional legends. Appropriations Committee members, simply put, expected to be treated like royalty. They could and did withhold money when the military failed to treat them accordingly, and everyone knew it. Charlie Wilson was enraged when his girlfriend was not allowed to board a Defense Department plane in Islamabad, Pakistan. The U.S. embassy's military attaché told Wilson that Annelise "Sweetums" Ilschenko could not board; only a congressman's spouse could. Wilson started cursing up and down. Why couldn't Ilschenko fly when all of his previous girlfriends had been allowed to board?

Back in Washington, Wilson told his colleagues on Defense Appropriations, "Gentlemen, the honor of the coequal branch of government has been challenged. They have insulted the Committee on Appropriations, they have insulted me, and they have insulted my true love, Sweetums. I want you to give me revenge." The Defense Intelligence Agency plane that Wilson's girlfriend couldn't board and one other were permanently removed from the agency's fleet. To ram the point home, the two planes were reassigned to duty with the Texas Air National Guard.

The intoxicating nature of such power rubs off on congressional staffers. Jason Alderman, a twenty-seven-year-old staff member for the second-highest-ranking Democrat on Appropriations, got into a dispute with a policeman after he was stopped for walking his dog without a leash at a park near his home. In retaliation, Alderman added language to a House Appropriations bill ordering the National Park Service to build a dog run at the park "as expeditiously as possible."

Buried in a 2005 omnibus spending bill, a three-thousand-page monstrosity of a package that included among other examples of waste $25,000 for the study of mariachi music in the greater Las Vegas area, were a few lines that revealed just how powerful appropriators believed themselves to be in 2004. Language in the bill gave the chairmen of the House and Senate Appropriations committees or their "agents"—a vague term that could mean virtually anyone—the authority to read the income tax returns of any American without violating any criminal law. Alaska Republican Ted Stevens, one of the old bulls, who chaired the Senate Appropriations Committee and was known for slipping an Incredible Hulk tie around his neck during political battle, apologized for what he called a mistake by an exhausted staffer of his who had worked long hours to get the bill finished before the Thanksgiving recess. Democrats in the Senate who discovered the language didn't buy it. "Does anyone believe, really, that some staffer, without any permission, thought up a scheme by which a chairman's 'agent' could have access to every IRS facility anywhere in this nation, and every IRS filing of every citizen in this nation?" asked an incredulous Senator Dianne Feinstein of California.

Shortly after Cunningham joined the committee, friends began to notice he was developing a taste for the finer things life had to offer. The Capital Grille, whose power scene he had once been wary of, now became one of his favorite restaurants. He developed a taste for fancy wines, fine furnishings, and luxury homes. He acquired a huge symbol of his newfound power. Cunningham had attended a gathering in Washington aboard the *Kelly C,* a boat owned by Sonny Callahan, a Republican congressman from Alabama. Cunningham was impressed by the sixty-five-foot houseboat, custom-built for Callahan, who had lived aboard it in Washington for five years. "He saw it and liked and wanted it, so I sold it to him," Callahan said. Cunningham paid $180,020 for the *Kelly C* and started living in the yacht at the Capital Yacht Club on the Potomac River.

Some of Cunningham's friends and associates felt something was wrong when they heard about the boat. When Ronald McKeown, Cunningham's former Top Gun commander, popped by his congressional office one day, Cunningham told him about his new boat and invited McKeown to come aboard.

"Can you get a martini aboard that boat?" McKeown asked.

"Hell, yes," Cunningham told him.

McKeown went down to the Capital Yacht Club and visited with Cunningham. The boat was so big McKeown joked that Cunningham could have invaded Honduras with it. Cunningham led McKeown into the salon and made him a good martini.

"Okay, want to see the boat now?" Cunningham asked.

"Duke, let's get something straight," McKeown said. "I don't want to know anything about this boat. I don't want to know its length, its draft, its beam. I don't want to know anything about it."

"Why not?"

"Five or six years from now, when the FBI comes around and asks me what I know about this boat, I'll say, 'All I know is I got run over by a gin truck.'"

Cunningham laughed and made another martini.

On another evening Cunningham invited a defense contractor named Tom Casey onto the *Kelly C* and the two shared a bottle of wine. The congressman put on a recording of himself giving a patriotic spoken-word performance set to dramatic music and sat listening to himself with obvious pride. With a few glasses of wine inside him, Cunningham revealed to Casey how poorly he felt the Pentagon had treated him after he became an ace, and that he was so upset that he never received the Medal of Honor he felt he deserved, he almost didn't accept the Navy Cross. Well, here he was on the Defense Appropriations subcommittee. Cunningham told Casey that he was expecting to become chairman of that subcommittee soon enough. When he did, he would be far more powerful than all those Pentagon pencil-pushers, the desk jockeys who had failed to show him the proper respect.

5

That's Not the Way
We Do Things

Congressman Bill Lowery, the man Randy Cunningham had muscled out of a job in 1992, took stock of his twelve years in the House of Representatives and was not pleased with what he saw. Lowery had lost touch and become too comfortable with the privileges and perks of high office. It happened so slowly that he hadn't really noticed. He accepted the overseas junkets, the luxury condo, the trips on private jets and yachts, and soon he didn't know any other way to live. Time after time, he was linked with whatever scandal was brewing in Congress. Too late, he realized that he had become part of the problem in Washington.

Following his withdrawal from the primary against Cunningham, Lowery used the final eight and a half months of his final term in Congress to take some time for himself and consider his prospects. He spent several days camping in Yosemite National Park with his closest advisers, and he flew down to Belize in the company of Brent Wilkes, an old friend from San Diego. Wilkes was furious at Cunningham for snatching away his friend's seat in Congress. "That goddamn asshole," Wilkes told a friend. "How can he do this to someone who has seniority?"

Lowery's sprits seemed to revive during the trip to Belize when Lowery and Wilkes stopped in for a visit with Eugene Scassa, the U.S. ambassador. Scassa welcomed Wilkes and the congressman to his home, which was just short of ostentatious by Belizean standards, and the three sat outside and chatted. At one point, Lowery asked Scassa how much it cost him out of pocket to be an ambassador. Lowery heard the figure and remarked, "You need a chuck wagon."

Scassa wasn't sure what Lowery meant. Lowery pointed at Wilkes and said, "He is a chuck wagon. If you have expenses, they pay. If you go out to lunch, they pay. If you need a pair of boots, you go out to the chuck wagon to get them."

"That's not the way we do things," Scassa replied icily.

Wilkes and Lowery had known each other for years. The two had met when Lowery, a city councilman and rising political star, first ran for Congress in 1980. Although Wilkes was fresh out of college, he used his business acumen to operate at a higher level than his twenty-something contemporaries who slaved away on campaigns to earn their entrée into party politics. "You wouldn't see him on the steering committees of candidates' campaigns, like Lowery's kitchen cabinet group. That wasn't Brent. He was kind of one half-step above. He was with the top-layer guys who write the checks and get the phone calls answered," said Pat Shea, a San Diego lawyer who has known both Wilkes and Lowery for years.

With green eyes and blond hair parted to one side, Wilkes, at thirty-seven, was working as a stockbroker in San Diego. In addition to the Belize trip, Wilkes arranged for Lowery to give a talk at his firm, Aimco Financial Management, in the summer of 1992. The congressman was one of a host of speakers Wilkes had brought in, including Alan Keyes, a black Republican and Reagan administration official who was running to be a U.S. senator from Maryland, and the woman who would become San Diego's next mayor, Susan Golding. Wilkes also brought to Aimco Gray Davis, the California state controller, who was running for U.S. Senate.

Around the time of Davis's visit, Wilkes had called on an old high school friend, Ralph Nieders, and asked him for help with a party Wilkes was organizing in Tijuana, Mexico, for Davis's staff. "We need some hookers," Wilkes said. He specifically requested "clean" hookers, such as a secretary who had sex for money on the side. Nieders looked into it, but finally told Wilkes to talk to the maître d'. Nieders never heard from Wilkes again.*

Garry South, Davis's former campaign manager and chief political adviser, said there was no staff party in Tijuana. Furthermore, Davis didn't remember Wilkes and a search of campaign records dating back to 1992 found no contributions from him. The whole thing was ludicrous, South said. "Somebody who's saying this either has a badly flawed recall or is making up shit to tag people along with Wilkes," he said.

Wilkes grew up one of seven children in a small home in Chula Vista, California, a southern suburb of San Diego, with a pet monkey in the backyard named "King Louie." His parents were Mormons from Idaho, and his father, Gaylen, was a fighter pilot and a Navy lieutenant commander assigned to Fighter Squadron 126 at Miramar, the same squadron Cunningham would command three decades later.

---

*Wilkes denied this conversation ever happened. He never threw a party in Tijuana for Davis, and the only staffers he dealt with were women.

On May 1, 1959, with Brent's fifth birthday less than a month away, his father took off in an FJ-4B Fury from the deck of the carrier USS *Lexington* off the coast of Hawaii. The catapult malfunctioned, not giving the plane enough speed to fly, and it hit the water and was lost at sea. Despite a search, Gaylen's body was never found. An official investigation found the cause was an accident. Two days later, commanding officer Jack C. Stuart typed a letter home: "With his vast experience, judgment and outstanding leadership qualities, he was a valuable aid to me during our short turn-around period. It was my pleasure to have served with him. I regret that he was unable to spend more time with his family during the past few months."

Raised by his mother, Brent attended Hilltop High School in Chula Vista, where he graduated in 1972. The students were almost all white sons and daughters of middle-class parents, many of whom worked in the military. Wilkes did well academically and formed part of the cool crowd at the school. He devoted himself to the football team and, despite his slender build, impressed his teammates with his hard-nosed play at center. He dated a sweet, demure cheerleader, Edie Hartin. With his strict Mormon upbringing, Wilkes worried about Hartin's parents, who smoked cigarettes and drank alcohol.

One day, his voice filled with concern, Wilkes told her, "Edie, your parents are going to go hell because they smoke and drink."

"No," she replied, "they're not because they're really good people."

In college, Wilkes started drinking during weekend jaunts to Tijuana, Mexico. Wilkes's friends noticed that he was soon imbibing quite a bit. Years later, Hartin went over for dinner with Wilkes and his wife, Gina. When Wilkes poured her a glass of wine, Hartin couldn't help but tease her old boyfriend, "So now who's going to hell?" Hartin explained the story to Gina, who remarked, "If you're going to hell, he's definitely going to hell."

Wilkes graduated with an accounting degree from San Diego State University in 1977 and went to work at Arthur Andersen. He began establishing political contacts through Republican Associates, a well-connected group of young business professionals. Future California governor Pete Wilson was an executive director and future San Diego mayor Dick Murphy was an active member at the time. Wilkes seemed to be doing well, but he was restless, unable to stay in one job or one place very long. He moved to Washington in the early 1980s, where he joined the accounting firm of Deloitte, Haskins & Sells as a tax manager.

Through Deloitte, Wilkes did some work for a private group working to restore the USS *Sequoia*, the former presidential yacht that President Carter had ordered sold as an unnecessary luxury. Wilkes befriended the crew and would bring friends and dates by to impress them with the yacht where President Kennedy reportedly bedded Marilyn Monroe.

Wilkes left Deloitte to start his own financial services firm in 1985, World Finance Group Ltd., which leased an office on Pennsylvania Avenue and did some consulting work for a Washington real estate developer renovating historic properties. Fred W. Thompson, a former Senate staffer who had launched a budding acting career, had an office down the hall from Wilkes, and the two would share a beer and shoot the breeze at the end of the day. But World Finance Group was short-lived. Wilkes kept telling a colleague that he was over his head in debts and saw no way of repaying them. One day, Wilkes packed up and left town without so much as saying good-bye. He was off to Honduras, where an old friend from high school, Dusty Foggo, was working for the CIA and playing a role in the agency's growing covert war in Nicaragua.

Wilkes would spend the better part of two years in Honduras, a time he would come to look back upon fondly, and he would sometimes wistfully wish that he'd never left. He was an eligible bachelor in a country where Americans were at a premium, and he dated members of the Honduran elite, daughters of some of the highest-ranking members of the government. Wilkes's natural talent for networking came in handy. Although he didn't speak the language, Wilkes used a series of contacts to arrange a meeting with the man in charge of the Honduran military, who helped him arrange a government-to-government deal to support the country's dairy industry. When an acquaintance asked what he had been doing in Honduras, Wilkes replied, "Selling bull semen." He also represented a company to sell cattle and fertilized embryos and bull semen, but the deal never came to fruition.

During his time in Honduras, Wilkes returned home and visited an old friend, Tim Richardson, who asked him what he was doing for women. Wilkes had been best man at Richardson's wedding, and he told his friend how fathers in the poor Central American country would sell their daughters for "virtually nothing." Wilkes also told him about a young woman he had picked up at an airport. Wilkes wanted oral sex and the woman said no. "Ho, ho, ho, you've gotta do this for me, baby," Wilkes told her, and she did.

At the time Honduras was the busiest CIA station in the world, a staging area for covert operations in neighboring Nicaragua, where the contra rebels that the United States equipped, supplied, and trained were trying to overthrow the Sandinista government. Wilkes insisted that he never worked for the CIA in Honduras, but he told a different story to a former Aimco colleague. Mickey Michaud had hired Wilkes as a lobbyist and flew in for a meeting in Washington in March of 1997. The conversation drifted onto the subject of Oliver Stone's film *JFK*, which implicated the CIA in Kennedy's assassination and the subsequent cover-up. Wilkes told Michaud he didn't think the CIA had anything to do with Kennedy's death and began discussing his own work for the agency in Central America. Wilkes told Michaud he had worked on the accounting side of the CIA's operation, but he did make some revealing comments.

It was a different mind-set, working for the agency, Wilkes said. He told Michaud "we"—apparently referring to the CIA—had to "take care of some priests" who were causing trouble. He didn't go into much detail, and whether Wilkes had actually gotten his hands dirty in any operations was unclear. But he did seem troubled by what had happened. "It's like he had some past sins," Michaud said. When Iran-contra figure Oliver North came to San Diego in 1992 to promote his book, *Under Fire*, Wilkes helped him sign books.

By 1989, Wilkes had returned to San Diego and had gotten his license as a registered stockbroker. He worked for a variety of firms before reaching Aimco, where he was hired as a consultant to bring in municipal bond business. By the summer of 1992, Wilkes was open to a new opportunity, especially one that would put him back in the center of the political world. His time in Central America had made a huge impression on him. Sitting in his Aimco office, Wilkes told a colleague that his ambition in life was to become an ambassador to a Central American country. If he could accomplish that, it would be his life's crowning moment.

Wilkes was presented with a new opportunity shortly after Tom Casey paid a visit to Aimco to talk about his company, which sold computer software to the military. Casey, a large man with curly, blond hair, needed help getting things done in Washington, and he had heard of Wilkes. Casey was impressed by Wilkes, finding him to be smooth and charming, with a good sense of humor. He asked Wilkes if he wanted to do some lobbying for him, and, on June 22, 1992, Wilkes resigned from Aimco and soon began working for Casey's company, Audre Recognition Systems.

At the time, Wilkes was flat broke, so constantly pressed for cash that it began to wear on Casey. He owed more than $20,000 in state and federal tax liens in 1992. When he went out to dinner at Marie Callender's with his old high school girlfriend Edie Hartin, her father, a stockbroker who knew Wilkes, told her to bring her wallet because "Brent never pays for anything." He carpooled to work in an old car with his wife, Gina, a beautiful and intelligent blond Texan, and the couple lived in a rented house with her children from a previous marriage. Most Audre employees were reimbursed for their expenses at the end of the month, but Wilkes demanded up-front payment for all his expenses. If Wilkes was on the road and incurred any expenses, he would send Gina over to pick up his expense check.

In 1992, Wilkes headed to Washington, and Congressman Lowery took it upon himself to school Wilkes in the ways of Capitol Hill. Lowery told Wilkes to rent a suite at the Hyatt Hotel near the Capitol and instructed him to bring envelopes for several congressmen, each containing between $5,000 and $10,000 in campaign checks. Lowery had set up a series of meetings with a half dozen or so members of the House Appropriations Committee, including Steny Hoyer, the future House majority leader; Jack Murtha, the powerful chairman of the Defense Appropriations subcommittee; as well as Charlie Wilson, Norm Dicks, Jerry Lewis, and Julian Dixon.

The meeting was Wilkes's initiation into the way fund-raising for members of the Appropriations Committee truly occurred. Lowery instructed Wilkes never to mix fund-raising and requests for appropriations—a mixed message itself given the way the meetings the congressman had arranged clearly blurred the line between the two. To drive home the significance of who was doling out the contributions, Lowery personally handed over the checks, sometimes, Wilkes noticed, in the elevator in the hallway that led to the suite.

Wilkes and Casey made their first lobbying foray to Washington in January 1993, shortly after the new Congress was seated. Lowery took Wilkes and Casey to his close friend Congressman Jerry Lewis, another Southern California Republican, who chaired the Republican Conference. Lewis seemed to know Wilkes well, and he encouraged Casey to hire Lowery, who had decided to join the growing ranks of former congressmen turned lobbyists. "This is perfect for both of you. You can work with Bill, and Bill then can get his start with you," Lewis told Casey.[†]

Casey asked Wilkes how he knew all these congressmen. Wilkes told him a story from his time in Honduras with the CIA's Dusty Foggo. Wilkes proudly told Casey that he was a "handler," whose job it was to take care of visiting U.S. congressmen. The Honduran military leaders would offer the visiting dignitaries special services at a general's ranch. Soldiers would go out into the villages to round up young girls at gunpoint. They would be brought to the ranch, where guards would be posted so the girls could never run home. Although more than one person claimed they heard Wilkes tell this story, he said it was absolutely false. "I have never been in Honduras with Bill Lowery—not when he was a congressman, not before or after he was a congressman, never," Wilkes told me. "I have never been with, or in the presence of, a congressman in Honduras under any circumstances."

On April 3, 1993, Casey met Randy Cunningham for the first time during a party he hosted at his mountaintop home in Rainbow, California, to celebrate his company's tenth anniversary. Other guests included Wilkes, Lowery, and Boris Kogan, a Soviet scientist who had

---

[†] "I have never insisted on the hiring of a lobbyist by any constituent, contractor or anyone seeking federal funds," Lewis said in a statement in response to an NBC News report. "It is outrageous and false to suggest that I might have supported a program in order to provide some illicit benefit for a friend. This technology was primarily supported by the two Congressmen who represented the area, and had been endorsed by top members of the Defense Appropriations Subcommittee—including the Democratic chairman. Although I was a junior minority member of the subcommittee at the time, I felt it was worthwhile to join in that support because the technology appeared to have promise."

been awarded the Stalin Prize for his work on the Soviet Union's first analog computers. Cunningham went wild over Kogan, whose technology had played a role in the development of the surface-to-air missile that had shot him down over Vietnam. Cunningham, unlike Congressman Lewis, wasn't then part of the inner circle of the Appropriations Committee who could help Casey's company.

In the spring, Congressman Lewis asked Casey to write his own earmark for the program he wanted, a Pentagon-sponsored competition to determine which software could provide the best value for the military. Casey followed one of Lewis's staffers, Letitia White, to a basement computer room used by the House Appropriations Committee in the Rayburn Office Building. When he arrived in the computer room, it occurred to Casey that he wasn't the first visitor; nobody else seemed surprised to see him there. Casey sat down and typed in a paragraph that called for a test for the type of software his company made that converted archival drawings and weapons systems specifications into digital format.

Soon, the congressman started letting his guard down around Casey, who got the feeling he was being groomed for what the congressman called "the Lewis family," his friends who helped raise money and whose interests he supported in exchange. Lowery and Lewis invited Casey to join them for dinner one night, and during the meal, Casey heard the two discussing the case of Joe McDade of Pennsylvania, the ranking Republican on the powerful Defense Appropriations subcommittee. Earlier that year, a federal grand jury had indicted McDade on charges of racketeering, conspiracy, and accepting $100,000 in cash, gifts, and services from military contractors and an industry lobbyist. (He was ultimately acquitted of all charges.) Lewis, a fellow member of the Appropriations Committee, said he needed to lower his profile by putting distance between himself and lobbyists like Lowery, as well as defense contractors like Casey. Lewis told Casey that he needed to work with Lowery, who, as a former member of Congress, had "floor privileges" and was permitted use of the congressional gym. Lewis and Lowery could meet without generating any record that would reveal what they had talked about or even that they had met. "Believe me," Lewis told Casey, "I'll be there working for you, because I'll work for you through Bill."

In January, Lowery called up Casey and invited him to go with Lewis and him on a scuba-diving trip to Belize. "We're hooked up with the Belizean Navy, but we'd like you to be our dive master," Lowery said. "Come on out. It would be great." Casey was tempted. He was an accomplished scuba diver and had heard about Belize's spectacular reef system, but he said he would have to think about it, and the more he thought about it, the more he didn't like the idea. He didn't think much of congressional junkets and thought the trip sounded like a joke. Casey called back and told Lowery he wasn't interested.

Unbeknownst to Casey, Lewis and Lowery brought Wilkes down to Belize with them. They met with Ambassador Scassa, who knew Lowery and Wilkes from their visit the year before. Also with them was the chairman of Rawlings Sporting Goods, who donated some basketballs, nets, uniforms, and backboards for a night basketball league intended to give Belizean youths an alternative to the streets. The group also spent a day and a half diving and two days in El Salvador before returning home.

Less than two weeks after he turned down the Belize trip, Casey received a call at his mountaintop home in Rainbow, a small community in northern San Diego County, from Representative Lewis. Lewis started by saying he wanted to discuss Casey's hiring Lowery as a lobbyist. Lewis thought it would be perfect for Lowery and Casey. Then he shifted gears and told Casey he wanted him to set up Lowery with stock options in Audre. "It would be good for you, good for him. He's dedicated his life to public service. The appropriation language is together now. It looks like it's going to go forward. So before that becomes public information, I'd like Bill to get in early, so he can get the maximum benefit from the transaction," Lewis told Casey.[‡]

Casey said he didn't want to have anybody think that he only got his earmark because of Lowery. Casey was concerned about the appearance of granting Lowery, a former congressman, stock options in Audre as Congress was considering an earmark that would benefit the company. In addition, Lowery wasn't even allowed to lobby his former committee for a year. "I don't want to lose the significance of this by having it become some political deal," Casey said, but added he would consider giving Lowery options if he would serve on Audre's board of directors, something Lowery himself had expressed interest in.

Casey explained the process of selecting board members to Lewis, but the congressman feared the appropriation would become public before Lowery's nomination to the board could be approved by Audre shareholders. He then suggested that Casey could issue the stock options through the Canadian holding company that controlled Audre. Casey replied that he would still have to put Lowery's name down on the stock option ownership forms that he would file with the U.S. Securities and Exchange Commission and its Canadian equivalent.

"Well, Bill could be the beneficial holder but he would be able to give you other names of record," Lewis replied. Casey said he wasn't comfortable with that. He was still required to identify the beneficial holder. Lewis said he understood and appreciated Casey's time and ended the conversation. Casey never hired Lowery as a lobbyist.

The defense bill containing Casey's earmark was introduced in the House in September. The language called for a $14 million software

[‡] In the NBC News statement, Lewis provided the following response: "I have absolutely never told anyone to provide 'stock options' or any other sort of compensation to someone who is their advisor or lobbyist. To do so would be extremely unethical, and it goes entirely against all of my principles of good governing."

testing program that was literally spare change in the $240 billion Defense Appropriations Bill of 1994. It was overlooked by all but a handful of people paying close attention. On November 3, Letitia White, the Lewis staffer who had led Casey to the basement computer room, reportedly bought stock in Audre. The bill passed Congress the following week.

Getting the earmark was only one stage of the Byzantine funding process, and in some ways it was the easiest part. The money Congress had appropriated was doled out by contracting officials in the Defense Department, which decided how much money Audre would receive. Of the $14 million for the software testing program, only $2 million went to Audre.

Casey did find someone in the House of Representatives whom he felt he could work with, Congressman Duncan Hunter. To Casey, Hunter seemed to be the opposite of people like Lowery and Lewis. The two had met during one of Casey's visits touting his software, and the hawkish, deeply religious congressman and the race-car-driving businessman had somehow hit it off. Hunter would take Casey along and go searching for a fund-raiser to eat hors d'oeuvres. "I had all the money in the world but I kind of liked that because here was a guy who never asked me out to dinner, anything," Casey said. "What clothes he was wearing didn't matter. What he was going to eat didn't matter. Where he was going to sleep didn't matter." According to Casey, Hunter was not fond of Wilkes, who had once brought a case of beer to "liven up" a fund-raiser Audre was throwing for Hunter, who was a teetotaler. When Casey once kidded him by reminding him that even Jesus drank alcohol, Hunter replied, "I'd like him a lot more if he didn't."

Befriending Hunter didn't endear Casey to Lewis and Lowery,

who made no secret of their contempt for Hunter. Lewis and his wife openly mocked Hunter in front of Casey, but Casey found Hunter to be a man of principle, while Lewis was off on congressional junkets to Belize. During a dinner with Congressman Lewis and his wife, Casey excused himself to watch a boxing match. Julio César Chávez was fighting, and Casey, an avid fan, wanted to watch the match at Bullfeathers, a bar near the Capitol. Lewis sounded interested—until Casey told him that Hunter had been invited, too. Lewis drove Casey to the bar and made him check in the window to see whether Hunter was inside. Casey signaled that Hunter was there waiting, so Lewis waved and drove on.

Trying a different tack, Wilkes came up with the idea of having Casey sponsor card games with congressmen, including Charlie Wilson, the flamboyant Texas Democrat on Appropriations. Wilkes wanted Casey to rent a hotel suite and pay for liquor to host the game, but Casey wasn't interested. As an inducement, Wilkes decided to introduce Casey to his friend from high school Dusty Foggo, now in his eleventh year with the CIA, which was grooming him for upper management. The CIA sent Foggo to Harvard to study at the Kennedy School of Government's midcareer program for a master's degree in public administration.

Wilkes and Foggo had remained extremely close over the years. As a sign of their intimacy, Foggo had told the agency that Wilkes knew he worked for the CIA—a process known as witting. Typically, only the closest people in one's life know—a spouse or parents. In another sign of their closeness, Wilkes and Foggo named their sons after each other. "Don't you guys think you're taking this a little too far?" Wilkes's old high school girlfriend Edie Hartin asked when the two stopped by for a visit at her home.

Wilkes and Foggo took Casey to a Georgetown strip club. There was a line, so Foggo showed the security guard at the door his CIA badge and his gun. Casey found this odd; he thought CIA employees were supposed to be discreet. Foggo told him it would get them a good seat, which was true. The three were seated in the front row next to a group of Saudis. Casey listened as Foggo spent the night lusting after women. "All he talked about was fucking girls in the ass—all night long," Casey recalled. Foggo told Wilkes about a woman at Harvard who he felt might be ready for a threesome. Casey soon found himself disgusted and wanted nothing more to do with Foggo. "He seemed to be completely, utterly obsessed with it," Casey said. Wilkes, too, reveled in Washington's sleaze. "I love this town," he told Casey. "You get in bed with someone in Washington, you're sure to get fucked."

The pair reminded Casey of two fraternity brothers who had never grown up. Wilkes and Foggo had known each other since Hilltop Junior High School days in Chula Vista. Foggo arrived at the school in seventh grade, a nerdy boy with a shock of extremely curly, blond hair who introduced himself as Kyle Dustin Foggo the Third. Those words had barely left his mouth when a group of boys, including Wilkes, immediately started teasing him. In 1969, Foggo was written up in the school newspaper for being selected as the outstanding ninth-grade boy of the year. "Everyone likes Dusty for his courteous, friendly manner," one teacher observed.

By high school, Foggo had shed his nerdy persona. He had grown into a tall and handsome young man. With his mop of curly, blond hair, Foggo was attractive to the girls at Hilltop High, and his pleasant personality made him popular with boys. He and Wilkes became inseparable. Like Wilkes, Foggo was raised by his mother, as his father wasn't around. Foggo once told a close friend, "You've been more of a father to me than he ever was." Foggo and Wilkes always seemed to be in on a secret with each other. They loved to clown around together, scaring girls during nighttime strolls through cemeteries.

Wilkes and Foggo grew even closer after graduation. They both attended Southwestern Community College in Chula Vista for two years after high school. They met with their friends and girlfriends for Friday-night poker games, a tradition that had begun in senior year of high school. The two then transferred to San Diego State. Foggo, who had an interest in law enforcement, majored in criminal justice administration. He graduated in 1976, a year before Wilkes, and applied for a job with the San Diego police force.

Foggo seemed to get off on the authority and power that came with law enforcement. To earn some extra cash, Foggo and Wilkes worked in the summer as security guards at Sears Roebuck & Co. in Chula Vista. Foggo was aggressive, chasing down suspected shoplifters in the parking lot, and he was sued twice for falsely accusing customers of shoplifting. In 1977 he was hired by the San Diego police. Tim Richardson, a friend who was also trying to become a police officer, recalled that Foggo would walk in to the poker game, unstrap his weapon, and slam it on the table.

Foggo soon developed a reputation on the police force for being a little rough or "badge heavy," as Wilkes once put it. Foggo did have an us-versus-them mentality. Foggo used "Foggo fluid"—Wite-Out—to correct his police reports. He told a county prosecutor that he used his "Foggo fluid" to alter the motto YOUR SAFETY IS OUR BUSINESS, emblazoned on the door of his squad car, so it read OUR SAFETY IS OUR BUSINESS.

Richardson and Rick Foss, another friend and fellow police officer, thought Foggo was a good officer, but Richardson found Foggo's attitude toward his work troubling. Foggo said he loved taking his flashlight and beating it on the door when he served a warrant. Foggo felt it was "almost Gestapo-like" and gave him a thrill. "You're a sick puppy," Richardson told him. "He loved to show off this power he had, which would terrify me in the position he was in," Richardson said.

One night when Foggo was home in San Diego from Honduras, he picked up Richardson in a fancy rental car. Foggo had been drinking and wanted to go to San Diego's Loma Prieta neighborhood to "troll for hookers." On the way, a San Diego police officer pulled them over. Richardson thought they were in deep trouble, but Foggo flashed his CIA credentials. The officer glanced at them and said, "See you later. Bye," leaving the obviously drunk Foggo to get back behind the wheel.

Some friends found that Foggo's behavior had crossed the line in other areas. In July 1982, the year he joined the CIA, Foggo decided to get married. Wilkes organized a bachelor party at the Hyatt Regency Islandia in San Diego, attended by some officers Foggo knew from his years on the San Diego police force.

During the party, Foggo made a series of startling revelations about his time on the police force. He revealed he had a female partner whom he was constantly hitting on. Foggo apparently wouldn't take no for an answer, and one day his partner drew a gun on him. Startled, Foggo pulled out his own gun. The two officers sat in a squad car with their guns pointed at each other before Foggo backed off. Foggo also said he was suspended for three days when he drove back to the home of a young man he had booked in jail and taunted the family with the loudspeaker of his squad car.

As he listened to Foggo, Bruce Inniss, a former high school football teammate, wondered what had become of his friend, but what happened next floored him. Don't bring a camera, Wilkes had told Inniss before the party. And bring some money. Wilkes had arranged a special treat for Foggo, a prostitute.

The woman arrived at the party, disrobed in front of the group of two dozen or so men, and sat naked in a chair. Foggo kneeled in front of her and started performing oral sex on her. Disgusted, Inniss, who was married at the time, walked out, joined by a few others. "It crossed the lines of values and taste," Inniss said.

Wilkes and Foggo continued their long-standing tradition of weekly card games in Washington. Foggo would invite along friends from the CIA, and Wilkes would bring the congressmen. One of the congressional guests was Charlie Wilson, who had in 1993 received the CIA's Honored Colleague medal, the first time it was ever awarded to anyone outside the agency. At one game, Wilson invited along his friend from Texas Joe Murray, a columnist for *The Atlanta Journal-Constitution*. Murray met Wilson in the hotel lobby. "I'm not sure how they chose the Watergate," Murray wrote in a May 20, 1994, column, a few days after the poker game. "Perhaps because of a sense of history. Either that or a sense of humor."

Murray followed Wilson into the suite, which was filled with cigar smoke. Wilson knew a few of the CIA personnel at the game. One was Brant Bassett, a well-regarded agent who spoke fluent Russian, German, and Hungarian. Bassett was known as Nine Fingers after a motorcycle accident had cost him a finger. Wilson brought gifts, a sack full of guns that included a Soviet automatic used by Russian paratroopers. Wilson had a special pen for everyone, one that with a click fired a .32-caliber bullet. Everyone in the room started clicking his pen.

"Boy, I wish I'd had it this afternoon," someone said.

"If only Aldrich Ames were here."

Murray and Wilson stayed only a short while, and as they were leaving, one of the agents offered Murray one of his cigars, a Dominican. Murray offered the agent one of his, a Cuban. The agent told him, "You know, of course, this is considered contraband. But you've done the right thing as a good citizen. You've turned it in to the proper government agency. Be assured that very shortly it will be destroyed by fire."

Wilson insisted there was no hanky-panky the night he was there.

"The only activities that took place there that would be considered illegal and unlawful was cigar smoking on a nonsmoking floor," Wilson said. Cunningham was the only other congressman who ever attended the poker games, according to Wilkes.

In the summer of 1994, Wilkes showed up in Casey's office at Audre and told him he had solved a big problem. Casey had been having trouble with John Karpovich, a Defense Department procurement officer who had a big say in determining whether Audre would get military contracts and how Casey's software fared in tests that were crucial to winning contracts. Casey claimed that Karpovich seemed to have it in for him.

"We got Karpovich," Wilkes told Casey.

Wilkes told his boss that Foggo had set up a sting operation and secretly recorded Karpovich. On the tape, Casey said, Karpovich could be heard vowing to destroy Audre and to make sure the company never succeeded. Was this legal? Casey asked. Wilkes told him that an attorney for Audre had cleared the operation. Foggo had hired a few off-duty Fairfax, Virginia, police, including an especially attractive female officer. At a bar Karpovich frequented, the female officer, pretending to be from Jacksonville, Florida, expressed an interest in Karpovich and gave him her phone number. While they chatted, another officer sat nearby recording with a directional pen microphone. Foggo bugged a room in Jacksonville, Florida, and flew the attractive officer down to meet Karpovich. The female officer offered him drink after drink and got him to unload his feelings about Casey. As Casey listened to the tape, Karpovich, sounding drunk and slurring his words, could be heard promising to get even with Casey.§

§ Wilkes said he did not recall this incident.

"Isn't it great?" Wilkes told his boss. He asked Casey to pay for the $24,000 in expenses Foggo had incurred arranging the "sting." Casey agreed and told Wilkes he planned to hand the tape over to Defense Department criminal investigators as evidence against Karpovich.

"What are you, crazy? You don't do that!" Wilkes said. Sure, turning the tape in would get rid of Karpovich, but someone else could take his place and possibly make things even worse for Casey. "You keep that tape, you use that tape right, and you control this guy for the rest of his life."

When Casey insisted on taking the tape to military investigators, Wilkes withdrew his offer to sell it to him. If Casey turned over the tape, Wilkes worried it could compromise Foggo. He put the tape in his pocket and walked out.

Following the incident over the secret taping, Casey's relationship with Wilkes grew increasingly strained. Things came to a head at a trade show in Long Beach at the end of 1994. At dinner, Wilkes laid out Casey's problems. By not playing ball, Casey had ruined all the contacts Wilkes had made for him in Congress. But Wilkes had a plan to fix things. He wanted to set up an office in Washington, D.C., and make the donations he needed to make on Casey's behalf. "I'll make it right, but you can't be involved," Wilkes said. He asked for $148,000 in expenses per month to set up the D.C. office and said he didn't want Casey approving any of his expenses. Casey insisted on a breakdown, but Wilkes refused and finally threw down his napkin. "That's it. I'm out of here," Wilkes said, and stomped out.

6

At the Watergate

For students of political scandal, Washington's Watergate Complex is one of the stations of the cross, looming from across the Potomac like a stack of old records with its curved façade of alternating white and black. The Watergate is part hotel and part shopping center, but the curious come to the office complex to feel some connection to one of history's darker moments. It is one of the few buildings in the world to appear in the dictionary, forever linked with the 1972 break-in at the Democratic National Committee and the events that led to the resignation of President Richard Nixon.

In the mid-1990s, passersby might be forgiven for shaking their heads and wondering if strange things always happened in the Watergate. From a balcony in the hotel that formed part of the complex, a glimmering white disk would shoot out into the sky, spinning like a

Frisbee, soaring over the roadway that ran behind the Watergate. It would have been difficult, if not impossible, to tell that the disks were not made of plastic, but were plates that the hotel staff had used to serve a regular guest who was running his new company from a suite in the Watergate Hotel.

Brent Wilkes would pick up plates and, after making sure no cars were coming, would fling them off the hotel balcony to see if he could reach the Potomac. No one around him would say a word. That was just Brent, they would say. During one angry conversation with staff in a Long Beach, California, hotel, he picked up fruit from the complimentary basket at the front desk and started hurtling it across the lobby. With Wilkes, there was a sense of not knowing what he would do next, and that made things interesting, even a bit dangerous. He took his employees to a Las Vegas strip club and handed out dollar bills so everyone could tip the girls. "No rest for the wicked," he liked to say.

After his fallout with Casey, Wilkes had decided to start his own document-scanning company. Casey's company, Audre, had self-destructed when it was forced into bankruptcy as a result of a bitter divorce proceeding. As a result of the bankruptcy, the Securities and Exchange Commission sued Casey for directing the falsification of corporate records to conceal a $908,000 personal loan from the company.

Wilkes decided to put his considerable political connections to use. Over the years, he had collected a number of contacts in Congress. In addition to Congressman Lewis, Wilkes was close with Ben Gilman, a New York Republican who chaired the House International Relations Committee. And more recently, Congressman Cunningham had taken an interest in Wilkes's new company.

Wilkes had first met Cunningham shortly after Duke left the Navy and was giving speeches about his ace legacy and selling aviation memorabilia through Top Gun Enterprises. Wilkes had always had an interest in aviation. His father had been a Navy pilot, and Wilkes himself was a licensed pilot, and the two men had become friendly. As Wilkes told one of his associates, there wouldn't be any problem getting more funding out of Congress—Cunningham could help them out. "He's not the brightest guy up there," Wilkes told Randall Kerley, who had joined the new company.

Cunningham enjoyed spending time with Wilkes, who was twelve and a half years his junior. The two men would share a meal at The Capital Grille, where the congressman would order his trademark Courvoisier stingers. Unlike Lowery, who always seemed to have his hand out in Congress, Cunningham seemed to feel a little guilty about expecting things. At the end of one meal in 1996, a former acquaintance of Wilkes's recalled that Cunningham tossed a wadded ball of cash on the table, which he gave to Wilkes. Cunningham, in turn, invited Wilkes over for a meal of Costco lasagna or elk chili. Wilkes's colleagues would hear the congressman tell his stories about Vietnam and the "fact" that he was the inspiration for the film *Top Gun*. "They became very close, just like two old buddies getting together for a night on the town," Kerley said.

ADCS, the name of Wilkes's company, stood for "automated document conversion system," and the business was as dull as it sounded. Wilkes competed against Casey, his old boss, in the business of selling software that converted paper engineering drawings into a digital format. On a flight back from San Diego, Wilkes had met Dennis Wise, the husband of a wealthy heiress. It wasn't long before Wise agreed to put $1 million of his wife's money into the venture in 1995.

The company was a political animal, a reflection of its owner. It had lobbyists before it had a product to sell, with Lowery continuing to provide Wilkes with key guidance and strategy even when the company was only an idea in Wilkes's mind. ADCS depended both on sales and on earmarks. The business plan had two parts. The first part involved selling software to the military, which Wilkes left to others. Wilkes handled the second part, which called for convincing Congressmen Randy Cunningham and Duncan Hunter to earmark money so the military could buy his company's software. Wilkes was becoming adept at winning support for his business in Congress. The trick to Washington, he came to realize, was convincing members of Congress that whatever project he was working on was going to happen anyway. Then they would all climb aboard.

Wilkes believed that he had to spend money to make money. "If you want to be the big dog, you better look like the big dog," Wilkes would say. He acted like the starving man who had hit the lottery. In Washington, he rode around in limousines driven by Christopher Baker, a recovering heroin addict who had spent time in prison. In San Diego, Wilkes started living in a $3,500-a-month rental home in Poway and driving a brand-new Hummer. The Hummer's license plate was MIPR ME—a reference to Military Interdepartmental Purchase Requests, the forms the Pentagon uses to pay its contractors. He threw a cocktail party at a convention in Long Beach with a Hawaiian theme that cost around $15,000. He had ADCS printed on expensive Ashworth golf shirts.

When San Diego played host to the Republican National Convention in August 1996, ADCS rented a three-bedroom apartment near the convention center, paid for by Wise. Complete with a well-stocked bar, the apartment was a "hospitality suite" where congressmen could get away from the hubbub of the convention and relax over stunning views of San Diego Harbor. The primary focus of Wilkes's attention was Congressman Gilman. Wilkes had rented a few Cadillacs, and Gilman claimed one for the duration of the convention. Wilkes considered Gilman a friend, although exactly what the New York congressman involved in international relations could do for a San Diego businessman selling software to the military was never clear. Congressman Jerry Lewis also visited the suite, as did Frank Collins, Cunningham's chief of staff.

According to prosecutors, Wilkes had begun to give Cunningham the first of many bribes. In July 1997, Wilkes had one of his employees buy a fourteen-and-a-half-foot Sea-Doo Speedster jet boat for $11,225, which was made available for Cunningham's use. Wilkes also paid his limousine driver to transport the congressman around Washington and bought him the first of thousands of dollars' worth of meals at The Capital Grille, The Palm, Ozio's, and others.

When ADCS secured $5 million worth of contracts from the Pentagon in 1997, Cunningham beamed. "The success achieved by ADCS Inc. is an asset to the San Diego business and technology communities," Cunningham said in a company press release. ADCS's software saved money for taxpayers and contributed to "a stronger, more efficient national defense." Competitors were upset that Cunningham was working behind the scenes to secure money for a new company that didn't have the best software for the job, but the congressman brushed critics aside. Anyone who thought he was doing anything underhanded "can go to hell," Cunningham told reporter Dana Wilkie of Copley News Service. "I'm on the side of the angels here."

When a defense contractor competing against Wilkes for a scanning contract visited Cunningham's office, he noticed plaques on the wall that Wilkes had given the congressman. "I don't know what this guy has on Cunningham, but he's got to have pictures of this guy with his pants down," the contractor whispered to his companion, a retired Navy admiral.

In 1997, a Defense Department program manager approached Wilkes about working on a contract to scan documents related to a military weapons system. But then the government came to him and asked if he would put that work off to take on a bigger, more ambitious project in Panama. The military wanted Wilkes to scan and digitize every blueprint for the Panama Canal and every facility that the United States had built in Panama over the years, a massive archive of more than 1 million documents that included French maps from the eighteenth century. The project would be the largest digitization ever attempted and required Wilkes's company to scan plans for hospitals, offices, schools, and housing, even the bases's dog kennels. Everything had to be finished before the United States handed the waterway back to Panama at the end of the millennium. It was a coup for such a small, relatively inexperienced company.

The idea of scanning documents of the Panama Canal was the brainchild of an analyst named Steve Jenkins at the Army's National Ground Intelligence Center in Charlottesville, Virginia. Jenkins thought it imperative for the military to have a copy of every blueprint and engineering diagram of the canal's unique set of locks. If the military had to move in and retake the canal in the future, the blueprints would be the key to getting the waterway running again.

Defense intelligence officials also saw the Panama contract as a way to test out a concept for a new intelligence database. The Facilities Infrastructure and Engineering Systems database, or FIRES, was a collection of blueprints of sensitive infrastructure—buildings, bridges, and key commercial facilities—from around the world that were of potential military or intelligence value. The blueprints were scanned into the database and could be sent electronically to troops or spies in the field. If, for example, the military was planning to invade a foreign country and needed to know whether the hospitals in the area could treat U.S. casualties, a check with the FIRES database could show that the hospital had no electrical generator, making surgical treatment of the wounded impossible.

Cunningham believed the Panama contract to be important for U.S. national security. Some in the defense intelligence community feared that China could sabotage the canal or seize it once the United States handed over control at the end of 1999. Such a move would strangle the U.S. economy. Panama Ports Company, a subsidiary of a Chinese company, had won concessions to operate ports on both ends of the canal after the United States transferred the waterway to Panama. Cunningham and Congressman Hunter had gotten language inserted into a defense authorization bill that prevented a Chinese company from taking over an abandoned naval facility in Long Beach, California.

In one lengthy floor speech Cunningham linked the Chinese presence in the canal to allegations that the Chinese government had illegally funneled money in 1996 to Democratic Party coffers, allegations that the Chinese denied. "Hutchison Group, also owned by Communist China, recently purchased both ends of the Panama Canal. This would give the Chinese control of the Panama Canal, it would give them control of Long Beach Naval Shipyard, and all of the access to and from and who sees what and where it goes. We feel that this would be a major national security threat," Cunningham said.

Others in the intelligence community did not seem terribly concerned about the presence of the Chinese subsidiary in Panama. "Any potential threat posed by the presence of a pro-Chinese corporate entity in the Panama Canal Zone is indirect," a declassified Defense Intelligence Agency report from October 26, 1999, stated. "It is unlikely that PPC (Panama Ports Company) officials or employees would overtly sabotage or damage the canal on orders from Beijing, as it would be contrary to their own financial interests and would undoubtedly elicit an immediate response from the US and the international community." The report did note that the Chinese corporate presence could provide a conduit for illegal shipments of technology or prohibited items back to the People's Republic or facilitate the movement of arms into the Americas.

The way Wilkes's company operated on the Panama Canal project made government officials suspicious. ADCS submitted a $2.9 million bill for scanning equipment needed for the project. The bill was based on the equipment list in the proposal for the project that the government had handed Wilkes, but the contracting officials overseeing the project had promptly rejected it. The bill included extremely precise, costly scanners, an $85,000 LCD flat-screen monitor, $34,000 worth of chairs, several $4,500 laser printers, and a few $2,000 paper shredders, prices that the contracting officials thought were wildly inflated and for which Wilkes did not provide invoices. Government contracting officials were not sure what exactly was going on, but they held up payment on Wilkes's bill until, at the very least, he showed them what he had actually paid for the equipment.

The government contracting officials found that holding Wilkes accountable was a unique challenge. In November 1998, Gary Jones, a Pentagon program manager, arranged for a meeting with Wilkes. Wilkes showed little deference to government people like Jones, who found Wilkes arrogant, a man who believed he didn't need to play by the rules. He arrived at Jones's office in Falls Church, Virginia, in a huge limousine with an entourage. According to Jones, Wilkes took out five invoices for payment and threw them across the table to Jones. "Here," Wilkes told him, "just sign these and we'll be on our way."

Jones told Wilkes to hang on while he took a look at the documents. The invoices that Wilkes wanted him to sign totaled about $750,000 for work on some scanning project that was never completed. Jones wasn't sure whether Wilkes knew the invoices were fraudulent, but he wasn't going to accept them.

"You don't want to give these to us," Jones said, and handed the documents back.

Wilkes reluctantly took the documents back and departed with his entourage in the limousine. About a half hour after Wilkes left, the phone rang on Jones's desk.

"Hey, Gary, this is Duke." Congressman Randy Cunningham was calling.

"Oh, hi, Congressman Cunningham," Jones said. It was highly unusual, to say the least, for a program manager to receive a phone call from a member of Congress. Such contacts are deliberately kept at arm's length to ensure that contracts are awarded fairly. Typically, congressional staff work with legislative liaisons in the Defense Department who relay messages back and forth and serve as a buffer to avoid the kind of conversation Jones was having with Cunningham.

"No, no, no, between you and me, this is Duke," the congressman told Jones.

Cunningham then said he understood that Jones had just had a dispute with Wilkes over some invoices.

"Yeah, matter of fact, he tried to get me to sign about three-quarters of a million dollars' worth of fraudulent documents," Jones told the congressman.

Cunningham went extremely cold and cut the conversation short. He told Jones that if he ever needed anything, he should not hesitate to call. Later, Jones would hear that Cunningham had called Jones's boss to complain about how Wilkes was being treated.

Nor was Jones the only Defense Department official receiving calls from Cunningham. Paul Behrens had been assigned to oversee Wilkes's work on the Panama contract. In 1998, Behrens was summoned to the Watergate Hotel for a meeting with Wilkes. Behrens was escorted up to the suite, where Wilkes was sitting in the corner of the room in a large, leather lazy chair, puffing on a cigar. Filtered light poured in through the window blinds behind him, casting Wilkes in shadow. All Behrens could see was the cigar smoke that surrounded him in a blue haze.

"Paul, come have a seat," Wilkes told him. "I think we've got a problem."

Wilkes explained that he was having severe money problems. He had spent more than a million dollars on all the equipment he needed for the job, but had not received a penny in return. He needed $1 million in cash to make a balloon payment to buy out a former owner of ADCS. Although Wilkes didn't give Behrens all the details, Dennis Wise, whose wife had provided the start-up money for Wilkes's company, had filed for divorce and his ex-wife now wanted the ADCS money back. Wilkes wanted Behrens to release the government's money for the equipment on the Panama contract. If Behrens didn't, Wilkes could lose his company.

Wilkes told Behrens he was expecting a call from Congressman Cunningham, and sure enough, Wilkes's cell phone rang. He greeted the congressman and then passed the phone to Behrens. Cunningham told Behrens that the Panama work was a national security project of great importance. The congressman told Behrens he knew the government wasn't signing invoices but stressed that the Defense Department had to keep the project moving forward. Behrens replied that all he could go by were the contracting regulations that Cunningham and his colleagues had passed.

"Gosh," Cunningham said, "I even get lobbied by my fellow government employees."

Cunningham continued to pester Behrens with phone calls. The congressman called Behrens at his desk in Huntsville, Alabama, and on another occasion Cunningham also phoned Panama to reach Behrens. Each time, it was the same message: scanning documents in Panama was vital to national security; the Defense Department had to keep things moving. Cunningham was always cordial. He never lost his temper, but he didn't need to with Behrens. There was no doubt what Cunningham wanted him to do, and if Behrens failed to deliver, who could tell what revenge a member of Defense Appropriations might exact on him or his department's budget? Shortly before Thanksgiving, the government paid $1.95 million of Wilkes's $2.9 million invoice.

Federal prosecutors would later make an issue of Cunningham's contacts with Jones, Behrens, and many other Defense Department officials who felt extreme pressure to sign invoices and do the congressman's bidding. While Cunningham maintained that he acted in the national interest, prosecutors, citing Jones and Behrens as examples, wrote, "The evidence indicates that Cunningham's motivation was to ensure that his co-conspirators gorged themselves at the national trough, regardless of the national interest.

"Shamefully, he did this not knowing on all occasions what specifically the money he was delivering would be spent on, but only that one of his co-conspirators would receive it," prosecutors wrote. "Shamefully, he did this knowing that the contractors would extract such exorbitant profits from our nation's taxpayers that they would happily continue to ply him with millions of dollars in illegal payments and benefits."

Congressional meddling with the automated document conversion program was not limited to Cunningham. Gary Jones, the program manager, wanted to bring some new ideas to a program he saw as outdated and inefficient. Jones held an industry briefing in the Fort McNair Officers' Club, which he advertised in the hopes of opening up the competition for document conversion. Afterward, Congressman Duncan Hunter let Jones's superiors know that he didn't ever want to see that sort of industry day ever again. Even though the event was held in a government facility, Hunter insisted it was a waste of taxpayers' money. By then, Wilkes had hired lobbyist Tony Snesko, a process server, antiporn crusader, and former Poway, California, city councilman for $3,000 a month. Snesko's main qualification appeared to be he was a close friend of Hunter's.

But it was Cunningham, not Hunter, who was fiercely protective of

Wilkes's document-scanning program. After two or three years of watching the program grow as large as $50 million a year, a Senate staffer grew curious and called over to the Pentagon to see if they had any use for the program. "Hell, no" was the response. The whole thing seemed totally outrageous. What was going on? When the staffer started raising questions, Congressman Cunningham's staffers would insist on keeping the program in the bill. Clearly, Cunningham's staffers couldn't go back to their boss and tell him that they had lost his pet program.

When Cunningham got his $50 million appropriated for the document-scanning program, he went an extra step to ensure that Wilkes got his money. According to federal grand jury transcripts, Cunningham gave his staff marching orders to secure the maximum amount of money for Wilkes's company. In 1998, Cunningham requested a meeting with Senator Richard C. Shelby of Alabama to discuss the program. Intergraph Corp. in Huntsville, Alabama, had gotten what Cunningham viewed as more than its fair share of document-scanning money. During the meeting, Cunningham was, in the words of a spokesman for Shelby, "very insistent" that the money should be re-awarded, a move that struck Shelby as interference with the process. Shelby declined to participate. According to federal prosecutors, Cunningham convinced the Defense Department to direct $25 million of the $50 million to Wilkes's company.

Cunningham's incipient abuse of power came as he was experiencing a major upheaval in his private life. Following a routine physical, the fifty-six-year-old congressman had been diagnosed with prostate cancer that summer. His reaction, which he recounted later at a congressional hearing, was revealing. "You have the wrong test. I am invincible. It happens to the other person. I can't have cancer. I am Duke Cunningham; I just can't have it." He did, and on August 5,

Cunningham underwent a radical prostatectomy. The cancer reoccurred following the surgery, and Cunningham underwent radiation therapy. Released from the hospital two days later, his staff put out a press release: "Duke 1, Prostate Cancer 0." At a news conference attended by Speaker Newt Gingrich, Cunningham declared, "I have engaged the enemy and won."

The battle, however, left him frayed and ill-tempered. During a visit with a group of prostate-cancer survivors in San Diego the following month, Cunningham made a series of offensive remarks and behaved crudely. The congressman described a rectal exam as "just not natural, unless maybe you're Barney Frank," referring to the openly gay Massachusetts Democrat whom Cunningham continued to lampoon. His talk then shifted to politics, a poor choice for an audience of cancer survivors with whom he was supposed to be commiserating. Cunningham launched into his opposition to military spending cuts in Congress, saying that the defense budget was at its lowest point in twenty-five years.

Charles Cotton, a seventy-four-year-old retired World War II veteran seated in the audience, was getting increasingly upset by Cunningham's talk. Cotton, a Democrat who lived in Cunningham's district, interrupted to say he disagreed with the congressman and believed the defense budget was "not low enough." Cunningham exploded, flipped Cotton the bird, and said, "Fuck you." During the question-and-answer session, Cotton told Cunningham he had been offended and Cunningham apologized several times. (Cunningham later claimed that Cotton had flipped him the bird first and interrupted him four times.) *The San Diego Union-Tribune*, in an editorial, called Cunningham "an embarrassment to San Diego." It was past time, the newspaper wrote, for Cunningham to conduct himself in a manner befitting his office. Come election time, the newspaper endorsed him nevertheless.

Another personal problem for the congressman involved his

twenty-nine-year-old son, Todd, now a bartender, who had been arrested the previous year and charged in federal court with marijuana possession and distribution. Todd's drug use had gotten him involved with a group of dealers who shipped tons of marijuana cross-country. Fortunately for him, prosecutors viewed Todd's role in the operation as minor; he was a "worker," paid $100 to ship small packages of marijuana. He had gotten arrested for driving a van loaded with four hundred pounds of pot in Lawrence, Massachusetts. He pleaded guilty shortly after his arrest and testified before a federal grand jury in Massachusetts, and his testimony helped lead to the indictment of eighteen others. While out on bail, he tested positive for cocaine on three different occasions. When federal probation officers in San Diego tried to arrest him following the third test, Todd jumped out a window to avoid them and fractured his leg.

Todd was still wearing a cast when he appeared in U.S. district court in Boston for sentencing on November 17, 1998. Seated in the courtroom was his father, who had flown up from Washington to attend the hearing. A few months before Todd's arrest, Cunningham had published an essay in the *Union-Tribune* that called for an increase in the number of drug-enforcement agents, additional drug-interdiction efforts, more drug prosecutions, and longer mandatory minimum sentences for drug trafficking. He had also railed against "soft on crime" liberal judges. The congressman asked for permission to address the court.

"This is . . ." Cunningham's voice trailed off. "This is difficult." He began to cry. "I'm sure you see people from broken homes and cases every day of your life. My son has made some bad decisions, and he has to take responsibility for those, and I have told my son the same thing. But I think there are some things that I don't know if it will help the court or not. I didn't have access to my son. He was adopted. I was shot down on my three-hundredth mission over North Vietnam, and I didn't have a lot of time with him at a young age. When I came back, his mother took him to St. Louis, and I only had him for a month at a time and it was difficult on him them.

"He would cry and not want to go back, and then my son, we haven't had a whole bunch of time together, but I know that, unlike a lot of young men, he has got a good heart, and he works hard, and if you talk to anybody that he ever worked with, he does better than an average job. He will never set the world on fire. He won't become a doctor, lawyer, or judge. He wants to go back to school and work this out. I would ask that if he does go to jail, that he goes somewhere at Lompoc, California, where my wife and I can have access to him, to visit with him and to do that, but I thank the judge for recommendation of downsizing. He's never been in trouble before. He has been a good son. He has made some bad decisions, and I thank the court for at least hearing me, Your Honor."

Cunningham put his hands on his son's shoulders, sat down, and wiped away a tear. Judge Reginald C. Lindsay, who by virtue of being a Clinton appointee might have fallen under Cunningham's definition of soft on crime, said he recognized in Todd a young man with no prior criminal record who still had something to contribute to society and sentenced him to two and a half years in prison.

7

———— ◆◆◆ ————

Fat Fingers

A few days before a trip to Panama in March in 1999, Gary Jones, the Pentagon official overseeing the document-scanning program, came home from work to find his wife looking shocked and ashen-faced. "I just got a phone call that said that 'you need to tell your husband to watch his back while he's in Panama,'" Jones's wife told him. Before leaving, Jones wrote down a whole bunch of names and put them in an envelope and told his wife that if anything happened to him while he was gone, she should open the envelope and get hold of the people whose names he had listed.

By that time, the Panama contract Wilkes was working on had turned into a major headache for the government. To straighten things out, the government officials involved in the contract flew down to inspect things firsthand. Jones was impressed by Wilkes's operation:

"They were doing a pretty decent job." He was reasonably happy that the government would get what they were paying ADCS for.

Jones didn't think anything more about the strange phone call his wife had received until he went out to dinner one night at a restaurant with the rest of the group attending the meeting in Panama. At dinner, Jones was seated next to a man he didn't know. "You know," the man told Jones, "I don't know if you're aware of this, but we have ways to keep people from ever leaving Panama. No one would ever know where they went." When he wasn't in his meetings, Jones spent the remainder of his Panama trip behind the locked door of his hotel room, too scared to venture out. "I was in the government for thirty-two years, and I never came across anything close to this," Jones said.

Paul Behrens, another government official who flew down to Panama, had a similar story. He was met at the airport by Wilkes and his entourage. As they walked out of the airport, Behrens heard Wilkes say, apropos of nothing, "Boy, you guys know that people can just disappear in foreign countries?" Behrens took it as a clear threat, and he relayed the remark to the Defense Inspector General's Office and the Army's Criminal Investigative Division, but was told that no action could be taken since it did not constitute a "specific threat."

Gail Cotton, the lone woman in attendance in Panama, has taken to calling the sessions her "twelve angry men meetings." The meetings were arranged to resolve a dispute between Wilkes and Rollie Kimbrough, another defense contractor involved in the project. Kimbrough was the prime contractor on the Panama contract, and Wilkes worked for him as a subcontractor. The two men were in a bitter dispute about money. Wilkes believed that Kimbrough had been stealing money that was rightfully his, and as a result ADCS was close to going out of business. Unless he got paid, Wilkes announced at a meeting, he would halt work and keep all the equipment that he had purchased and never been reimbursed for. Things got so heated that the two men were on the verge of blows. Gail took Kimbrough aside and told him he needed to work things out. She urged him to walk away from the Panama project and put an end to things with a minimum of hassle.

Wilkes had been asking his friends in Congress for help in getting Kimbrough kicked off the Panama contract. He drafted a letter to the Defense Department, complaining that the setbacks in the project had forced him to lay people off. Copies of the letter went to two San Diego congressmen, Duncan Hunter and Ron Packard. In February 1999, Wilkes met with Jeff Shockey, a longtime aide to Congressman Jerry Lewis, Wilkes's diving partner in Belize, who had risen to the chairmanship of the Defense Appropriations subcommittee. Wilkes asked Shockey if Congressman Lewis could do anything to help get Kimbrough kicked off the contract. "I offer you this information in hopes that your office can intervene in these matters and help restore the project that ADCS, Inc. has so diligently tried to maintain," Wilkes wrote Shockey, who followed up with his own letter to Veterans Affairs.

In the end, Wilkes got what he wanted. Kimbrough reluctantly agreed to walk away from the Panama project. Gail Cotton terminated Kimbrough's company from the contract and immediately issued a new contract to Wilkes's company, which agreed to complete the remainder of the work for $1.25 million. Still, Wilkes remained furious at Kimbrough. At the end of the meetings, Wilkes, joined by his new consultant, Mitchell Wade, paid a visit to Kimbrough in his hotel room in Panama City, a scene that Kimbrough recounted in a 2000 deposition.

Q. Did there ever come a time when ADCS or any of its personnel threatened you?

A. Yes. I was in Panama. I was sitting in the hotel and Mr. Wade, who was a consultant of, I believe, of Brent Wilkes, the two of them met me in my hotel room after this meeting in Panama and demanded that I give them $400,000 right then.

I told them I couldn't do that. They told me that if I didn't do that, they would never let me go and that at some point and time someone with fat fingers would walk up to me and that would be it. And I take that as a threat.

Q. What did you think that meant?

A. That they were going to attempt to assassinate me.

Kimbrough later said Wade made the threat, and told the FBI about the exchange, but nothing ever came of it. Wilkes said he laughed when he heard about Kimbrough's claim, and both he and Wade separately denied the incident ever took place.

Wilkes had hired Wade as a consultant for the Panama project based on the recommendation of government officials. Before he signed on with Wilkes, Wade had helped a defense contractor develop a proposal on how to do the work and spelled out in detail exactly what equipment and manpower would be needed for the job. Paul Behrens, one of the government officials involved in the Panama contract, knew Wade from his work for the National Security Agency and had mentioned his name to his Defense Department colleagues as someone who could help out.

Wilkes initially had low hopes for how useful Wade would be. He came away less than impressed from their initial meeting. Wade seemed arrogant, but Wilkes put him in a position where he felt he could work with him. Wade started working for ADCS as a consultant in July 1998, earning between $10,000 and $20,000 a month, which Wilkes thought was reasonable given how useful Wade turned out to be in Panama.

Tall and imposing with dark, wavy hair, Wade, at thirty-five, ran a one-man firm called MZM Inc., which served the intelligence community. He had a reputation as a take-charge, get-it-done kind of guy. "He had the balls," said a former contractor who hired him in the mid-1990s. "He could get things done."

Born in Washington, D.C., Wade was the son of an executive at a local ironworks company, while his mother worked in the banking industry. Shortly after graduating from George Washington University in 1985, Wade had joined the Pentagon as a newly married man with a baby on the way. He rose quickly through the Pentagon hierarchy and became a program manager in an office that specialized in "black projects" in the Office of the Secretary of Defense. Wade wanted perks from the contractors he worked with; one complained that Wade pressured him for a first-class upgrade on a trip to Europe.

He began making deeper contacts in the intelligence world through the naval reserves, which commissioned him as an intelligence officer in 1987. His first duty assignment the next year was at the Defense Intelligence Agency in Washington, D.C. He attended Basic Intelligence Training School in San Diego and continued to work for brief periods at the Defense Intelligence Agency. According to intelligence analyst Steve Jenkins, Wade had been sent down to Panama after U.S. forces invaded in December 1989, as part of a document exploitation team, and he scanned papers of Manuel Noriega's regime to determine what the dictator knew about the weaknesses of the U.S. military.

Wade left the Pentagon in 1992 and started MZM Inc. out of his apartment in Arlington, Virginia. As a contractor, he possessed badges or identifications that allowed him to get in and out of the National Security Agency, the Central Intelligence Agency, and the Defense Intelligence Agency. In 1996, Wade had allowed his top-secret security clearance to lapse, although Army intelligence kept a top-secret clearance for him at the National Ground Intelligence Center in Charlottesville, Virginia, according to MZM's former security officer.

Wade's contacts throughout the government made him indispensable to ADCS in Panama. He knew how to make the slumbering Defense Department bureaucracy come to life and make things happen with incredible speed. If five pallets of equipment needed to be sent to Panama on short notice, Wade could make it happen. Ditto if ADCS needed some additional office space. The contract was a large one for such a relatively inexperienced company as ADCS, and without Wade, the company might not have been able to pull it off.

Wilkes was impressed, and Wade gradually became part of his inner circle. At Wilkes's direction, Wade gave thousands of dollars in 1998 and 1999 to various congressional campaigns. Through Wilkes, Mitchell Wade met Congressman Randy Cunningham over dinner one evening at The Capital Grille and began a relationship that would have devastating consequences for both men. Wade even got invited along to a poker game Wilkes hosted in Washington hotels. Wade bet too much in what was a low-stakes game, however, and didn't get invited back.

One of Wade's principal contacts in the Defense Department was Robert Fromm, a small, paunchy man with fading hair who worked at the Army's National Ground Intelligence Center in Charlottesville, Virginia. In 1999, according to Wilkes, Wade wrote a letter to get rid of Paul Behrens, a government contracting official who was becoming a thorn in his company's side. Behrens was replaced by Fromm.

To key government contracting officials, Fromm seemed to be too close to ADCS and Wade. "Once Bob got involved, all I knew is that everything was acceptable. There were no problems. He would sign off on every invoice. Everything was happily ever after," Gail Cotton said.

During a trip to Panama, Steve Jenkins joined Fromm and Wade for dinner at a restaurant by the presidential palace. They dined on lobster, venison, and sirloin tips, and Wade ordered a $400 bottle of red wine. Wade swirled the wine around in his glass and sniffed it, then called out the chef to pour him a glass. Jenkins, who drove a Nissan Sentra, was no connoisseur, and to him the wine tasted bitter. Fromm, however, seemed impressed with the wine and taken by the whole occasion. Later, Fromm showed up at the twelve angry men meetings in Panama. He behaved oddly. He followed Gail Cotton to the bathroom and stood outside waiting for her to finish. "He was just like this little spy guy," Cotton said.

In May 1999, Fromm approached Jones and told him that he wanted more money for FIRES. The Panama project, he told Jones, was a test case for the database, and Fromm needed $15 million to continue the program. Cunningham and Hunter followed up by putting pressure on Jones's superiors. Jones said he would only authorize money for a program with a "strategic purpose." Fromm agreed and Jones authorized $5.3 million, money that would go directly to Wilkes's company.

Still, Wilkes wanted more money. He faxed Cunningham a set of "talking points" on July 6 and asked the congressman to demand the full $15 million for the FIRES program. "We need $10m more immediately," Wilkes wrote in his script for Cunningham, a document that would later fall into the hands of federal prosecutors. He instructed Cunningham to tell Jones's superiors that the money should, if necessary, come out of another program Jones had managed at the Defense Advanced Research Projects Agency, a unique Pentagon agency chartered to bring radical innovation to the Defense Department.

Jones felt the document-scanning program at the Defense Advanced Research Projects Agency actually delivered something of greater value. But the pressure from Cunningham worked. Against

Jones's better judgment, he moved an additional $5 million to Wilkes's company in September. The total of $9.77 million that ADCS received from the Pentagon's scanning program in 1999 was the largest single award under the entire program.

In an e-mail, Gary Jones told Gail Cotton what had happened.

Gail,

Great to hear from you. Unfortunately, all is not well in the world of ADCS. We had Congressman Cunningham come down very heavy on the program and force us to withdraw money from one of my projects and send it to ADCS, Inc. (indirectly of course). Bob Fromm does not keep me informed at all. Believe he feels he will be protected from "DoD oversight" by his contractor now. So that relationship is going to take some work.

How are things with you? How does it look like ADCS, Inc. is performing?

Gary

In her reply, Cotton expressed her frustrations with the whole affair and said she looked forward to closing out the Panama contract: "My 'gut instinct' still says this whole affair is bad news. Now that the Panama piece is complete, I don't know that you are getting much of value, but I hope so. I'm sorry you had to 'give' them more money. It's that kind of congressional interference that really turns my stomach."

Cunningham continued to push for ADCS to get every cent he had squeezed out of the Defense Department. When the money didn't move fast enough, Cunningham vented his frustration with Gary Jones and his boss, Louis Kratz, to Army Secretary Louis Caldera when he appeared before a Defense Appropriations subcommittee hearing. "I want Lou Kratz removed from office," Cunningham said. "I think he's incompetent. And I'm calling for his removal. I've had it.

I'm tired. And I want the money identified. I would like it released. This is for an intelligence program that is critical."

Jones helped bring increased scrutiny on the document-scanning project, which led to an audit by the Department of Defense Inspector General. Investigators found the program rife with congressional influence. The report noted that Jones had put millions into the program at the insistence of two members of Congress. The meddling by Congress was not without its price. Four other projects Jones's team had recommended for funding got nothing. As a result, the Inspector General found that a project involving the Blackhawk helicopter was delayed and costs rose for spare-parts procurement at an Oklahoma City base, among others.

Partly as a result of what they were hearing, the Pentagon Inspector General launched three separate investigations into ADCS's work on the Panama Canal contract. The investigations examined, among other things, whether ADCS had complied with State Department requirements for contractors working overseas. In his 2000 deposition, Wilkes claimed that investigators determined the company wasn't required to obtain the clearances. Another investigation looked at the prices ADCS was charging in Panama. Wilkes said in deposition that no improprieties were found. "They were all wrapped up and everything was finished and clean and fine and done," Wilkes said.

The investigation into the Panama contract had a number of people in the Pentagon Inspector General's office worried. The allegations weren't substantiated, but they weren't refuted either. The Inspector General isn't allowed to do fishing expeditions, so the case withered on the vine. Some of these matters should have been more thoroughly examined by Pentagon investigators on the East Coast, but they couldn't figure it out. "In hindsight, I cringed," said a senior investigator with the Pentagon Inspector General.

ADCS continued to wring as much money as it could out of the government. In a June 2, 1999, e-mail titled "Remaining Funds," Wade wrote to Wilkes and others that $264,356.24 was left to be spent on the Panama contract and instructed company officials to prepare a bill of materials for that amount. "More blood from the turnip!!!" Wade wrote.

By December 14, ADCS had still not finished all its work under the contract. The Panama contract also covered smaller projects, including a digital library at Camp Pendleton, a sprawling Marine base north of San Diego, and with one day left on the contract, the company still had more work to do. Things were getting dicey: if government contracting officials learned that the company had not finished its work at the Marine base, it could be trouble. "We don't want the government 'talking' with them [Marines] for fear it would delay and complicate things," ADCS Vice President Mike Williams wrote in an e-mail.

Wade had a solution. He instructed Williams to draft a letter for a Marine official to sign stating that ADCS had completed its work. "Signed . . . muckity muck," Williams wrote. "That's all that needs to be said." The muckety-muck, a Marine colonel, signed the letter a few days later, praising the company's outstanding services. The letter went to Bob Fromm, and ADCS quietly finished its work after the contract deadline had passed.

After Panama, Wilkes's company continued scanning documents for the military, only now ADCS was no longer under the direction of Gary Jones and others at the Pentagon. The program now had a new name, Global Infrastructure Data Capture, and millions of dollars earmarked by Cunningham. Instead of scanning documents onto compact discs as Wilkes had done in the Panama project, he was now scanning blueprints for the FIRES database at the National Ground Intelligence Center.

The switch had been engineered with Wade's friends at the National Ground Intelligence Center and Cunningham's help. At the end of 1999, Bob Fromm asked for a private lunch with Cunningham to, among other things, explain the FIRES program and ask for money to support the program in the future. The meeting was held in Las Vegas on December 21, 1999, at the Four Seasons Hotel. According to prosecutors, Wilkes paid Cunningham and his chief of staff, Trey Hardin, to fly over from San Diego. When the meeting ended, Wilkes treated the group to a $4,000 meal at Andre's French Restaurant. Later, according to a source, Wilkes, Cunningham, and Hardin went out gambling. Wilkes pulled out a large pile of cash and peeled off some bills for Hardin to go play blackjack with while Wilkes and the congressman went to play craps. When they were through, Wilkes took Hardin out on the town.

An entirely new program was created in 2000, giving ADCS a fresh start away from the scrutiny from the Defense Department Inspector General's office. Changing the nature of the program held several advantages for Wilkes. Too many people were involved in the previous program, too many members of Congress with an interest in squeezing money out of it. It also meant avoiding oversight from pesky government officials like Gary Jones and Paul Behrens.

Although Wilkes couldn't see it yet, the real advantage belonged to Wade. The program was now in the hands of his friends like Robert Fromm and others at the Defense Information Systems Agency, who Wilkes felt were willing and able to do his bidding. Wilkes had no choice but to rely on Wade as his guide in the world of military intelligence. Wade was the go-between, running interference for Wilkes with the government program officials, which gave Wade control of the information flow. He began to charge six-figure fees, and Wilkes had no choice but to pay. "Wade played me," Wilkes said. "He'd create problems so he could earn value by solving them."

Wilkes claimed that he received several e-mails from Fromm pressuring him to give Wade what he was asking. "He's basically saying I hope you understand how important this is to the project and you're doing everything you can to ensure he continues to work with us. I don't think this project could continue without his services," Wilkes said. It wasn't an explicit demand for money—no dollar amount was mentioned—but the message was clear.

Army intelligence officials preferred to talk with Wade, who spoke their language. Wilkes dragged his feet when it came to getting classified clearances for his employees, which meant ADCS couldn't do classified scanning, so military intelligence people started dealing with Wade. "When we talked about opportunities for getting documents that were available, Mitch immediately understood how we could do certain things and the cost-effectiveness and made it happen from his end," said Steve Jenkins, the analyst at the National Ground Intelligence Center who worked on the FIRES program. "Brent didn't have the same understanding. He didn't care what he did for the money. He could be shining shoes as long as the money was coming in as copious amounts as it was."

Acting at Fromm's direction, Wilkes packed up his operation in Panama at the end of 1999 and shipped it at government expense to Winchester, Virginia, where he began working on scanning projects for the FIRES program. ADCS scanned blueprints and documents of overseas military facilities built by the U.S. Army Corps of Engineers. These included military facilities in Pakistan and Iran, a road system in Afghanistan, port facilities in Somalia, and a $14 billion construction program in Saudi Arabia for air and navy bases, military barracks, port facilities, hospitals, military training centers and schools, and associated utilities and roads.

———

Scanning documents for the government had made Wilkes a wealthy man. He moved his family into a $1.49 million home in 1999 that he had purchased from former Chargers quarterback Stan Humphries. He surrounded himself with a group of businessmen who lived in Poway, an affluent San Diego suburb. "He was like a rock star with his Poway friends," said Patrick Shea, an attorney and friend of Wilkes's. With his tales of Washington, his friends in the CIA, Wilkes seemed like an otherworldly figure to the crowd in Poway.

And business was booming, or at least it looked that way. To show he had arrived, Wilkes created a whole host of new companies. Group W Holdings Inc., which had been in existence for several years, was joined by Group W Transportation, Group W Outfitters Inc., Group W Media Productions Inc., Group W Events Inc. (which had four catering divisions, including W Catering), and Group W Advisors Inc. That didn't include The Wilkes Foundation, Wilkes Corporation, and Wilkes Technology Group Inc., to name but a few others. It sounded impressive, but most of these companies existed principally in name. Group W Transportation, for example, managed fractional shares in corporate jets.

ADCS had purchased Wilkes's one-sixteenth shares in a Lear 60 and a Lear 31 in September 2000. The cozy planes could fly coast to coast without stopping, and Wilkes used the plane to give members of Congress a ride home. Cunningham boarded the first of many flights aboard a Wilkes jet in February 26, 2001, for a flight from Palm Springs to San Diego, and then on to Washington. In the air, Cunningham and other guests dined on a cold seafood platter, grilled chicken or filet mignon, a side salad, six bottles of Silver Oak cabernet, and three bottles of Cakebread chardonnay. Group W Transportation covered the $17,000 cost of the trip. Congressmen Ben Gilman and Jerry Weller, whom Wilkes counted as his friends, also flew on the plane. Much of the Republican House leadership would fly on a Wilkes plane: Speaker Dennis Hastert, Majority Leader Tom DeLay, and Majority Whip Roy Blunt.

That DeLay flew on Wilkes's plane would lead to much speculation, which was somewhat unfair, given that successful government contractors routinely fly members of Congress on corporate jets. While Wilkes clearly was a well-connected man, no evidence has ever surfaced that the majority leader ever did anything for the defense contractor in return. "I never heard Tom discuss Wilkes or bring up anything he had ever talked to Wilkes about," said a former DeLay chief of staff. DeLay also told his lawyers that he had never had any dealings with Wilkes, according to his former top aide. Wilkes was known to DeLay's staff principally as someone whose name was in the press and was involved in fund-raising for the majority leader, but De-Lay's former aide said he was never able to establish any contact between the two. However, Wilkes's contributions to DeLay's political action committee, Texans for a Republican Majority, would become part of an investigation into the majority leader by a Texas district attorney.

The burgeoning Wilkes empire settled into a new and impressive headquarters in Poway. Completed at a cost of $11 million, the building showed off Wilkes's tastes for expensive high-end design. Visitors entered into a stunning vaulted, steel-and-glass lobby with granite tile floors buffed to a high sheen. Receptionists answered phones at desks wrapped in beautifully milled cherrywood. A 9,600-square-foot venue called the W Pavilion hosted fund-raisers and other corporate events, with food for up to three hundred provided by an on-site industrial kitchen. Wilkes's private office suite had a warm, cozy feel. Cherry-wood panels lined the walls of the president's suite, which included a pool table and a gas fireplace. In a small rear-projection theater lined with acoustic tiles, guests could settle into comfortable chairs and join Wilkes to watch movies. At nearly one hundred thousand square feet, about the size of a typical branch of The Home Depot, the headquarters was more space than Wilkes's small operation needed. He called it his "expansion space." Visitors described large rooms that housed only a photocopy machine, and the feeling that there wasn't as much to the company as it seemed.

Much of Wilkes's success was owed to Cunningham. As a way of saying thanks, Wilkes sponsored a lavish "Tribute to Heroes" in 2002, honoring the congressman and other local veterans. A few days before the event, Republican Bob Ney of Ohio read a proclamation into the *Congressional Record*, recognizing "Tribute to Heroes" for "its worthwhile efforts for servicemen and their families, emergency workers and children's health care." (Ney would later plead guilty to performing a variety of official acts for lobbyists in exchange for campaign contributions, expensive meals, luxury travel, sports tickets, and thousands of dollars in gambling chips.)

Wilkes's charitable foundation spent more than $35,000 on the military-themed gala held at the Aerospace Museum in Balboa Park, which featured a troupe of dancing children and an auction to raise money for various charities. Wilkes gave generously to the United Way and a local YMCA, which named Wilkes Man of the Year in 2002, but two organizations who said they were promised funds by the foundation never received any. One was the Air Warrior Courage Foundation, and the other was the Vision of Children Foundation, which was run by Cunningham's friend Samuel Hardage, who had a son born with a rare genetic eye disease. "We never got a penny. Not a nickel, not one thin dime," Hardage said. "To promise funds to charities and then not deliver is just bizarre behavior. You just don't do that. You don't mess around with foundations. Particularly foundations like the Vision of Children Foundation that are benefiting children. That's just low."

8

Lost in Washington

As the new millennium dawned, Cunningham seemed bored. He was virtually guaranteed reelection in his solidly Republican district, he had his seat on Appropriations, but ambitions still stirred in him. An earlier attempt to climb up the ranks of the Republican leadership in the House had gone nowhere. His House colleagues had turned back his bid for chairmanship of the House Republican Conference, with only forty-two members supporting him.

In 2000, according to Nancy Cunningham, Randy was at his wit's end about his lack of role in the leadership. He vented his anger in Speaker Dennis Hastert's office and, in Nancy's view, came completely unhinged. "He thought he should be at the top, and when Speaker Hastert promoted people over him, Mr. Cunningham became very, very disturbed," Nancy told Kitty Kelley. Unable to get into the ranks of the House leadership, Cunningham sought a chairmanship instead, and he had a new chief of staff who promised to make it happen.

Dewitt Talmadge Hardin III, known as Trey, had taken over Cunningham's office in August 1999, bringing with him little experience and, unlike his two predecessors, no prior relationship with Cunningham. But Cunningham and Hardin had an agreement. Hardin was going to work the political angles, start a political action committee, spread money around, and work on getting Cunningham a committee chairmanship. Tom DeLay, the House majority whip, instituted a new system whereby committee chairmanships were, in part, distributed based on a member's fund-raising prowess. House GOP members with safe seats like Cunningham's were expected to contribute to the party as a whole. Cunningham told his staff that he intended to raise $1 million.

Hardin quickly went to work on Cunningham's PAC. He brought in Barbara Bonfiglio, an attorney with the Washington lobbying firm of Williams & Jensen, who had set up PACs for DeLay, Charlton Heston, Senator Rick Santorum, and other Republican bigwigs. Cunningham's American Prosperity PAC held a kickoff fund-raiser in February 2000 at a posh La Jolla restaurant overlooking the Pacific Ocean. In August, Cunningham hosted another event at the high-end Coeur d'Alene Resort in Idaho. The PAC also hosted an annual event in May—a golf tournament at Torrey Pines followed by a deep-sea-fishing expedition off the coast. Small amounts of money started flowing to other congressional campaigns, but Cunningham wasn't able to raise the big sums needed for a chairmanship, the prize that continued to elude him.

It soon became apparent to others in Cunningham's office that Hardin was not up to the job of chief of staff. Hardin, at thirty-eight. He had jumped to chief of staff after serving as campaign manager, spokesman, and policy director for Representative Tom Davis. He lacked attention to detail; there were various flights he didn't reimburse properly. In addition, Hardin had his own problems. His marriage was breaking up. At his first meeting with a Cunningham district director in San Diego, he hit on the waitress who was serving them lunch. Then he missed a dinner appointment in order to go out with the waitress.

An excellent golfer, Hardin would take defense contractors out on the links and play against them for money, beating them almost every time. During a visit to San Diego, he went out to dinner at an expensive restaurant with a number of other chiefs of staff and, as they finished their meal, called up the employee of a local defense contractor who was home in bed at 11 p.m. Could he please come down and pay for the dinner?

With Hardin in charge of the office, deals that other chiefs of staff would have quashed managed to get through. In May 2000, Wilkes wrote Cunningham checks totaling $100,000 to buy his boat, the *Kelly C.* The sale was a "gentlemen's agreement": no paperwork would record the transaction, and Cunningham would continue to live on the boat. The first check for $70,000 went into his personal bank account; the second, he deposited in his account at the Congressional Federal Credit Union in Washington, D.C., which serves members of the House and Senate. Wilkes also started making regular payments on Cunningham's mortgage on the boat. The timing of the boat sale was suspicious. Two weeks earlier, Cunningham had submitted a $16 million earmark for the Global Infrastructure Data Capture program to benefit Wilkes's company.

It would be months before Hardin and other staffers learned that Cunningham had "sold" his boat, the *Kelly C,* to Wilkes. According to a former Cunningham aide, the deal was halted when Nancy Cunningham called her husband's Washington office and shared her concerns about the impropriety of the boat deal. Staffers were alarmed. Even if the transaction was legal, it was highly inappropriate, to say the least, for a congressman to sell his boat to a defense contractor and close friend. Cunningham, however, was determined to go ahead with the deal. He even drafted a letter to the House ethics committee to get them to bless the deal, although it is unclear whether the letter was ever sent. The committee never provided a response.

When the aide asked Trey Hardin, Cunningham's chief of staff, what had happened, Hardin replied that both Cunningham and Wilkes were told the deal had to be "unwound." Hardin told another staffer that the checks had been torn up, which wasn't true. The sale was halted, but Cunningham kept the money. Accounts differ over what happened. Wilkes either asked for the money back and Cunningham refused, or the congressman tried to give the money back but his friend told him to keep it. The boat transaction would later become the first overt act in Cunningham's plea agreement.

It must have seemed unfair to Cunningham that he was earning $141,300 a year in 2000 while his former aides were making a fortune. Frank Collins, his first chief of staff, did well enough as a defense lobbyist to buy a spectacular $1.25 million home in January 2000 located on a cul-de-sac in Alexandria, Virginia, a stone's throw from the Potomac. The four-level home had hardwood floors and palladium windows that looked out over the river, and where *Washington Life* magazine gushed that Collins was "living in the lap of luxury." During a visit, Cunningham was impressed by the house; according to a former staff member, he seemed somewhat jealous.

The boat sale wasn't the only sign that Wilkes would bring trouble for Cunningham. Cunningham had another close call, thanks to Wilkes's lawsuit against Rollie Kimbrough, his former partner on the Panama contract. Kimbrough had filed for bankruptcy in March of 2000, claiming he was driven out of business by Wilkes. To Wilkes, however, Kimbrough's bankruptcy was an "escape plan" to get out of paying the $1.66 million that he claimed Kimbrough owed him. So determined was Wilkes to get his money that he failed to realize or simply didn't care that he was giving Kimbrough's lawyers an opportunity to explore his relationship with the congressman.

Buried in the government's file on the Panama contract was evidence that was described by Kimbrough's attorney, Paul Sweeney, to a federal judge in August as "severe political interference." Especially troubling, Sweeney told the judge, was the e-mail from Gary Jones complaining that Cunningham had "come down very heavy" on the program. Sweeney asked the judge to order ADCS to produce documents that explained what benefits and money the company had received through Cunningham's efforts. "They are hiding the ball, Your Honor," Sweeney said. Kimbrough "has been sued for fraud and misrepresentation, his company has been destroyed and put into bankruptcy, and it is a witch hunt against him. And, in fact, based on the e-mail traffic, I think it's more appropriate that this matter be referred to the Inspector General."

On September 6, 2000, Wilkes arrived in Sweeney's offices in Silver Spring, Maryland, for deposition. Knowing Wilkes's reputation as a man with only hard edges, Sweeney went at Wilkes as forcefully as he could with the bits and pieces he had learned about Wilkes's relationship with Cunningham. By the end of the second day of deposition, Sweeney struck a nerve. Wilkes lost his cool and started cursing at Sweeney during a break in the questioning. When Wilkes's attorney accused Sweeney of conducting a fishing expedition, Sweeney turned to the subject of Wilkes's close relationships with members of Congress:

Q. Since your counsel brought it up, let's talk about fishing expeditions. Do you have a close personal relationship with Mr. Lewis, the congressman?

A. We're acquaintances.

Q. Do you take vacations together?

A. No.

Q. Have you ever gone on vacations, fishing trips, that sort of thing?

A. I was on a trip once that involved an official delegation going to Belize for a meeting with the ambassador down there, and Mr. Lewis made a presentation to the government of Belize and we went diving for a day and a half after that.

Q. No fishing?

A. No. Well, we fished from the boat between dives.

Q. Was Mr. Cunningham present on that trip?

A. No. . . .

Q. Have you gone on any trips with Mr. Cunningham?

A. Vacations?

Q. Let's just say trips of any sort.

A. I have been in his presence on flights back and forth to Washington.

Q. Traveling with him?

A. Traveling on the same plane.

Q. For the same sort of meeting?

A. No.

Q. Did your travel at that time with Mr. Cunningham relate in any way to the ADCS initiative?

A. No.

Q. Did you ever go on any—

A. No, and it wasn't something coordinated, he was just on the plane at the same time that I was.

Q. Did you ever take any vacations, fishing trips, diplomatic missions, anything like that with Mr. Cunningham?

A. No. I've attended some official functions and fund-raisers and things like that with him, but nothing that could be construed as a diplomatic mission or whatever else you said. . . .

Q. Are there any loans between Mr. Cunningham and yourself or the company?

A. No.

Q. Any gifts between you and Mr. Cunningham and/or the company?

A. No.

Convinced there was more going on, Sweeney subpoenaed the congressman for trial. Sweeney had recognized that Cunningham was a source of Wilkes's power. It was another bluff, and Sweeney hoped it would encourage ADCS to reach a settlement. Instead, the other side seemed only to stiffen their resolve. Trial was scheduled for October 4. Sweeney's witness list included Congressmen Cunningham and Jerry Lewis, as well as Lewis's aide Jeff Shockey.

Subpoenas were a problem for the congressmen. Under House rules, subpoenas are a matter of public record for members of Congress. Any problem, however, was headed off when the House Office of General Counsel contacted Sweeney and told him that congressional immunity protected Cunningham from having to answer any questions. Sweeney let the matter drop, and a few months later a federal judge dismissed the case against Kimbrough. The subpoenas, however, made Cunningham's staff nervous. The appearance of a congressman pressuring Defense Department officials on behalf of a friend who made a living off Cunningham's earmarks was troubling.

Hardin met with Patrick McSwain and Frank Collins, his predecessors as chiefs of staff, and discussed the possibility that perhaps Cunningham should not run for reelection in November 2000. He had served five terms in Congress, and it might be time for him to go into the private sector and work as a lobbyist. Lobbying, however, required subtlety and persuasiveness, and Cunningham was as smooth as sandpaper, as subtle as a hammer. Cunningham ran for reelection instead and won easily.

By 2001, Cunningham seemed completely lost, unable to find his way out of Washington's ethical swamp. He had stopped coming back to his district. Local groups started to complain to his district office: when were they going to get a chance to talk to the congressman? As a freshman legislator, district staff members recalled, Cunningham had enjoyed meeting with his constituents, and he returned home virtually every weekend. Unlike other representatives, Cunningham would sit down with individuals for meetings that lasted a half hour or so to hear their problems. Now, he didn't want to leave Washington, and the staff did nothing to force him to come back.

In an especially embarrassing episode, Cunningham missed a fundraiser held on his behalf in Rancho Santa Fe. Three or four days before the event, a staff member noticed that the event wasn't on Cunningham's official schedule. Hardin had forgotten about it, and in the end Cunningham didn't leave Washington; he wanted to stay in town to take people out on the *Kelly C.* His wife was forced to cover for him, and she was livid and embarrassed, a former staffer said.

Cunningham was also absentminded about his widowed mother, Lela, who lived near San Diego. The congressman's parents had moved west shortly after their son was elected to Congress, but Cunningham's father had passed away in 1994 at the age of seventy-six. Staffers were fond of Lela Cunningham, who would call up her son's district office and wish his employees a happy holiday. Her son the congressman spent more time with Nancy's parents; her father helped run Cunningham's aviation memorabilia business. Staffers had to schedule visits between Cunningham and his mother when he returned to the district.

A new Republican administration took office in January of 2001, ushering out the Clinton regime, which Cunningham had so long detested. The day George W. Bush took the oath of office, the Cunninghams showed up at the Capital Yacht Club in a 700-series BMW. Nancy exited dressed in a mink coat that reached her calves. Other members of the yacht club looked at her and wondered, why does she need a mink coat in San Diego?

With his own party now in charge, Cunningham saw the opportunity to grab an office that he had always coveted: secretary of the navy. Hardin, once an intern in the George H. W. Bush White House, said he would help Cunningham develop contacts with the incoming president. Staff had for years dealt with Cunningham's desire to run the Navy or the Defense Department as a whole. In another display of his staggering naïveté, Cunningham submitted a résumé to the incoming administration, edited by the staff in the Washington office. The post went to Gordon England, a genial Baltimore native serving as an executive vice president at General Dynamics.

Still, Cunningham's sixth term in office began with a new committee assignment at what would prove to be a critical time in the nation's history. Speaker J. Dennis Hastert named him to the House Permanent Select Committee on Intelligence. The move made Cunningham the only member of Congress who sat on both the Intelligence Committee and Defense Appropriations subcommittee. He could now authorize new intelligence programs and capabilities on the HPSCI and then, on the Defense Appropriations subcommittee, vote to put more money behind them.

"As the speaker's newest designee to serve on the House Permanent Select Committee on Intelligence, I feel fortunate to represent the nation's top technological talent in the 'black' world," Cunningham wrote to Wilkes in a letter obtained by *The San Diego Union-Tribune.* "I have long benefited from your expertise on major defense issues before Congress, and have appreciated the opportunity to work with you on key service funding priorities. With my new assignment, I see even greater opportunities to work together in support of our national security and intelligence communities."

Still acting out of a misguided sense of loyalty to Wilkes, Cunningham continued to browbeat Defense Department officials on his behalf. John P. Stenbit, an executive vice president at TRW Inc., had been asked by Defense Secretary Donald Rumsfeld to become assistant secretary of defense for command, communications, control, and intelligence. ASDC3I, as the job was known, is one of the more powerful jobs in the Pentagon, with oversight for intelligence, counterintelligence, and weapons in space, among other responsibilities.

About a month before his confirmation hearing on July 31, 2001, Stenbit received a call from Cunningham. The congressman told Stenbit that he must fire Cheryl Roby, a high-level Defense Department official. Stenbit told Cunningham he appreciated the information but he would not do anything until he had a chance to investigate what had happened. Roby's "sin" had been that she took money out of Wilkes's pocket, moving $3 million away from the Global Infrastructure Data Capture program. Roby believed that the money would be better spent on creating databases that would improve the Defense Department's ability to use the scanned images. When Wilkes complained, Cunningham asked his staff to investigate, then summoned Roby to his office. He berated the official for not spending all the $10 million on document scanning and directed her to move the money back to Wilkes's company. She refused. Cunningham was furious.

In August 2001, Speaker Hastert joined Cunningham and his wife for a flight aboard a Wilkes-leased jet to San Diego, where the Speaker was headlining a Cunningham fund-raiser at the U.S. Grant Hotel downtown. "I usually told my husband to check everything with Ethics, but it never occurred to me that there might be something wrong about flying with Speaker Hastert and his wife," Nancy Cunningham told Kitty Kelley. "How can it be illegal or unethical if the most important man in Congress is doing it?"

Tom Casey, Wilkes's former boss, attended the fund-raiser, along with his friend ultimate fighter Ken Shamrock, "the world's most dangerous man." Shamrock posed for photos with Cunningham and Hastert, a former high school wrestling coach. At the event, Cunningham's three chiefs of staff, Hardin, McSwain, and Collins, all came over to have a word with Casey. "You've created a monster," Collins told Casey. Wilkes, they told him, had always been searching for the perfect vehicle to play the game in Washington he had always wanted to play, and now he had it in his document-scanning business, which Casey had handed to him. Wilkes was pushing the boundaries unlike anyone else they had ever seen. "He had learned to play the game so hard and was doing it so relentlessly that they were astonished," Casey said.

A few weeks after the Hastert visit, Cunningham flew on Wilkes's corporate jet to Coeur d'Alene, Idaho. According to prosecutors, Cunningham stayed at the Coeur d'Alene Resort, where Wilkes paid for $2,286 worth of room charges as well as a $250 fully-automatic machine gun shooting session, and $802 worth of golf equipment. Cunningham returned to San Diego on board Wilkes's jet. Later, Cunningham flew back and forth from Manassas, Virginia, to San Diego on the Group W Transportation jet. And Wilkes flew Cunningham to Idaho again the following year and picked up the tab for Cunningham again at the Coeur d'Alene Resort.

But not all was going well for Wilkes. Mitchell Wade, his consultant, was outmaneuvering his old boss. With Wilkes's relationship with Cunningham raising alarms on the congressman's staff, Wade sensed an opportunity to get closer to the congressman and gain a powerful ally. It was a mutual opportunity: Cunningham, too, was looking for a relationship that was less trouble, while Wade had contacts throughout the Defense Department, but had no pull in Congress. "He'd gotten all the corners nailed down—the one he never had was Congress," Wilkes said.

Like a shark circling Cunningham, Wade had sized up his prey. He must have seen a congressman who would do anything—for money. And in Wade, Cunningham found someone perfectly willing to "help" him out with some of his needs, to scratch his itch for the life of luxury. A few weeks after the terrorist attacks on New York and Washington, events that would prompt a massive buildup in the military and intelligence world that Wade knew well, he got his chance.

November 16, 2001, was for Cunningham a fairly typical day of congressional business. He took to the House floor several times that day. He thanked the staff at an Alexandria, Virginia, health-care facility where he had spent some time recuperating from knee-replacement surgery. He also spoke in opposition to the tuna provisions in a South American trade pact. He read into the *Congressional Record* a tribute to the U.S. Capitol Police and the staff who kept the building running.

The same day, Cunningham also found time to go antiques shopping with Mitch Wade. At an antiques store in Kensington, Maryland, Cunningham picked out three nightstands, a leaded-glass cabinet, washstand, buffet, and four armoires. When it came time to pay the bill, Cunningham wandered to a different area of the store. Wade was clearly supposed to pay, and he wrote out a corporate check to cover the $12,000 bill. When he was finished, Cunningham returned to the counter and instructed that the antiques be shipped to his Arlington condo. Wade drove Cunningham back to his condo, and on the way, the congressman thanked him for buying the antiques.

Cunningham told him he was going to make him "somebody."

9

World Headquarters

New Hampshire Avenue near Dupont Circle is one of Washington's most distinguished neighborhoods, home to a dozen embassies. Wedged between the Slovenian embassy and the Cotton Council of America is a trim four-story town home that housed the new headquarters of Mitch Wade's company, MZM Inc. Cyndi Bruno walked under MZM's green awning as she arrived for a job interview in December 2001.

MZM was no longer a one-man show. The company had hired a half dozen people and had recently purchased its headquarters from the Regents of the University of California. The offices were under construction, but even so, they had a genteel, old-world character. The walls were painted butter yellow, and beautiful Persian carpets were scattered throughout the office. Bruno shook hands with MZM's general counsel and made her way up the stairs to Wade's enormous office on the second floor. Wade sat behind a huge, antique secretary's desk. A large bay window overlooked an alley, and Bruno glanced around and saw a fireplace with a white-painted mantel.

Bruno found Wade physically imposing and a bit intimidating. He was blunt and to the point at times during the interview, but gracious. He seemed to style himself after Gordon Gekko, the greedy stockbroker played by Michael Douglas in the Oliver Stone film *Wall Street*. Like Gekko, Wade wore his thick, black hair slicked back and dressed impeccably. He wore custom-made pin-striped suits, seven-fold ties, custom Brooks Brothers shirts, and Allen-Edmonds shoes.

When the interview was over, Wade sent Bruno to Starbucks for a half hour, then asked her to return and made her an offer for the job of assistant general counsel. Bruno became MZM's seventh employee, scheduled to start work on January 2. Her starting salary was $75,000. Within a year she was earning $165,000, a huge amount from such a small, relatively new company.

At thirty, Bruno knew little about the private sector. She had attended UCLA law school after graduating from college at the University of California, Irvine. For the past five years, Bruno had worked in the Navy as a defense counsel and staff lawyer in the Judge Advocate General Corps. Shortly before she was scheduled to leave the Navy, the September 11 attacks had filled Bruno with a strong desire to continue to help her country. A friend had e-mailed Bruno a job posting from MZM.

Attractive and petite, Bruno had curly brown hair, and her regimen of swimming and running helped keep her weight at just over a hundred pounds. She was no pushover, however. With her dark green olive eyes and a military background, Bruno was tough-minded and intense, attributes that men sometimes found intimidating. Despite her lack of experience in the corporate world, Bruno realized that she wasn't working for a normal company. Before beginning work, she had been invited to the December 2001 MZM Christmas party at the company offices, where, to her surprise, she received a bottle of Dom Pérignon as a gift, which came in a lovely box. Bruno had never seen a bottle of the famed French champagne before.

Guests at the party included Congressman Randy Cunningham, and he seemed to be enjoying himself. A Navy veteran herself, Bruno wasn't impressed by Cunningham. He seemed almost senile, a man living in the past, rambling semi-incoherently about Vietnam, and she wondered what, if anything, he had to offer. Physically, he appeared to be much older than he actually was.

Within a few weeks Bruno realized she needed to stay far, far away from Wade. He took Bruno and two of her colleagues out one January evening. The four dined at The Capital Grille, where Wade kept a wine locker stocked with $100-a-bottle 1996 Silver Oak cabernet sauvignon.

At The Capital Grille, lobbyists wined and dined congressmen in an endless round of merrymaking that not even the September 11 attacks could dampen. Two days after the attacks, Paul Magliochetti, a former House Appropriations staffer who ran a defense powerhouse lobbying firm, hosted nine Democratic congressmen at The Capital Grille. After spending the day listening to classified briefings, the congressmen caroused with three attractive Hill staffers, which proved especially embarrassing when the events were featured in the pages of *Vanity Fair* magazine.

The dinner Wade hosted at The Capital Grille four months later attracted less attention. Following a meal of fresh seafood on a bed of ice and well-aged steaks washed down with Silver Oak, the group headed to the MCI Center, where Wade had season tickets to the Washington Wizards in a section close to the floor. Michael Jordan had resumed his stellar basketball career with the Wizards that season and was on his way to scoring thirty points against the Philadelphia 76ers when Wade said he wanted to return to The Capital Grille. Back at the restaurant, Wade ordered "stoli-doleys"—Stolichnaya vodka marinated in fresh pineapple.

Around midnight, Wade started talking about Congressman Cunningham and his boat, the *Kelly C.* Wade told Bruno that he and the congressman had wild parties on the boat, and there was a Jacuzzi covered by a tent on top to protect Cunningham and his guests from intrusive reporters. Wade no doubt made the Jacuzzi sound like more than it was: a bacteria-laden hot tub covered with a tent made of the plastic painters used to catch drips. As he was talking, Wade pulled out his cellular phone and dialed Cunningham. Bruno thought she had entered the twilight zone. Who calls a congressman at midnight? And what kind of congressman answers the phone?

The two talked for a minute and then Wade quickly handed Bruno the phone. Cunningham offered to get out of bed in his Arlington condo, drive down to the Capital Yacht Club, and unlock the gate that led to the boat so Wade and Bruno could make use of it. "Do you want me to come down so you and Mitch can have some fun?" Cunningham asked. Bruno realized that the congressman thought she was some "arm candy" for Wade. Bruno was bewildered. Who was this congressman? What was going on? Was Cunningham pimping for Wade? Cunningham didn't say what they would do on the boat, but he didn't need to. What else would she and Wade be going to use a boat for at midnight?

Bruno thanked Cunningham, but she excused herself by saying she was tired and it was way past her bedtime. It was a Tuesday night, and Bruno, who woke every morning at 5 a.m. to go jogging, wanted to go home. Wade insisted she stay. He didn't want her to take the Metro home; he wanted to personally drive her back to Crystal City, Virginia, where Bruno's car was parked.

Bruno got into Wade's car, but before heading across the Potomac to Virginia, Wade insisted on going somewhere else first. He stopped at MCCXXI, a fashionable nightclub on Connecticut Avenue, where Wade told Bruno he had another liquor cabinet. The music was pounding inside, and Wade led Bruno upstairs where there were a set of couches. Wade started kissing, hugging, and fondling Bruno, who asked him to stop and told him she needed to go. "I wanted out," she said. She couldn't help thinking about Wade's wife, Christiane, who was eight months pregnant and would soon give birth to their first child, Abigail. "What's the matter with you? Are you that desperate?" Bruno asked, and reminded Wade that his wife was about to give birth. She would later learn that Wade intended the dinner with her two colleagues to be a "double date," despite the fact that everyone in the group was either married or in a committed relationship.

On Valentine's Day, Wade made another pass at Bruno. He took her to the Capital Grille for lunch, then told her he needed to stop by Cunningham's boat. There had been a wild party on the boat the night before, Wade told her, and he needed to change the sheets in the master bedroom. On the boat, Wade tried once more to kiss and fondle Bruno, who again told him no and insisted she needed to get back to work. She helped him change the sheets so she could leave as quickly as possible. Bruno had just left the Navy, a man's environment, and she had experienced flirtation in the workplace, but she had never before encountered the level of aggression that Wade showed. "He was unrelenting," she said. "He didn't care what people wanted or didn't want. He thought he could buy people or bully people into submission."

Bruno had started work almost immediately not at MZM headquarters, but at the offices of an upstart defense counterintelligence agency. Behind the dark glass towers in Crystal City, Virginia, a small operation that mostly crunched data was being transformed into a much larger defense agency. It was the job of counterintelligence agents in the military to thwart spies and terrorists who wanted to get their hands on U.S. military secrets, but it had long been a neglected backwater in the U.S. military, a view that began to strike some as a major weakness after the September 11, 2001, attacks. The Army, Navy, and Air Force all had their own counterintelligence branches, which all had agents running around acting independently of each other. The Pentagon's response was to build a new agency with sufficient resources and power to make sense of this confusing picture.

On April 5, 2002, a group of defense officials gathered on the tenth floor of an office building in Crystal City for a small ribbon-cutting ceremony marking the birth of a new military intelligence agency. The speakers, none of whom would be known outside the Pentagon, took turns extolling the virtues of the new agency that promised to root out spies and terrorists and bring much needed coordination to military counterintelligence. Then the agency's future director grabbed a pair of scissors and snipped a red ribbon, launching the Counterintelligence Field Activity.

Mitchell Wade had arrived for the ceremony together with Cunningham, who was the only congressman in the room. Cunningham had arrived at the last minute, and it wasn't entirely clear that the congressman was welcome here. He didn't stay long. He and Wade left together before the speeches had even begun, but not before everyone in the room understood the message. The president of MZM, which had Bruno and others working at the Counterintelligence Field Activity, had a powerful friend in Congress.

The Counterintelligence Field Activity would grow at an incredible clip over the next few years, gobbling up resources and programs in a push to become a full-fledged intelligence agency. The agency became sort of a hodgepodge of programs that had no formal home in the intelligence community, such as a training academy, a polygraph institute, and a behavioral sciences directorate with a staff of twenty psychologists analyzing the terrorist mind-set. According to two sources, the Counterintelligence Field Activity processed some of the information that was obtained by the National Security Agency's secret wiretapping program.

The Counterintelligence Field Activity would become best known for a database that collected reports of suspicious activity at defense facilities. The Cornerstone database gave investigators a way to detect a terrorist plot in the planning stages. An example that made the rounds at the agency was the story of the vehicle that had approached the Central Intelligence Agency in Virginia after the September 11 attacks. The driver claimed to be lost, and the incident might have gone unnoticed if the same car had not pulled up to the gate at the National Security Agency in Maryland.

The database created in May 2003 to gather raw "Talon" reports from around the globe was a sound idea in theory, but the execution was poor. About 260 reports out of 13,000 records in the classified database related to Quakers, college students, and other U.S. citizens taking part in peaceful antiwar demonstrations, some of which were far from any military installation. After NBC News broke the story, the Counterintelligence Field Activity was portrayed as a malevolent big brother spying on Americans. It seems more likely that the information on U.S. citizens was passed along by those who had no idea that an executive order from the president forbade it.

The problem, as was repeatedly the case at the Counterintelligence Field Activity, was that it grew with astonishing speed. According to *The Washington Post*, the agency spent $1 billion over four years, a staggering amount in the often-neglected counterintelligence world. One of the most serious problems involved a ten-year, $100 million lease for office space that was disguised as a service contract to avoid oversight. In its rush to grow, the agency touched off a feeding frenzy for defense contractors. And as the Counterintelligence Field Activity grew, so did Wade's company.

Like other MZM employees, Bruno couldn't help but notice that Cunningham and Wade were frequent companions. Wade would brag at Monday-morning meetings how he had spent the weekend with Cunningham or the two had gone out drinking. Wade and the congressman were often on the phone together. Cunningham showed up at company parties and dined at charity events Wade hosted. They shared countless meals together at The Capital Grille.

Cunningham and his wife, Nancy, joined the MZM top executives for an off-site meeting at The Greenbrier, a posh resort in West Virginia, where Wade and the congressman competed in a round of skeet shooting. Wade paid $2,731.33 for Cunningham's lodging and meals over two nights at the resort. He bought the congressman a $1,500 gift certificate, which Cunningham redeemed for a set of earrings for his wife, as well as a $400 Greenbrier charm and necklace. Nancy Cunningham and her daughter April both served on the advisory board of the Sure Foundation, a charity run by Wade's wife. Wade paid the Cunninghams' nineteen-year-old daughter, Carrie, $4,000 for two weeks' work and gave April Cunningham $2,500 as a wedding present, the girls' mother told Kitty Kelley.

Cunningham attended company get-togethers so often that many came to hear his stories over and over. In the year that Joe Romano spent at MZM he heard Cunningham tell the same war story three different times. Romano, a former member of the senior executive service at the Defense Intelligence Agency, was impressed the first time he saw Cunningham shed tears as he recalled watching a Navy comrade get shot down over Vietnam. The second time he heard Cunningham tell the same story, almost word for word, Romano noticed that the congressman cried at the same point. At the Greenbrier when Romano heard Cunningham tell the same story for a third time and the congressman started to tear up, Romano just laughed out loud.

Through his friendship with Wade, Cunningham began to grow accustomed to life's finer things, which he could never have afforded on the $150,000 salary he earned in 2002. When Cunningham wanted to go yacht shopping, Wade spent $12,975.22 to hire a private jet to fly the congressman to Miami. Cunningham's one-night stay in room 603, a one-bedroom suite at the Delano Hotel, a tony, oceanfront hotel in Miami Beach, cost $1,254.50, and the congressman's meals cost another $848.27. Wade was a master host, and being around him was incredibly seductive. The two men could most frequently be found at The Capital Grille, where Wade had his personal table and his personal waiter. At The Capital Grille, Wade kept his wine locker well stocked and kept his congressman well fed. "Cunningham grew to expect luxury," prosecutors wrote. "His co-conspirators eagerly plied him with it."

At Wade's invitation, Cunningham visited the home of the Shipleys, the parents of Wade's wife, Christiane, and a wealthy, patrician family that traced its ancestry back to an Englishman who arrived in Maryland in 1668. The Shipleys had a home on Maryland's Eastern Shore, where Cunningham and Wade hunted. The congressman reciprocated by taking Wade to a place where he liked to hunt. "He showers you with gifts, he pretended to be my best friend for 16 years," Cunningham lamented in a letter from prison.

Cunningham clearly had reason to suspect that Wade wasn't the most ethical of businessmen. In another letter from prison, Cunningham related that he was on his yacht one night when Wade showed up drunk, accompanied by two women. He asked Wade what was going on. Who were these two women and what were they planning to do? "Surprise," Wade told the congressman, by way of reply. Whether the women were prostitutes or not isn't clear, but Cunningham did go on to say that Wade went down to a stateroom with one of the women, apparently leaving the other behind for the congressman to enjoy. Cunningham says he wasn't interested and he left the boat that night.

As prosecutors would later say, Wade had quickly identified Cunningham as a congressman who could be bought, and he proceeded to do exactly that. In early 2002, Wade bought the congressman a leather sofa, a sleigh-style bed, and two antique French commodes worth nearly $14,000. The bill went to MZM and the antiques went to Cunningham's condominium in Arlington, Virginia.

Cunningham had a taste for antiques. An MZM employee recalled that Cunningham popped by the office one day and took offense when he noticed that Wade had spread some expensive prayer rugs on the floor and placed furniture on top of them. Cunningham pointed out that the rugs were works of art that were meant to be hung on the wall, not placed on the ground. You can tell the quality in a prayer rug, the congressman explained, by the number of knots.

After spending most of the past twelve years living on the opposite coast, Nancy Cunningham would spend sixteen months in Washington working for the U.S. Education Department. Her $114,200-a-year job as chief of staff for Assistant Secretary William Leidinger began on February 25, 2002. Nancy did not want to live on Randy's yacht, the *Kelly C,* because she got seasick, so in late 2001, Randy purchased a two-bedroom condominium in Arlington, Virginia, for $350,000. According to the government's sentencing memorandum, Cunningham's friend Thomas Kontogiannis quietly made the $200,000 down payment on the condo on the congressman's behalf.

In April 2002, Cunningham decided that he wanted a vintage Rolls-Royce and demanded that Wade give him $10,000 to buy it. The blue 1973 Rolls that arrived at the port of Baltimore was in awful shape, and Cunningham demanded thousands of dollars to restore the car. Richard Peze, an executive vice president at MZM, saw Wade driving it to get an exhaust system put on it. "If he had driven it more than fifty miles, the carbon monoxide would have killed him," Peze said. Wade couldn't resist telling Bruno about the Rolls. He wanted to take her for a ride in the Rolls, which he had bought in "partnership" with somebody. Later, she heard him say he was letting Cunningham drive the car. Bruno asked where it was. "It's in the congressional parking garage," Wade told her.

Cunningham's condo was stuffed with antiques, as one new MZM employee noted when she stopped by with Wade. Wade had driven her out to Arlington to introduce her to someone whom the company did a lot of business with. She noticed several armoires, including one that seemed out of place in the dining room, and one in the bedroom with clothes tumbling out of it, and she spotted Persian carpets lying on top of the white shag condo carpeting.

It has widely been assumed that Randy purchased the antiques for his wife. How else could a man of simple tastes have suddenly developed an appreciation for French provincial furniture? Nancy's attorney, Doug Brown, maintains that she never asked for the antiques, and she knew nothing of her husband's corruption. She said that her husband told her he had negotiated a deal on all the antiques. "In high school, Mr. Cunningham worked at a country club and always told me he wanted that lifestyle," she told Kitty Kelley. "He later learned about antiques from Johnny Cash, who had an extensive collection. But he grew tired of everything he collected and always wanted more."

By the summer, Cunningham had his eye on the *Buoy Toy*, the forty-two-foot boat at the Capital Yacht Club that belonged to Scott Schramm. Cunningham and Schramm shared the same mechanic,

Will Whitehouse, who told the congressman that Schramm wanted $165,000 for his boat, which was mechanically perfect. Cunningham was interested, and Whitehouse tried to find out the lowest price Schramm would take for it. Schramm wanted to hear an offer. Finally, Cunningham called and spoke directly to Schramm on August 30.

"If I bring you a cashier's check this afternoon, will you take one forty?" the congressman asked. Schramm asked if he wanted a sea trial first.

"No, I know the boat," Cunningham said. "Will says the boat's great. I'll bring you a cashier's check this afternoon. You hand me the title."

"Okay. You just bought yourself a boat. See you at two o'clock," Schramm said.

At two o'clock, Cunningham and his wife, Nancy, joined by Wade and his wife, Christiane, walked down the dock to Schramm's boat. Cunningham introduced Wade as his "business partner," something that is not all that uncommon in the boating world. They brought take-out sandwiches and a couple of bottles of white wine and sat on the back of the *Buoy Toy* and sipped wine to celebrate their purchase. Cunningham moved the *Buoy Toy* into his personal slip at the Capital Yacht Club, and he and Schramm grew to be friends. Schramm never saw Wade again.

"There was no question as to who was buying the boat," Schramm said. "I mean, it was being represented as Duke buying the boat, but Mitch Wade walked in with a cashier's check in his name. We had to put down a name on the title registry, and we titled it in Mitch Wade's name.

"That's just not the way you buy a boat," Schramm said. "We just knew it was dirty at the time."

The congressman also kept his previous boat, the *Kelly C.* In the fall, Cunningham demanded that Wade pay nearly $17,000 for a new engine for the sixty-five-foot houseboat. Cunningham was having the boat moved to New York. On September 25, Wade paid to have a crew member transport the boat where it was to be renovated by Cunningham's friend Thomas Kontogiannis, the convicted felon. Kontogiannis paid Cunningham $600,000 to buy the *Kelly C*, but the boat remained in the congressman's name. No title or contract ever changed hands.

Cunningham had intended to rename the boat the *Duke-Stir*, but didn't get around to removing the name *Buoy Toy* from the back of the yacht for several months. In April 2003, Cunningham attended a charity skeet-shooting event held each year on Maryland's Eastern Shore to benefit the Cancer Research and Prevention Foundation. The wife of another congressman mentioned that she had visited a friend at the Capital Yacht Club and had seen the congressman's new boat. Cunningham asked her what she thought, and she replied, *"Buoy Toy?"* A group of House members nearby roared with laughter. Shortly thereafter, Cunningham had the boat's name changed to the *Duke-Stir*. The congressman explained the change by saying, "I bought the boat, not the lifestyle."

As a defense psychiatrist would later note, Cunningham possessed an extraordinary ability to rationalize his own conduct. This was a congressman who saw himself as a foe of corruption in the District of Columbia. During a House floor speech on the way the city council dispensed leases along the waterfront where Cunningham kept his boat, he publicly accused the city's elected leaders of pocketing bribes. "The city council was at that time taking money under the table to support leases," he said. "We changed that."

He wore no outward signs of guilt or torment from his own conduct that his staff could detect. If anything, he seemed content. As

Cunningham's corruption neared its apogee, he turned over a new leaf in his private life. It was as if all the gifts and the luxurious living had somehow satisfied something that had been burning inside the congressman for years. He began to make amends to some of the people he had hurt over the years. One day he walked up to Congressman Barney Frank, the openly gay Massachusetts Democrat whom he had often mocked years earlier. "Look, I want to apologize," Cunningham told him. "I may have said those things to you in the past that were harsh. I shouldn't have said those and I'm not going to say them again."

Cunningham offered Frank no explanation, but he did divulge more of what had prompted his change of heart to Scott Schramm, who sold him the *Buoy Toy*. Schramm, who is gay, had a long conversation one day about the congressman's antigay rhetoric.

"You know, I used to be very antiwomen, antigay, and a lot of things in my life have changed," Cunningham told him. "And one of those big things was 9/11. That was a big part of my life. I now vote pro-gay, and it's because of you and Lee [Marcum, who was Schramm's partner at the time]."

"You're kidding," Schramm said.

The congressman continued, "I'm sure I've met lots of gay people, but I've never met two guys that you know were outwardly gay and . . . that I would consider drinking buddies and friends and boating buddies and people I want to spend time with. That also said, 'Oh, by the way, I just happened to be gay.'"

Cunningham's conscience may have been clear, but his body was showing signs of too much good living. All those steaks and drinks at The Capital Grille and elsewhere had caused his weight to balloon and his face to turn blotchy red like a suckling pig. He had let himself go and seemed to be in a daze and unable to pay attention during highly classified briefings on the House Intelligence Committee, which was taking up critical issues in the wake of the September 11 attacks.

A former staff member of the House Intelligence Committee re-called that Cunningham would begin speaking in the middle of a para-graph and end before he finished. His conversations often seemed surreal, and Cunningham seemed to have a hard time focusing on whatever issue was being discussed. When speaking, his eyes would lose focus and seem to drift off. "He struck me as almost a caricature of what I expected him to be like," the staffer said. "He struck me as being not really there. I felt sorry for the guy." Winslow Wheeler, a former Senate staffer who dealt in defense appropriations, had a simi-lar view. "He'd walk in badly overweight, a fleshy, sort of sleepy guy," Wheeler said. "To think he was a fighter pilot, you saw him walking around on Capitol Hill, you'd think, 'What happened to him?' A fighter pilot was a certain type, and he wasn't it."

He seemed uninterested in committee hearings, even when the subject was close to home. The House Intelligence Committee sched-uled a hearing on unmanned aerial vehicles, the pilotless drones that were swiftly sent into the skies over Afghanistan and Iraq, where they impressed commanders with their ability to keep a camera trained on a site for twenty-four hours. The main models in production, Predator and Global Hawk, were built in San Diego, but Cunningham said he would not be able to attend the hearing. Intelligence committee staff members begged him to be there, and Cunningham grudgingly agreed to change his schedule. When the day of the hearing arrived, however, he didn't show.

Cunningham would show signs of life when it came to his "top two priorities"—Brent Wilkes and Mitch Wade. A September 27, 2002, e-mail exchange between two Cunningham staffers sought to "scratch the itch" Wade had for defense dollars by obtaining $7 million for MZM through the Counterintelligence Field Activity. The committee reduced Cunningham's request, leaving Wade with $5 million. When Cunningham learned that the committee had tinkered with his fund-ing request, he stormed into his office.

"I might as well become a Democrat," he said.

The congressman emerged a while later and said $1 million should come off some "big-ticket item" and be given to Wade. The amount appropriated in the committee report was $6.3 million. Money in hand, Wade then proceeded to tell officials at the Counterintelligence Field Activity how the $6.3 million should be spent and decided almost all of it should be for data storage at a facility in Colorado Springs, Colorado.

The employees at Wade's fast-growing company didn't know the details, but the boss's close relationship with Cunningham made some employees uncomfortable. During a lengthy conversation in Wade's office, Richard Peze laid out his concerns with MZM's business model and told Wade that he felt the company was relying too much on congressional contacts. In his twenty years of work as a civilian in the Defense Department and as a contractor, Peze had had about a dozen contacts with members of Congress; in one year at MZM, he had personally seen Cunningham at least six or eight times. The company had tripled in size in the first six months of 2002, and if MZM was going to be successful, Peze told Wade, it needed to showcase its considerable talent. Wade got angry and yelled at Peze not to question the business plan. Shortly after that, Peze left the company.

Others knew better than to ask Wade about Cunningham. To most employees, MZM was a mystery, a reflection of its bizarre and secretive owner. Some had no idea that the company's name stood for Wade's children from his first marriage, Matthew, Zachary, and Morgan. The company was highly compartmentalized, and most employees knew only a small slice of the company's business, the one in which they worked. Wade would fly into a rage when he heard that two employees had been discussing with each other what they were working on. Staff meetings were a joke, with no sharing of ideas allowed. Wade stared at employees, discouraging them from revealing too much. More than one employee compared the climate of MZM to John Grisham's novel *The Firm*, about a deeply corrupt law firm hidden by a façade of success. When an employee noticed that someone from the Executive Office of the President had signed into the MZM visitor log, he asked Wade out of curiosity what was going on. "That's none of your business," Wade snapped.

Wade's paranoia bordered on lunacy. He opened mail addressed to his employees that arrived at the Dupont Circle office. He screened employee e-mails and railed about those who received personal messages on their MZM accounts. No detail was too small for him to obsess over, and nothing got done at MZM without his say-so. He personally approved expenses. He wanted to know what employees were doing at all times, requiring them to check in with him several times a day. The company was even organized to fit his need to know everything: more than one hundred executive positions were listed on the corporate chart, and they all reported to Wade.

Money was pouring into MZM, but Bruno and her coworkers were not quite sure where it was coming from. The company had a few contracts, but not the kind of revenue that would explain what Wade called "world headquarters"—the $2.3 million Dupont Circle office, and its expensive decoration. Christiane Wade ran her charity, the Sure Foundation, from the fourth floor of the building, and Bruno had often heard Wade say his wife came from a wealthy family, so perhaps the money was family money. Although few employees knew about it, Wade in 2002 purchased a full-floor luxury apartment overlooking the water in Panama City, Panama, where the company opened a business that provided independent inspections of cargo moving in international trade.

Wade was offering outrageously high salaries to new employees. In a typical job pitch, he told one of his earliest hires over lunch, "I don't want any further discussion. I want you to start next Monday. I'll double what you're making. What are you making?" When Scott Rubin, a computer engineer with a background in defense and intelligence, showed up for a job interview in the summer of 2002, Wade asked him how much he made. Wade leaned back, shook his head, and said, "That can't be done." Rubin thought to himself he was obviously too high. "I can't pay you that little," Wade said.

The large sums Wade was dispensing helped MZM attract a highly talented staff comprised of senior officials with the FBI, CIA, the Defense Intelligence Agency, and the military. As the company ballooned with talent, so did the number of vice presidents. One company chart listed eighteen senior executive vice presidents, twelve executive vice presidents, and sixty-nine vice presidents in a staff that numbered a few hundred.

And when money wasn't enough, Wade presented himself as a Christian businessman and pointed to his wife's work helping needy children in the third world. Some of his most senior executives were religious people, including Jim King, a Utah-born Mormon and a recently retired three-star general. King was highly respected within the intelligence community. He had run the National Imagery and Mapping Association. He helped reassure prospective employees who had doubts about the company, and gushed about Wade in an e-mail to a new hire: "Mitch has created an environment and ethos that cares for the people, our nation, and our clients. He understands the business better than any CEO or senior government leader I know. He is a master at bringing together requirements, resources, the right team, and delivering far more than clients ever expected." Wade, however, did not see King the same way and would bad-mouth the "three-star genius" behind his back.

Wade, had something of a dual personality, incredibly generous one moment, and vindictive the next. Wade would throw elaborate employee birthday parties. He paid for fertility treatments for an employee. Hospitalized ill relatives of MZM employees got flowers from the boss. One year, he sent everyone who worked for him a Christmas ham or a turkey.

"Many times, while I was there, several of us spoke about Mitch as being the best boss and the worst boss we ever had," Richard Peze said. "He was capable of incredible charm. He was capable of being extraordinarily generous. He would display patriotism. He would speak to religious belief, a faith. He would do the right things for people in that environment. He was capable of doing good. He was also capable of being incredibly demanding, demanding in ways that were not healthy. He would ask people to do tasks that were impossible to do. He had convinced himself that he had this tremendous presence and ability to dominate any situation and do things he wanted done. He expected the same of others."

Wade's kindness and graciousness made it all the more brutal when employees fell out of favor with him, and it seemed that everyone eventually fell out of favor with him. Employees would immediately be kicked out of the office, their names never to be spoken again. When one of his closest advisers questioned the way he treated his employees, Wade joked that was a trait passed down from the Lebanese on his mother's side of the family: "It's my Middle Eastern heritage." As time wore on, employees began to see less of the friendly Dr. Jekyll in Wade and more and more of the mean Mr. Hyde.

It occurred to more than one employee that Wade had deep psychological problems. His paranoia, his compartmentalization, and his secrecy were all traits that many of his employees recognized from their experience in the intelligence world. Suspicion and paranoia were a job hazard, particularly in the spy-vs.-spy world of counterintelligence that was MZM's specialty. Too much time spent wondering if your colleagues were really your enemies did tend to make people a bit loony. Some wondered if Wade's time in the intelligence world had warped his mind. "I don't think Mitch is evil. I think Mitch is very sick," Bruno said.

Another young woman who had joined the company soon became the object of his attention. Lindsay Peterson was visiting Washington in the spring of 2002 with a friend to interview for jobs when she met Wade at The Capital Grille. Wade had noticed Peterson, a strikingly beautiful, blond, twenty-five-year-old law school student, standing near the bar and kept walking past her on his way to the restroom. He then sent a waiter over to ask the two women if they would like to join him at his table. At first, they told him no, but the waiter returned and told them Wade and his guests were leaving and they could have his table. Relieved to have a seat in the crowded restaurant, the two women followed him over.

Wade was still seated at the table, along with three others, including Bruno, and immediately started to recruit Peterson and her friend to his company, which, he said, paid more than anyone else and was looking to recruit more legal talent. As she listened to him, Peterson felt that he was not as sketchy as he had seemed when he had been leering at her; he seemed more like a sophisticated D.C. businessman. Wade invited the two women to the annual pancake breakfast Duncan Hunter and Randy "Duke" Cunningham were to host the next morning in Washington.

Several weeks later, Wade invited Peterson back to Washington for a job interview, all expenses paid. Peterson accepted. Wade picked her up at the airport and took her to dinner at The Palm restaurant, where he had paid $10,000 to have his caricature drawn on the wall, a Washington status symbol of sorts. He paid for her to stay at the Ritz-Carlton before her job interview the next day. Wade made the job sound highly desirable, and Peterson was pleased. She was under the impression she would be doing legal work under the advisement of the company's general counsel, in addition to some corporate communications, but money compelled her to take the job. Her starting salary was $105,000, plus a $10,000 signing bonus. He also offered to pay off her student loans. "He made me an offer I couldn't refuse," Peterson said.

Wade told her he was interested in buying a corporate apartment to house the occasional out-of-town guest, and offered to rent it to her at what he said would be a reduced rate. He promised Peterson that her half of the condo would remain her private quarters, and guests would enter through a separate and secure entrance. After looking at a few sites, Wade bought a $425,000 condo on New Hampshire Avenue, just a few blocks away from MZM's Dupont Circle offices on August 21. Peterson's rent was $2,000 a month—a bargain, Wade told her. Wade wanted the condo to look as good as MZM's offices so he decorated it with antiques he and Peterson picked out together.

After a while, it became clear to Peterson why Wade had hired her. If they were in a cab on the way back from a meeting, Wade would touch her leg. Before the birthday of another MZM executive, Wade demanded that she put on a lot of red lipstick and sing "Happy Birthday" like Marilyn Monroe in front of a boardroom full of her colleagues, then kiss the executive on the check so he'd be marked with lipstick. Peterson felt she had no choice but to obey her boss, and the experience was humiliating. He insisted she do the filing in his office so he could look at her. He would ask her questions like "What's your definition of sex?" and "How far would you go before you considered it inappropriate?" On another occasion at MCCXXI, the same club where Wade had tried to romance Bruno, he asked Peterson if he could kiss her. She told him it was time for her to go. Another time he took her to what she thought was a normal restaurant lunch, but when they walked in, Peterson discovered her boss had taken her to a strip bar.

Peterson was hired on the understanding she would be working on congressional affairs and legal work, but in reality, she did whatever project Wade assigned her to do. Following an MZM fund-raiser for Senate majority leader Trent Lott of Mississippi in a private room at the Monocle restaurant on September 27, 2002, Wade assigned Peterson to help pick out a gift for the senator. Wade had heard that Lott liked ties and sent the attractive young lawyer out shortly thereafter to buy the senator the same $300 seven-fold ties that Wade liked to wear. He kept sending her back to different stores, unsatisfied with the ties she chose. Finally, she found ties at the upscale mall in Tysons Corner, Virginia, that Wade approved. He had them hand-delivered to Lott, who refused the gift, which clearly exceeded permissible limits. Similarly, Elizabeth Dole, who was running for the Senate in North Carolina, had declined to accept a bust of herself produced by a European artist following her tenure as president of the American Red Cross.

"If I can't use these guys, they're no good to me," Wade told his employees.

During MZM's 2002 Christmas party, Wade told Peterson to escort Cunningham to his private office and bring them drinks. Another time, she found herself seated between Wade and Cunningham during a dinner at The Capital Grille. Cunningham told her about his days growing up in Missouri, and then Wade sent her to the bar because the two men wanted to talk business.

Peterson found she was constantly looking over shoulder to see if Wade was coming. He could be intimidating, and she grew increasingly nervous because Wade had a set of keys to the condo and he refused to allow her to install an inside dead bolt on the door that led to her portion. He never molested her, but, over time, his words and actions became increasingly offensive. One day he had his assistant call Peterson into his office.

"Look at this," Wade told her.

On Wade's computer screen was a pornographic image that someone had e-mailed him of someone in the Navy having sex. Wade stared at her while she looked at it.

"Gross," Peterson said, and backed away.

Like everyone else at MZM, Peterson liked Wade's wife, Christiane, but couldn't understand why she stayed with him. Wade told Peterson that he had really cashed in when he married her. He told Peterson that his wife's family was involved in Chase Manhattan Bank. He also told her he was the youngest child and had grown up with more money than his siblings, who, Wade felt, always resented him for it.

Wade seemed unable to help himself around her. Intrigued that Peterson had been in a college sorority, Wade asked her to tell him pillow-fight stories. He started telling her wild tales from his own days in a college fraternity, Tau Kappa Epsilon. One time, he told her excitedly, he and his pledge class had taken advantage of a drunken coed by stripping her down and urinating all over her. While Wade laughed at the memory, Peterson felt sick. In the spring of 2003, Peterson had finally had enough of Wade and turned in her resignation after ten months at the company.

With Peterson gone, Bruno felt that Wade's attentions were being redirected at her. He invited her to stay at the posh Hotel Delano in Miami Beach, but she learned that he had booked only one suite. He took her to Hawaii to make a presentation to the Navy's Pacific Command. Wade stayed in the presidential suite at the elegant Halekulani in Honolulu, and she once again rebuffed his advances. After enduring fifteen months of off-and-on harassment, Bruno made an internal sexual harassment complaint to the company's general counsel. Wade refused to talk to her for weeks.

Bruno, too, decided she had had enough. She accepted a job working for Senator Dianne Feinstein, a California Democrat, on the Senate intelligence committee. Wade was furious. He called one of his newest vice presidents, a former Hill staffer who had good contacts on the committee, to his office and said he wanted Bruno's offer of employment terminated.

"I want you to stick a knife in it," Wade said.

The employee talked Wade out of it. If he tried to get her fired and didn't succeed, Bruno would then be in a position to hurt Wade and MZM on the Senate intelligence panel. Wade got the point.

Bruno soon found life on Capitol Hill wasn't to her liking. The intelligence committee was riven by disputes over the intelligence that had led to the war in Iraq, and the money was much less than she had been making at MZM. After less than four months, she decided to return to the company. Wade welcomed her back with a big pay increase and a new title.

10

The Dream Home

Behind the scenes, Cunningham had been using his position to help Wade's company by pushing for Project Fortress, a new program designed to get a handle on the foreign visitors who had been gathering intelligence on U.S. weapons systems. The concept of Fortress was to develop an analytical program that would provide an understanding of which foreign professionals visit labs and bases to observe military exercises. The program was being run jointly by the Counterintelligence Field Activity and the U.S. Air Force. MZM received the contract with the congressman's help in February 2003. Over time, the program grew into a $12-million-a-year contract that involved more than forty people gathering human and signals intelligence at bases around the country.

Cunningham has said he would have supported Fortress whether he had received gifts from Wade or not. From his experience in Vietnam, the congressman knew that the more the enemy learned about U.S. capabilities, the greater the danger to American forces. In a letter from prison he wrote that Fortress "will today save lives" and called it "the best aviation Humint [human intelligence] program in existence." According to Cunningham, U.S. Air Force chiefs of staff had written to him seeking more funds for the program. "[It] didn't matter whether or not I received gifts because I would have fought for it even if Nancy Pelosi had started the program," he wrote.

The congressman's belief in the Fortress program and others allowed him to erase any concerns that he was selling out his office to the highest bidder. Cunningham repeatedly consulted officials at the Defense Department, who assured the congressman and his staff that the programs were good for national security, and that the programs and the funding that Wade had requested had support from the Pentagon. If he supported the programs anyway, what was wrong with accepting gifts or presents from his friends? Built on a solid foundation of rationalization and self-delusion, the corruption steadily grew.

Although they didn't know the full extent of the congressman's wrongdoing, Cunningham's staff knew that things were going very, very wrong. In May 2003, Wade sold Cunningham his Chevy Blazer for $10,000, well below its market value. When Cunningham's new chief of staff, Dave Heil, found out about it, he was troubled by the sales price and the seller. In an effort to correct what was clearly a questionable transaction, Cunningham's staffers altered the California DMV vehicle title registration application to reflect a more accurate sales price of $18,000 and asked the congressman to make up the difference. He refused. When Heil spoke to Cunningham about the sale, he slammed his hand on his desk twice and yelled, "Stay the fuck out of my personal business."

In July 2003, Wade bought Cunningham two Laser Shot shooting simulators for $9,200, and Cunningham had one of the units installed in his congressional office. A computer projector displayed a hunting scene on a pull-down screen, and a rifle fired a red beam. The machine allowed Cunningham to select from a variety of programs including "Mallard Mania" and "Prairie Dog Hunt."

The game could be quite loud, and Cunningham didn't know how to lower the volume. While Cunningham showed the game off to one of his friends, his staff found themselves working over the sound of rifle shots and the squeaks from digital prairie dogs booming out of the congressman's office when someone hit the target. A staffer would slip into Cunningham's office and turn the volume down when the congressman wasn't around. "How do you turn the volume up on this?" Cunningham would later ask.

Wilkes, too, splurged on Cunningham in 2003, according to prosecutors. He gave Cunningham two tickets to his private box at San Diego's Qualcomm Stadium to watch the Oakland Raiders play the Tampa Bay Buccaneers in Superbowl XXXVII. In April, Wilkes paid for thousands of dollars in food, lodging, and entertainment on Cunningham's behalf during a vacation in Key Largo, Florida. And Wilkes rented a $6,660-a-night suite at the Hapuna Beach Prince Hotel on Hawaii's Big Island, where Cunningham spent three nights in August in one of the upstairs bedrooms.

On August 15, their first night in Hawaii, Cunningham, Wilkes, and other guests dined on shrimp, scallops, snapper, and lobster dumplings in the suite's private yard. Joining the group was Wilkes's nephew, Joel Combs, who worked at ADCS. According to sources, Wilkes instructed his nephew to hire two prostitutes for the evening and had given Combs $600 to pay for two hours of their services.

The women arrived with their "driver" around 11 p.m. Combs escorted the two prostitutes into the suite and paid the driver $600. About fifteen minutes later, prosecutors say, Wilkes and Cunningham escorted the two women upstairs to separate rooms. At midnight, prosecutors say, Wilkes tipped one of the prostitutes $500.

The next day began with a catered breakfast, followed by an all-day dive trip on a chartered boat. Wilkes hosted a cocktail party and dinner that evening attended by Cunningham and others. At 11 p.m., prosecutors say, two prostitutes again arrived at the suite. Combs again paid the driver $600. One of the women had been there the previous night, but the congressman must not have been happy with the woman he had the night before because he had specifically requested a different prostitute. Wilkes and Cunningham again escorted the two women up to their bedrooms. The same woman received another $500 tip from Wilkes.

Cunningham spent his final two days at the Hapuna Beach hotel golfing at the Mauna Kea Golf Course with its panoramic views of sea, lava beds, and the 14,000-foot volcano that gives the course its name. According to prosecutors, Wilkes told an employee to put the entire $21,159 hotel bill on his corporate American Express card. Through his attorney, Nancy Luque, Wilkes said he never paid for, arranged, or tipped prostitutes for Cunningham and the claims are pure fiction.

The Torrey Pines Golf Course, named after a rare, twisted tree, has earned a reputation as one of America's most beautiful public courses. The course, which hosts the PGA Tour Buick Invitational each year, allows anyone to play on greens that sit perched on a spectacular bluff overlooking the Pacific Ocean. Randy Cunningham's political action committee was hosting a fund-raiser here on May 29, 2003. At the course, the congressman bumped into a Realtor named Elizabeth Todd and mentioned that he was interested in buying a new home.

Cunningham knew Todd well. An attractive brunette and a crack golfer, Todd had once offered golf lessons as an auction prize during a Cunningham fund-raiser. Cunningham approached Todd and said he and his "partner" were interested in buying a condominium and had $1 million to spend. After a month or so, Cunningham mentioned that because he had a million dollars to spend, perhaps he would simply sell his home in Del Mar for $1.5 million and use the $1 million net profit to buy an even bigger $2 million house for himself. Cunningham said his partner, Mitch Wade, could simply have an office in the congressman's bigger house.

While Cunningham hunted for a new home in San Diego, Wade was hunting for cash back in Washington. In August, he called Christopher Rosché, MZM's director of communications, into his office. Wade told Rosché he needed him to get a $5 million congressional appropriation for the company. Wade seemed desperate. He needed the money now. "I don't care what you have to do to make this happen. Make it happen," Wade told Rosché. "If you don't, I will consider it a complete and utter failure."

Rosché was a former Senate staffer who knew how the Hill worked. The request for the type of appropriation Wade wanted should have been submitted to Congress months earlier. It had to be followed up with lobbying visits to various committee staff and members, all of which took a great deal of time. The longer one waited, the more difficult it would be. By August, it was already too late.

Rosché tried his best to work the Hill but had no luck. He certainly wasn't about to take his boss' hint that he should bend a few rules or twist some arms. A few weeks later, Wade had Rosché booted out of the company.

In the fall, Cunningham got another health scare. Despite the operation to remove his cancerous prostate, tests showed that he had elevated levels of an antigen that indicated the cancer had spread.

Cancer was found behind his bladder, and he underwent radiation treatment to try to control it.

Cunningham began to eye multimillion-dollar properties that were not even in the realm of possibility for a congressman on a salary of $154,700 a year. After scanning properties in a magazine called *Dream Homes*, Cunningham picked out a house at 7094 Via del Charro in Rancho Santa Fe, selling for well over $2 million. Cunningham told Nancy that the Del Mar house where they had lived for sixteen years was no longer appropriate. According to Nancy's lawyer, the congressman told his wife he needed a bigger house for entertaining. He was obsessed, Nancy says, with the citizens of Rancho Santa Fe. Nancy went over the numbers with her husband. It would be tight, but it was doable. He promised that he would soon retire and make the big bucks as a lobbyist. Cunningham eventually paid $2.55 million for the seven-bath house in Rancho Santa Fe. A company run by the nephew of Cunningham's old friend Thomas Kontogiannis agreed to write a mortgage of more than $1 million.

To afford the mansion, Cunningham sold his current home in Del Mar to Wade at a price far beyond what it was worth. Cunningham and Wade initially agreed on a price of $1.5 million. Within days, Cunningham had decided that he needed more money. He had another purchase agreement drafted, this time for $1.675 million, which both men signed again. In a last-minute, fateful move, Wade substituted the name of his limited liability company for his own as the home's buyer.

Wade had bought the house without ever having set foot in it. He found out only later that it was in sorry shape. As an example, Cunningham had an irrational fear of burglars in the wealthy coastal suburb and had bars installed over all the windows, including the skylight. The home languished for a year before Wade resold it at a $700,000 loss.

A few weeks later, Cunningham asked Wade for more money. He needed help to pay the capital gains on the proceeds of his Del Mar home. Wade wrote out a check for $115,000 to Top Gun Enterprises, Cunningham's aviation memorabilia business, and mailed it to the congressman's San Diego office. Wade wrote on the check that it was for public relations and communications expenses.

While details of the home sale were being finalized, Wade and his top executives flew to Martinsville, Virginia, on November 3 for the groundbreaking on another MZM facility to be built with congressionally earmarked funds. The Foreign Supplier Assessment Center was the creation of Congressman Virgil Goode, a Virginia Republican with a cornpone accent. Wade had hosted a Goode fund-raiser at his Dupont Circle office earlier in the year, which yielded more than $35,000, about $10,000 of which was illegally raised. Wade had reimbursed his employees and their spouses for $2,000 contributions to Goode's campaign. Goode has said he knew nothing about the illegal contributions and has never been charged with any wrongdoing stemming from his relationship with Wade.

After the fund-raiser, Goode inserted an earmark into the defense appropriation bill for the Foreign Supplier Assessment Center. The center was intended to screen foreign companies that sold products and services to the Defense Department for any possible national security beach. Cunningham, too, had shown an interest, writing his old friend Congressman Hunter in March to request $15 million for the program.

Goode inserted a classified provision into the bill to provide $3.6 million in funding for the center, which survived in the final bill. Goode wanted the center in his district and recommended the economically depressed town of Martinsville, well-known in the civil rights movement for the case of seven African-American men who were convicted and executed for raping the wife of a white store manager. Days after the bill was signed into law, MZM began talking with state and city officials about the center. Goode couldn't wait. He leaked word about the center to the local newspaper, and he maintained such a strong interest in the program that Virginia officials began describing it as "Project Goode" in internal e-mails.

Project Goode was being run by an organization Wade was intimately familiar with, the Army's National Ground Intelligence Center, in Charlottesville, Virginia. At MZM, Project Goode was being handled by Bill Rich, the recently retired director of the National Ground Intelligence Center, who, along with his son, had joined Wade's ever-growing staff. Rich explained to state and city officials that Defense Secretary Donald Rumsfeld was "not too happy" with equipment his troops were using in Afghanistan and Iraq. Particularly distressing were items of foreign origin, many of which were substandard, broke easily, or entailed security issues.

Rich said Congressman Goode had inserted the center into the defense bill "to allow Secretary Rumsfeld to do this project with MZM," according to an internal e-mail summary of the conversation prepared by a state official. "MZM will create databases on 'interesting' places around the world, including foreign companies and individuals that might want to supply products to the U.S. government." That way, Rich continued, the Defense Department could "track certain individuals" with a poor performance history and do no future business with them, as well as ensuring that U.S. security was not compromised by foreign-made equipment.

For Martinsville, a city with an 11 percent unemployment rate, the prospect of 150 new jobs, all filled locally and paying twice the region's prevailing wage, was irresistible. State officials saw it as a "huge win" for the town of fifteen thousand. Martinsville had built a building to attract companies like MZM; the state offered the company an economic development grant. Wade offered $400,000 for a building on which the city owed $1 million, then demanded an exemption from real estate and personal property taxes for five years. He gave the city a deadline of two weeks to respond and copied Congressman Goode on the message. With little choice, Martinsville relented. The city paid off the building with an economic development loan from the state that Wade had categorically refused.

Wade wanted to open a second facility in Goode's district, and on March 4, 2005, MZM hosted another fund-raiser for the congressman. Before the event, Wade reimbursed several employees and their spouses for $28,000 in campaign contributions to Goode. He also gave thousands of dollars in cash to pay for contributions in the name of MZM employees. In June 2005, Goode's staff told Wade that a $9 million earmark for the facility and a related program would be inserted into an appropriations bill.

Some time after that, Project Goode—the Foreign Supplier Assessment Center—was revealed as a waste of money, little more than a cash cow for MZM. The center duplicated work being done by other organizations, including the Intelligence Community Acquisition Risk Center, the National Security Agency, and the Treasury Department's Committee on Foreign Investment in the United States. In June 2006, the Pentagon decided to shutter the center.

Almost as important as the funding Cunningham and Goode generated for MZM was the influence they could wield over Defense Department officials. In this respect, Cunningham and Goode were little more than puppets for Wade, who would turn to them, just as Wilkes had, when he needed to squeeze money out of the sluggish Pentagon bureaucracy.

One of Wade's employees, Scott Rubin, spent nine months in the office of a senior defense official in the Pentagon's E-ring and got to see firsthand how this worked. Rubin had been detailed to the office of Deputy Undersecretary Carol Haave to help her out with her administrative work. Haave oversaw counterintelligence programs for the Defense Department, including the Counterintelligence Field Activity and the Defense Security Service, which was responsible for granting top-secret clearances. Her boss, Stephen Cambone, the undersecretary for defense intelligence, was widely viewed in the Pentagon as Donald Rumsfeld's henchman and was loathed and feared by the services.

Wade was happy to have his own people inside Haave's office. He dealt directly with Haave, although he wasn't the only military contractor who did so, and attended a number of meetings in Haave's office. Rubin would sometimes escort him into the Pentagon so he could meet with Haave to discuss congressional mandates for the programs Wade was interested in at the Counterintelligence Field Activity and the Defense Security Service. Wade's company was not only benefiting from these mandates, but he was arranging them through Cunningham.

A former special investigator for billionaire Howard Hughes's company, Haave had, before joining the Pentagon, run a defense contracting firm, Sullivan Haave Associates, with her husband, Terry Sullivan, who was well-known by senior officials at the Pentagon. The Center for Public Integrity, an investigative Web site, had discovered that Sullivan Haave had a contract to spend four months in 2003 in Iraq providing advice to various ministries being set up there by coalition and local authorities. Terry Sullivan said the contract had nothing to do with his wife's position at the Pentagon.

The Center for Public Integrity's findings on Sullivan Haave were part of a package of stories titled "Windfalls of War," which also included a report on MZM Inc. Wade bragged to the center that he expected to increase sales from $25 million to $120 million and hire 230 more employees in the next five years. To Wade, it seemed funny that he was getting rich off war. Following the publication of "Windfalls of War" in October 2003, Wade had a meeting in Haave's office. "Hey, Carol," he said, "how are you doing? Looks like we made the paper the same week."

Haave's deputy was a woman named Heather Anderson, the acting director of the Defense Security Service. Wade got impatient at the speed at which money for Project Goode was moving through the bureaucracy. Goode had added a brief description of the Foreign Supplier Assessment Center into the Defense budget, but Anderson pushed back and asked Congress to provide more clarity about exactly what the project was all about. The delay only seemed to infuriate Wade. He called up Haave's office and spoke with Rubin and told him to light a fire under Anderson. "You tell that dumb bitch to go fix it or she's done for," Wade said.

Rubin told his boss that he needed to be patient, but Wade didn't heed the advice. A few days later, a staffer from Goode's office called to speak with Anderson about the money for the Foreign Supplier Assessment Center. Rubin said Anderson was furious. "Your company's over its head," she screamed at him. Anderson says she was never pressured by Wade or congressional staff on his behalf. She denies making the remark to Rubin.

Wade was often frustrated with the Pentagon bureaucracy. A few months later, Rubin took a call from Wade, who asked if a multimillion-dollar appropriation for a classified program at the Counterintelligence Field Activity had moved through the Defense Department bureaucracy. When Rubin told him he didn't think so, Wade got angry and said, "It better goddamn happen or I'm going to have the congressman call and it's going to get very bad over there for some people."

Rubin told Wade he didn't need to do that. "Let me just check on some things before we start breaking out the cannon," he told his boss.

"No," Wade said, "I've run out of patience. I need an answer yesterday. This has to happen."

Less than two hours later, Rubin took a call on the main line in Haave's office.

"This is Congressman Duke Cunningham. I'd like to speak with Ms. Carol Haave, please."

Rubin placed the congressman on hold and ran around his desk to speak with Haave, who took the call right away. The conversation lasted a few minutes, and then Haave came out of her office, stopped at Rubin's desk, and told him to bring her two of her subordinates responsible for counterintelligence. Rubin brought the two men to Haave's office, and the three held an emergency meeting to figure out what to do. The meeting lasted a half hour and the two men walked out with actions items.

At the time, Rubin didn't think that Cunningham was doing anything wrong except perhaps paying too much attention to a bozo like Wade. Only later would Rubin learn that he had been taken in by the congressman. "You listen to the Duke talk of loving the country and caring about the war, caring about the troops, caring about the weapons," he said. "He was in the military once before, he had been on the front lines once before, and he probably thought to himself when he was a lieutenant commander/commander, 'I wish I had the power to rankle that jackass in charge.' It seemed that's how he was coming across. Not so much that Mitch was making him call. It seemed to me that Mitch was just kind of filling him in, stoking him. That's the way I saw it."

Just as Cunningham had predicted, Wade was becoming "somebody" in Washington. A few years earlier, Wade was running a company out of his apartment. Now, MZM's revenues were doubling along with the size of its workforce. The company was building new facilities, and as 2004 began, few parts of the government didn't have some association with his fast-growing company. MZM's customers included the U.S. Congress, the White House, and the Departments of State, Defense, Justice, Energy, and Commerce.

The National Security Agency had turned to MZM for help in obtaining $100 million that had been withheld by Congress. The House and Senate intelligence committees had fenced off the money for the agency's cryptology program until the National Security Agency could demonstrate that it was being well spent. Jim King headed MZM's work on the project. MZM also had its staffers working inside the Central Intelligence Agency.

King was one of several MZM employees who served on the professional staff of a White House panel that investigated the shortcomings of U.S. prewar intelligence that came to be known as the Robb-Silverman commission. Former top officials Kenneth Geide and John Quattrocki, both of whom worked for MZM, were also on the commission's professional staff.

At the Army's National Ground Intelligence Center, MZM was working on contracts including the Foreign Supplier Assessment Center and a classified contract involving roadside bombs. The U.S. Secret Service had turned to MZM for help in scrutinizing White House e-mails for any potential threats. The company had developed a "threat analyzer" to speed the scanning of the White House's huge backlog of e-mails for any indication of a threat to the country or the president.

A team of MZM translators was on the ground in Iraq providing support to the Coalition Provisional Authority, the transitional U.S. government in Iraq. Unlike other defense contractors, who hired translators by finding people with certain ethnic last names in the phone book, MZM found top-notch linguists, several of whom possessed highly sought top-secret security clearances. The company's translators were assigned to intelligence fusion cells in Baghdad and interpreted for Arab dignitaries when they came to visit the U.S. leadership. One MZM linguist appeared in the company newsletter shaking hands with Senator Hillary Clinton. Another translated for L. Paul Bremer and, when he wasn't translating, joined Bremer's team of bodyguards.

The contract also called for MZM linguists to take part in interrogations and produce written or recorded propaganda for use in psychological operations. The team of MZM linguists was led by Paul Rester, who would go on to head all interrogations at Guantánamo Bay Naval Station. MZM linguists would work in Abu Ghraib prison, translating for "high-value" detainees who were believed to possess critical information.

From the outside, MZM seemed like an American success story. In a few short years, Wade's company had made $150 million in Defense Department contracts. Cunningham had used his position on the House Intelligence Committee to authorize between $70 million and $80 million to Wade's firm. (Wilkes said his company did not receive any funding from the House Intelligence Committee.)

In the 2005 fiscal year, MZM had lined up at least $60 million in Defense Department contract sales, which put the company on the lists of some of the top information-technology defense contractors in the country. While MZM wasn't in the same league as giants such as Lockheed Martin or Boeing—it didn't sell costly weapons systems—Wade's firm was something of a player in the information and technology sector of the defense industry.

In 2003, Wade had successfully outmaneuvered Brent Wilkes, the man who had introduced him to Cunningham. According to Wilkes,

Wade had kept him in the dark about MZM. Wilkes said he knew nothing about the Dupont Circle headquarters and the true size of the company.

Wilkes realized he'd been had when Wade took over the Global Infrastructure Data Capture program in fiscal 2003. The document-scanning project had gone to Wilkes for the previous two years. Now, Wilkes learned, the contract was being awarded to Wade, and Wilkes would be working for *him* as a subcontractor. Wade had broken the news by saying there was a "problem" with the contract. When Wilkes asked what had happened, Wade told him it was what the government wanted. "I had nothing to do with it," Wade said.

Wade did throw Wilkes a bone, however. According to court documents, Wade paid ADCS $5.48 million as a subcontractor to purchase about $700,000 worth of off-the-shelf computer equipment for the Counterintelligence Field Activity. The subcontract earned Wilkes a profit of $4.7 million, but the computer system his company purchased was never installed and remained in storage in Arlington, Virginia.

When the Global Infrastructure Data Capture contract, worth $16.15 million, was again awarded to Wade in fiscal 2004, Wilkes angrily complained to Cunningham. Wade was stealing his business away from him, spreading lies at the Defense Department to get him kicked off the contract. The congressman asked his staffer, Nancy Lifset, to investigate. On December 10, 2003, Lifset contracted Stephen Cambone, the undersecretary of defense for intelligence, who was Carol Haave's boss. She left a voice message demanding to know whether Wade or Wilkes had been awarded the money. "I'm hearing stories that I sure hope are not true. Please reply ASAP," Lifset said. When a Defense Department official returned the call, Lifset, acting on Cunningham's instructions, told the department to hold off on awarding money to Wade's company. According to an e-mail message released by prosecutors, Lifset claimed that the money belonged to

ADCS, and MZM was "trying to take this funding which is not theirs." Cunningham had helped MZM get a separate $10.5 million award for another program and Lifset wanted "to send a message to MZM," the Defense Department official reported in an e-mail.

Less than an hour later, however, Lifset had to backtrack. She had spoken to Cunningham, who, to her surprise, told her the money should be awarded to MZM as planned. The congressman had also spoken to Wade. Wade told Cunningham that Wilkes had been underperforming on the contract by, among other things, failing to obtain security clearances for his personnel. Lifset sheepishly called back the Defense Department to "eat crow," as one official put it in an e-mail. The money goes to MZM, she said.

Amazingly, until this point, Cunningham had not had the intellectual wherewithal to realize that Wilkes and Wade had opposing interests. The two men had been working together on the document-scanning program for years, and Cunningham believed they still were. It was now painfully clear that the two men were bitter rivals — and Wilkes despised Wade.

Wilkes asked Cunningham to freeze Wade out from the document-scanning program. Cunningham refused to do so. The $16.1 million document-scanning contract was going to Wade. There was nothing Cunningham could do about it, he told Wilkes — it's what the government wanted to do. According to prosecutors, the two men worked out a solution to the problem. Cunningham demanded $525,000 from Wilkes, who agreed on the condition he receive $6 million in government funds.

Cunningham pressured Wade into issuing a subcontract to Wilkes. Shortly after he received the $6 million subcontract from MZM in May 2004, Wilkes, at Cunningham's urging, wired $525,000 to Parkview Financial Center Inc. in New York, a firm controlled by Thomas Kontogiannis. Wilkes would claim he had wired the money at the urging of Cunningham, who had been nagging him to participate in what the congressman described as a "short-term investment." Prosecutors called the payment a bribe and the investment a thinly veiled one.

The money would be used to pay down one of the mortgages on Cunningham's Rancho Santa Fe mansion held by a company controlled by Kontogiannis's nephew. The mansion had not come without its share of worries. One was the $1,095,000 in mortgages Cunningham owed on the house. Here he was, a sixty-two-year-old man with a history of cancer. What if he lost his ongoing battle with cancer? His wife, Nancy, would be saddled with a huge debt.

The congressman still owed another half million dollars on the house. In August of 2004, he came to Wade and demanded that he eliminate the remaining mortgage. "Nancy doesn't want any debt," Cunningham explained to Wade. In return, Cunningham promised to support a defense appropriation request for MZM. Wade wrote two checks totaling $500,000 in different amounts. He made the checks payable to Top Gun Enterprises, the congressman's aviation memorabilia business, and intentionally dated them on different days.

The checks, however, were never deposited into Top Gun Enterprises' bank account. They went into Kontogiannis's financial services company, along with a $70,000 personal check from the congressman. Kontogiannis simply assumed the congressman's $3,529.65 in monthly payments on the mortgage. Cunningham owned the house free and clear. He could rest easier about what might happen to his family if he was gone. In little more than three months, Cunningham had collected $1.25 million from Wade and Wilkes—the largest bribe in modern congressional history.

Prosecutors have called this a "sophisticated" scheme. Indeed, it was the most complicated of all the transactions involved in the case, and it took investigators some time to unravel where all the checks went. The congressman understood that the Internal Revenue Service treats a pay-down of a mortgage as income. Cunningham reported income in 2004 of $121,079, and that he was due a refund of $8,504.

But there was little sophisticated about this transaction or any other of Cunningham's many deals. The scheme was laughable compared to the multilayered transactions federal investigators in San Diego saw in criminal tax frauds and other more complex financial frauds. There were no offshore accounts, no deposits of less than $10,000 to avoid federal reporting requirements. Sophisticated laundering schemes sometimes involved hundreds of layered transactions, rendering illicit profits almost impossible to trace. There was none of that in Cunningham's case. It was simple greed—money went from defense contractor to congressman.

The Randy Cunningham who had first been elected to Congress, the decorated war hero and patriotic American, and the greedy representative he had degenerated into were so different by 2004 that if they'd met in a bar, they would have seen each other as enemies.

In Washington, it was Cunningham's custom to take his staff out on May 10 for lunch on what he called "MiG day"—the anniversary of the 1972 battle in the skies over Vietnam that had made him an ace. On May 10, 2004, he drove back to his congressional office in the Chevy Blazer he had acquired from Wade. In the garage, Cunningham slammed into a car that belonged to Congressman Lincoln Diaz-Balart, a Florida Republican who, coincidentally, counted Wade among his campaign contributors. (Wade had given $2,000 to Diaz-Balart in 2002 and discussed the possibility of hosting a fund-raiser for the congressman.) At first, Cunningham blamed the mishap on the staffer who was driving Diaz-Balart's car. The staffer insisted on summoning Capitol Hill police to settle the matter.

Later, Cunningham found Diaz-Balart on the House floor and pulled out a huge wad of cash in an effort to settle the matter with a minimum fuss. The report of the accident was scrubbed from the files of the Capitol Hill Police Department the following day.

In his first congressional campaign in 1990, Cunningham had mailed out a hit piece blasting his Armenian opponent for accepting campaign contributions from Arab oil interests. In 2004, Congressman Cunningham took the House floor and championed Saudi Arabia as a valuable U.S. ally in the Middle East, declaring that Crown Prince Abdullah Aziz and King Fahd—whose face had adorned his nasty 1990 campaign mailer—were "visionaries."

Cunningham visited Saudi Arabia courtesy of Ziyad Abduljawad, a wealthy, Saudi-born constituent who had become a U.S. citizen. Abduljawad, a neighbor of Cunningham's in Rancho Santa Fe, graduated from Pepperdine University in Malibu and became a successful Southern California land developer. Abduljawad had met Cunningham several years earlier, and when he offered to take the congressman to Saudi Arabia to show him the progress his native country had made, Cunningham accepted.

Wade learned that Cunningham was going to Saudi Arabia and tried to get one of his many vice presidents, an Arabic translator named Haig Melkessetian, to accompany him on the trip. "I have a good deal for us," Wade said as he filled him in on Cunningham's travel plans. Wade's employee said he had spent years battling the Saudis and their influence in the Middle East, and he didn't want to be on "both sides of the fence."

"Don't start that ideological crap with me," Wade snapped, according to Melkessetian's account. "I'm not here for ideology. I'm here to make money."

Cunningham made the trip without assistance from Wade and was quite taken by Saudi Arabia. He met with the country's ministers and legislative leaders in the Shura Council, toured Saudi banks, the country's legislative body, and met with a wide spectrum of Saudi society. He was even willing, as he put it, to "lay out political capital" to heap praise on Saudi Arabia during a special-order speech on the House floor.

In May, Patsy Samson, a widowed neighbor of Cunningham's in Rancho Santa Fe, threw a fund-raiser that raised more than $80,000 for the congressman, much of it from supporters with Middle Eastern backgrounds. The event wasn't handled by Cunningham's usual fund-raiser, but was organized by Samson, who was unfamiliar with campaign finance law. Cunningham seemed concerned. "Just make sure those Arabs are U.S. nationals," Cunningham told Samson. Abduljawad, the man who had flown Cunningham to Saudi Arabia, gave $2,000.

In December 2004, Cunningham and Abduljawad arranged for a second trip to Saudi Arabia. Before leaving, Cunningham pleaded with Congressman Pete Hoekstra, the Republican who chaired the House Intelligence Committee, to join him. Hoekstra didn't join the trip, but Cunningham did bring along Ken Calvert, a Southern California Republican. According to Calvert, the plane stopped in Athens, where Cunningham's friend Thomas Kontogiannis boarded and came along for the trip.

As he ended the year living free of any payments on his Rancho Santa Fe mansion, Cunningham joined Wade as the guest speaker at MZM's 2004 black-tie Christmas party held December 8 at the Four Seasons Hotel in Georgetown. Even by the standards of MZM's corporate events, this event was over-the-top. Cunningham, who sat at Wade's right hand, celebrated his sixty-third birthday and blew out candles on a chocolate birthday cake decorated with blue stars. Cunningham told some of his war stories and handed out silver dollars to wounded Iraq War veterans MZM had invited to the event. A nineteen-piece band serenaded the nearly four hundred employees and guests. The menu included a pâté appetizer and an entrée of filet mignon and lobster. Top-shelf liquor, champagne, and wine flowed freely.

In a 2004 end-of-the-year letter to employees, Wade announced that the company's staff had nearly tripled to more than four hundred employees. Revenues, too, had nearly tripled and the company had added new facilities across the country. "If one is bold, fearless, aggressive, and focused on expansive goals, *anything can be achieved*," Wade wrote.

11

———◆———

A Preliminary Investigation

On June 8, 2005, Randy Cunningham sat down in his office and took a call that would forever change his life. Marcus Stern was calling the congressman to ask how Cunningham had come to sell his home to Mitchell Wade. Stern was a news editor covering Washington for the newspapers owned by the Copley family, including *The San Diego Union-Tribune*. Stern had been at Copley News Service since 1983 and had known Cunningham since he came to Congress.

Stern's interest in Cunningham's lifestyle dated back to the fall of 1997, when a source related to Stern a conversation she had had with the congressman. Cunningham had met Stern's source at The Capital Grille and invited the woman and a friend of hers back to his yacht, the *Kelly C*. There, the congressman had changed into pajama bottoms and a turtleneck sweater and offered the two women champagne in a room lit by a Lava lamp. Cunningham told Stern's source of a hunting lodge on Maryland's Eastern Shore that Cunningham claimed he was building. He also revealed that a defense contractor had offered to buy another boat and "rent" it to Cunningham. Stern went down and staked out the Washington, D. C., waterfront with his dog, Amanda—he would draw less attention walking his dog, Stern figured—but could learn nothing further, so he set the matter aside.

Eight years later, Cunningham's trip to Saudi Arabia had renewed his interest. That trip struck Stern as curious, so he conducted a "lifestyle audit" of Cunningham, comparing the congressman's expenses to his income, and began examining his real estate holdings. That Cunningham had sold his home to 1523 New Hampshire Avenue LLC grabbed Stern. If the home had been sold to an individual, Stern might not have given it much attention. But the sale to a limited liability company was curious.

Through a series of searches on the Internet, he had established that the company was owned by Mitchell Wade, a defense contractor and campaign contributor. Even more alarming, Wade had later sold the house for a $700,000 loss in one of the hottest housing markets in the country. Within fifteen minutes, Stern understood what was going on. The facts were all there, in plain view for anyone to see.

When Stern got Cunningham on the phone in June 2005, the congressman told him he had just come out of an intelligence hearing with the head of the Counterintelligence Field Activity and had only a few minutes to talk. According to a transcript of the conversation, Stern told Cunningham that he wanted to clarify things so there were no misunderstandings. "I don't want any either," Cunningham said, laughing. Stern relayed what he had found: Cunningham had sold his house to a company owned by Wade, who paid a high price for the home. Then the home was on the market for 261 days before it sold for far, far less than what Wade had paid for it.

Cunningham explained that Wade had expressed interest when the congressman had told him he was selling his home. According to the congressman, Wade had been looking for a place in San Diego and had asked Cunningham to have an agent send him some comps from the Del Mar area. "And the agent actually set the price. Said I can get this for it. And Mr. Wade agreed, accepted. And I think today it's probably worth more than I sold it for," Cunningham said.

The congressman couldn't explain why Wade had put the home up for sale less than a month later. Cunningham didn't have a clue. Had Wade ever talked about the home again? No, the congressman said, it was none of his business. He had just been trying to get the most money he could for his house.

Cunningham said he didn't treat MZM any different from any other defense or intelligence program. MZM's programs, the congressman insisted over and over, were a national asset and he relied on what the military wanted.

"What do you say to some skeptics who might say, hey, this transaction occurred, the congressman ended up with a huge windfall?" Stern asked.

"Listen, that's a fair question," Cunningham said. "All I can tell you is, Marc, I think you know me, and my whole life I've been aboveboard. I've never even smoked a marijuana cigarette. I don't cheat. If a contractor buys me a lunch and we meet a second time, I buy the lunch. My whole life has been aboveboard, so this doesn't worry me. It's a fair question, but I don't see why Mr. Wade sold his property at that expense. I do know he's looking for other properties."

Cunningham then veered onto the subject of Saudi Arabia and a book about a former congressman, *Charlie Wilson's War*, before ending the conversation.

———

Four days later, on June 12, Maurice Hattier awoke before six o'clock and picked up the Sunday newspaper that lay coiled in front of his home outside San Diego. He carried the paper to the kitchen and sat down. Hattier was watching his two sons while his wife was out for an early-morning exercise class. As he unrolled the paper, he was struck by a headline on the front page: "Lawmaker's home sale questioned: Cunningham defends deal with defense firm's owner."

Stern's story got Hattier's mind whirring. It raised disturbing questions about Congressman Cunningham's home sale to Wade and was backed up by the public record, not anonymous sources and leaks. For Hattier, the article was like a slap in the face. Tall, thin, and dark-haired, Hattier, thirty-five, had spent much of the past decade tracking sophisticated financial crimes and money-laundering scams as one of a dozen FBI special agents assigned to Squad Three in San Diego.

Hattier couldn't read the story fast enough. First and foremost, it involved a federal elected official with seats on key congressional committees who had sold his house to a defense contractor. Most glaring of all was that the house had been sold and then resold at an enormous loss. As anybody living in San Diego knew, the market had been making double-digit-percentage gains for several years. That someone had lost money on the deal was even more suspicious than Cunningham's huge gain. To Stern's credit, it was all laid out in the story, in plain English. If any of this was true, it was going to be a huge case.

All FBI agents want to work on the big cases, and Hattier was no exception. With the exception of terrorism, few cases are more exciting for an FBI agent than public corruption. When Hattier finished with the article, he picked up his cellular phone and dialed his supervisor, Ken Boschen. Like Hattier, Boschen was an early riser and had already read the article. "I want to be a part of it," Hattier told him. Boschen agreed to make him the case agent, which meant Hattier would have key decision-making responsibility about how the investigation should proceed. When his wife returned home from her exercise class, Hattier told her about the story, and for the rest of the day the case was on his mind and he jotted down a few notes in preparation for work. "I couldn't wait for Monday to roll around so I could get down and get started," he said.

That Monday, the FBI decided to open a "preliminary investigation," a six-month inquiry that gave agents authority to use a broad range of investigative techniques, short of wiretapping and opening mail. Under U.S. Justice Department guidelines, an investigation of a public official is considered a "sensitive criminal matter," requiring Hattier to notify the U.S. attorney as soon as possible. Hattier had a phone conversation the same day with prosecutors at the U.S. attorney's office in downtown San Diego about the case.

Like Hattier, prosecutor Phil Halpern had read the newspaper story the previous day. Halpern had been prosecuting cases in the U.S. attorney's office in San Diego for more than two decades, but no newspaper story had ever piqued his interest as much as Stern's story about Cunningham's home sale. The Monday after the story ran, he walked into the office of George Hardy, his supervisor in the general crimes section, and told him, "This is a case." Hardy told him he could work on it, but he would have to check with Jason Forge, a taciturn prosecutor who had already expressed a desire to take on the case. A third prosecutor, Sanjay Bhandari, who was in Germany visiting his in-laws, had read the newspaper over the Internet, and he, too, had e-mailed Hardy and expressed an interest in the case.

Halpern, a compact, intense man who looked younger than his fifty-two years, was the most experienced of the three, having spent two decades as a federal prosecutor. A native of Long Island, New York, with a master's of philosophy degree from Cambridge University, Halpern had joined the U.S. attorney's office in San Diego in 1984. He had worked on a variety of challenging cases that attracted national attention, including the prosecution of two state judges convicted in a racketeering conspiracy of taking bribes. Halpern was a competitive runner and cyclist, and his aggressive nature carried over to the courtroom.

Cunningham's name had come across Halpern's desk before during an investigation of a local defense contractor accused of federal campaign violations. Employees and associates of Science and Applied Technologies Inc. had given more than $30,000 to Cunningham's campaign to help generate business for the company's experimental guided-missile program. Contributors, who also gave large amounts of money to Congressman Hunter and Senator John Kerry, were often reimbursed with cash, checks, company funds, or inflated billing hours on military contracts.

Defense attorneys took the unusual step of suing Halpern and federal agents during the investigation. The defense claimed that Halpern ran an overly aggressive investigation by, among other things, intimidating potential witnesses and sued, unsuccessfully, to have him removed from the case. The defense claimed that Halpern had "demanded" that the company president sign a proposed plea agreement the prosecutor had written without any input from the defense. "I would appreciate it if you would explain to your client that the specifics contained in the information are not really open to negotiation," Halpern had written. After a three-and-a-half-year federal investigation and a two-year legal proceeding involving sixty thousand pages of legal discovery, the company's president pleaded guilty in 2004 to two counts of illegal campaign contributions. Cunningham, who cooperated with investigators, was never charged.

As he got to work on Cunningham, Halpern phoned two investigators and told them he wanted them on the case. One was Jamie Harrison, a young investigator with the Internal Revenue Service. Allegations of corruption and bribes meant the possibility of unpaid taxes, which interested the Internal Revenue Service. He was a veteran Los Angeles police officer's son, and his father had once threatened to break his knees if he ever joined the police. Harrison had in his senior year of college chosen a path in federal law enforcement instead, for which he turned out to be well-suited. Only twenty-six, Harrison possessed skills far beyond his years.

Halpern also left a message for Sam Medigovich, whom the prosecutor knew from the Science and Applied Technologies case. Medigovich was an investigator with the Defense Criminal Investigative Service, the Pentagon Inspector General's investigative squad. Medigovich, forty-six, happened to be on his honeymoon in Las Vegas when Halpern called, and Harrison was in Texas on another case, but they, together with Hattier, became the three lead investigators on a fast-moving case.

Prosecutors agreed to take Cunningham or Wade to trial if the allegations on the home sale were substantiated. Hattier drafted an electronic communication laying out the allegations and their investigative plans and submitted it to Ken Boschen, who forwarded it to the Public Corruption Unit at FBI headquarters in Washington, D.C., With that, Hattier and the team of agents he quickly assembled from the FBI, Internal Revenue Service, and Defense Department's Office of Inspector General were off and running. "From that day on, that Monday, the foot never hit the brakes," he said.

In the early days, investigators struggled to keep up with the news reports on the Cunningham case. On Tuesday, the *North County Times* in Escondido reported that Cunningham lived in Washington aboard a yacht named the *Duke-Stir*, a boat that was owned by Wade. Cunningham continued to insist the arrangement was perfectly appropriate. FBI agents were incredulous when they read the story. How deep did this case go?

———

The day after the story about his home sale ran in the *Union-Tribune,* Cunningham contacted attorney K. Lee Blalack II. A native of Memphis with a warm demeanor and keen mind, Blalack was a partner at O'Melveny & Myers, one of Washington's top law firms, and specialized in high-profile criminal defense work. His clients had included a mix of business and political figures including Senator Bill Frist, the Senate majority leader; Jeff Skilling, the former chief executive of Enron; and Ford Motor Co. during the congressional investigation of a massive tire recall.

Blalack had represented Cunningham in a 2004 ethics inquiry examining whether the congressman had taken part in an unprecedented effort to muster enough votes to assure passage of a bill proving prescription-drug benefits under Medicare. After the customary fifteen minutes of voting on the bill, the tally showed it was headed for defeat. That would mean a defeat for President Bush, for whom the Medicare bill was a major social-policy initiative. Undaunted, GOP leaders held the vote open for nearly three hours while they twisted arms of Republican members to switch votes from no to yes. It was the longest roll-call vote in modern House history.

One of the holdouts was Republican Nick Smith of Michigan. Smith was retiring from Congress, and his son, Brad, was running for his seat. House majority leader Tom DeLay offered to endorse Smith's son if Smith switched his vote. Smith told House ethics investigators that Cunningham had reportedly walked up to Smith on the floor of the House chamber, waved a billfold at him, and said, "We've got ten thousand dollars already . . . to make sure your son does not get elected." Cunningham didn't recall whether he made reference to the money, but he conceded that he told Smith, "If your son is as hardheaded as you, I will be damned if I will vote for him or help him." As he walked off the House floor, Cunningham said he remembered thinking that he had gone too far, and he later apologized to Smith. A House investigative panel concluded that DeLay and one other member should be admonished, but found Cunningham had not violated House rules.

While a federal investigation was reason for concern, Cunningham had no cause to fear that the newspaper report would lead to an inquiry by his House colleagues. The House ethics committee had been shuttered all year as a result of a partisan stalemate. Speaker Dennis Hastert had purged the committee of the chairman and two members who were viewed as disloyal to the majority leader, Tom DeLay, who had been admonished three times by the committee the previous year. In January 2005, Republicans pushed through a series of new rules that made it harder to launch an ethics investigation without the support of at least one Republican on the panel. Democrats refused to participate in protest of the new rules, and the panel would not meet again all year.

To his staff, Cunningham didn't appear bothered by the stories about his lifestyle. During a meeting in his office, the congressman calmly assured his staff that the whole affair was being unfairly portrayed and he had done nothing improper. He had the paperwork to prove that he paid rent for the *Duke-Stir,* and his house was worth its full sale price. He seemed a bit defensive, but he spoke in an even-toned, matter-of-fact way. "He didn't seem all that worried, to tell you the truth," said Gregg Parks, a young legislative assistant in Cunningham's office. "I guess that's why he seemed believable, because he didn't seem concerned by it." No one on the staff believed that Cunningham was guilty of anything—at least, they didn't say so publicly. There were two schools of thought in the office. Some felt Cunningham was being railroaded, and others believed the congressman had acted foolishly, but had not done anything deliberately wrong. Everyone seemed a bit apprehensive, but nobody was faxing résumés.

As reporters caught a whiff of a major scandal brewing, Blalack showed up at the office at the end of June and explained that Cunningham's office had been subpoenaed by a grand jury in San Diego. A member of Blalack's firm copied every computer hard drive in Cunningham's office. The following day, Parks stayed until midnight to copy the office's computer server and shipped it Federal Express to O'Melveny & Myers.

On June 23, Cunningham told his constituents what he had told his staff. Against the advice of his attorneys, the congressman issued a four-page "personal statement" assuring his constituents that he had acted honorably and honestly. He did, however, concede that he'd showed "poor judgment" in selling his home to friend who did business with the government and should have given more thought to the perception it would create. "I have always felt a duty to this country and its people—a duty that motivated me to volunteer for the Navy, serve in combat in Vietnam and run for office. I would never put the interests of a friend or a contractor above the interests of my country. I trust that the facts will bear this out over time," the statement read.

Reports that he had secured contracts for Wade's company were false. Cunningham said he did not have the authority or the ability to award a contract to Wade's company. He welcomed the investigation. "My constituents know me to be the same fighter that has always fought for this nation, whether in uniform or in the halls of Congress," he said.

From day one, federal agents and prosecutors viewed the Cunningham investigation as a bribery case. They began by confirming the basic facts of the home sale. Agents collected public property documents, gathered background from real estate professionals, and spoke to people in the neighborhood of Cunningham's former Del Mar home. Like the agents themselves, neighbors, too, thought there was something suspicious about the sale. As they gathered material, federal agents and prosecutors began drafting what would become a lengthy affidavit in support of a search warrant.

A picture swiftly emerged of a congressman who had stepped over the line to support Wade and his company. In interviews, Defense Department officials reported how they had been pressured by Cunningham, who had bullied, harassed, and threatened to get them fired if they didn't deliver contracts and money to Wade's company. The congressman would personally call low- and midlevel Pentagon employees. If he couldn't get satisfaction, he would then call their superiors. He would lambaste them when they came before the committees he sat on. Before long, federal agents began hearing about Brent Wilkes, another contractor who seemed to be too close to the congressman.

The more they learned about Cunningham, the more troubling it was that he remained in office. As a general rule, the Justice Department seeks the resignation of any member of Congress who has abused his or her office, but Cunningham's committee positions made the need for his ouster even more acute. For a corrupt lawmaker to hold seats on the House Permanent Select Committee on Intelligence and the Defense Appropriations subcommittee was more than alarming to prosecutors; it was potentially dangerous. Those two committees authorized and appropriated billions of dollars for the U.S. intelligence community, and Cunningham's limitless greed made him ripe for blackmail. Once they understood the enormous scale of his misdeeds, the overriding priority for investigators was to remove Cunningham from office as swiftly as possible.

Reports soon reached federal agents that forced them to accelerate their plans for a search in the Cunningham case. MZM employees reported that Wade had been shredding documents. On Friday, June 17, Wade's last day in the office, he had shown up for work early. An MZM official who worked closely with Wade shredded a large stack of documents on the third floor of the company's Dupont Circle office. A Post-it reading "Keep Out" was slapped on the door where the shredder was located. Exactly what got shredded isn't clear, but prosecutors didn't feel it was significant enough to file obstruction of justice charges. Before too long, Wade gathered up all his personal papers and belongings and exited the MZM building through a back-door in the basement that led to an alley. Employees never saw him set foot in the building again.

There was some discussion about searching Cunningham's congressional office, but there were huge hurdles. The search of the office of a member of Congress was without precedent, and although elected representatives were not immune from criminal laws, the question of whether the Constitution allowed a search of their offices had never before been tested in the courts. Representatives like Cunningham were protected by the "Speech or Debate" clause of the Constitution, which granted a broad immunity for legislative business. In the end, the idea of searching Cunningham's office was dropped.

Federal prosecutors and investigators hurried to put together a search warrant application they could bring before a judge. Maurice Hattier, Jamie Harrison, Sam Medigovich, and prosecutor Sanjay Bhandari had all traveled to Washington and they worked late into the night to finish the paperwork. When the others had gone to bed, Bhandari remained at his computer until four o'clock in the morning. The hotel where they were staying was the Hyatt near the Capitol, the same spot where in 1992 Congressman Lowery arranged meetings with Appropriations Committee members for his friend and protégé Brent Wilkes.

The newspaper story about the home sale had shaken MZM to its foundations. Wade had quickly retained the firm of WilmerHale, another top Washington law firm with a client list that includes Daimler-

Chrysler, Fannie Mae, General Electric, and Pfizer, to name a few. Howard Shapiro, a former general counsel of the FBI, led the firm's representation of Wade, while Reginald Brown, a graduate of Yale University and Harvard Law School who had served in the White House counsel's office under President George W. Bush, handled the enormous media interest in the case and tried to salvage what was left of Wade's tattered reputation.

Wade's attorneys swiftly realized that he had little legal room in which to maneuver, and his best course of action was to cooperate with the government and work out the best deal possible. Wade faced a range of potential charges, including bribery, money laundering, fraud, and conspiracy, that carried stiff penalties. But Wade held an attractive trump card: he could help the government land a far bigger fish, a corrupt congressman who was the government's main target. On June 27, Shapiro contacted a prosecutor in the Washington, D.C., public integrity unit and said he wanted to talk.

Before Wade began cooperating with the government, federal agents on July 1 raided his $3 million home in Washington's exclusive Kalorama neighborhood, not far from Donald Rumsfeld's residence, as well as MZM's Dupont Circle offices. Along with the simultaneous searches of Cunningham's boat and mansion, agents also descended on the offices of the Counterintelligence Field Activity. And agents walked into the office of Defense Deputy Undersecretary Carol Haave, Wade's contact at the Pentagon, to inform the leadership of what was happening. Agents told her of the raids, and that they would need to speak with Secretary Rumsfeld immediately.

Sometime after the raids, Wade had the first of many meetings with the government, and signed a cooperation agreement. Wade essentially agreed to investigate himself. All the financial information, the secrets, Wade had so zealously guarded, he put to use. He and his lawyers gathered up every corporate check, credit card statement, every receipt, that revealed in stunning detail the more than $1 million in payments he had showered upon Cunningham.

In his interviews with investigators in Washington and San Diego, Wade played his hand to the fullest in the hopes of keeping his prison sentence to a minimum. He handed over a photo he'd snapped of a grinning Cunningham standing beside his Rolls-Royce. He recounted the story of Cunningham promising to make him "somebody." He also gave prosecutors a piece of evidence that would come to symbolize what the congressman had become.

On board the *Duke-Stir*, the boat Wade had purchased for Cunningham, was a handwritten series of numbers on a piece of congressional stationery. Federal agents hadn't realized the significance, but Wade recognized the chart as one Cunningham had drawn up over dinner.

The two men had been discussing contracts when Cunningham started to jot down a menu of possibilities. As Wade explained it, the congressman wrote out two columns of numbers, indicating how much a certain contract would cost. One-half of the paper represented the amount of money that would be paid to Cunningham, which translated into the millions of dollars' worth of contracts listed on the other side of the paper. The figures started at the top with the $140,000 for the yacht, which translated into a $16 million contract. For each additional $50,000 that Wade handed over to Cunningham, the congressman would increase the value of the contract by $1 million: a $190,000 payment would yield a $17 million contract, and so on.

Cunningham offered Wade an incentive to keep paying. Once the contractor had paid the congressman $340,000 in bribes, the rates dropped. The congressman would charge only $25,000 for each additional million dollars awarded to MZM. A $25 million contract could be had for the discounted price of $440,000. When he was finished,

Cunningham put the piece of paper away and the two men finished their dinner.

Prosecutors were deeply impressed by Wade's account, and they would come to describe the document as the "bribe menu."

Wade also implicated his friend Bob Fromm. Wade claimed that Fromm had helped him land a $225 million blanket purchase agreement by writing favorable performance reviews of MZM. According to Wade's plea agreement, he and Fromm had conspired together to help MZM's business. Fromm had recommended that MZM receive defense contracts and had sent Wade an e-mail that Wade could use to tailor a proposal for additional government work. In exchange, Wade had hired both Fromm and his son, Sean.

It has been widely reported that Wade told investigators that Wilkes had provided prostitutes to Cunningham in the Watergate and other Washington hotels. The story first appeared in an article in *The Wall Street Journal*, which reported that Wade had said Cunningham periodically phoned him to request a prostitute, and that Wade would pass the request on to Wilkes. A limousine driver working for Wilkes then picked up the prostitute as well as Cunningham, and drove them both to Wilkes's hotel suite.

This claim, the most salacious allegation that has emerged from the case, appears to be wildly inaccurate. Not only had Wade never helped with the arrangements for prostitutes, but Wade never said anything about prostitutes at the Watergate, and no credible evidence has ever emerged to support this claim. Although investigators ran down every rumor of prostitutes being provided for congressmen, they were able to substantiate only the allegations involving the 2003 trip to Hawaii.

The facts, however, could not get in the way of the story of prostitutes at the Watergate. "Boring Ol' Congressional Corruption Case NOW WITH HOOKERS," trumpeted the racy political blog *Wonkette*, which seemed to aptly sum up the unspoken attitude of the entire press corps. Inexplicably, sources confirmed the reports for follow-up stories in the *The Washington Post, The New York Times,* and *The San Diego Union-Tribune,* which described the hotel rooms as "hospitality suites" for lawmakers. The allegations were repeated so often that they are now accepted as fact.

Wilkes firmly denies it. "Not only am I not aware of it ever happening under any circumstance, I didn't have a 'hospitality suite,'" he told me. "I kept a hotel room that doubled as my D.C. office, and did a limited amount of entertainment, usually involving employees and associates. In fifteen years, I hosted fewer than a dozen poker games there—only a few included a congressman; none included prostitutes." Wilkes believed the leaks were part of an intentional campaign by the federal government to coerce him into pleading guilty to avoid further embarrassment.

If he did provide prostitutes as prosecutors have alleged he wouldn't be the first lobbyist to do so. Former Senate staffer Roy Elson told author Ron Kessler that a "cathouse" was once located right across the street from Senate offices. "They were mainly housewives who were making a little extra money. Some members went across to it [courtesy of lobbyists]," Elson said. And Paula Parkinson, an agricultural lobbyist who later posed nude for *Playboy* magazine, claimed she had sex with eight members of Congress.

After the raids on his home and his boat, Cunningham no longer had a home in the capital. His attorney refused to let him back on the *Duke-Stir.* Reporters were staking out the Capital Yacht Club. Cunningham spent a night or two in his congressional office, which offered only a small couch for sleeping. Members of the Capital Yacht Club say he found a place to stay at the Virginia home of his boat mechanic. Wherever he was, he wasn't around the Capitol much, only showing up for the occasional vote.

The *Duke-Stir*, meanwhile, was cleaned up and prepared for sale. A source who was aboard before the sale said he was sickened by what he found, which included sexy underwear and more than one bottle of sexual lubricant. Also found was a small handwritten card that seemed to be some sort of sex ad. Though partly illegible, the writing that can be made out states "sex boyfriend" and "Coby Briant," apparently a misspelled reference to basketball star Kobe Bryant, and "no violence—gentleman."

On the morning of July 14, two weeks after the raids, Cunningham's staff gathered again for a meeting in the chief of staff's office. Cunningham, who was on the West Coast, spoke over the phone. He assured his staff that he was innocent, but he had to work on clearing his name, and Cunningham said it would be too difficult to clear his name and run for office. Gregg Parks, the legislative assistant, found Cunningham convincing and continued to believe him. "It's kind of like a member of your family," Parks said. "Until they either admit to it or get convicted, you kind of give them the benefit of the doubt."

At 3 p.m., Cunningham called an impromptu press conference outside the library of California State University, San Marcos, about an hour's drive north of San Diego. He again assured his constituents that he had acted honorably and honestly. "The truth will be evident in time," he said. Cunningham said he had always served his country honorably in the Navy and in Congress and was confident he would be vindicated, but acknowledged the government's investigation would stretch into the election season. "The time has come for me to conclude the public chapter of my life," Cunningham said. "After talking with my wife Nancy and our children, I have decided that I will not stand for reelection in 2006."

Cunningham again conceded that he had shown "poor judgment"

in selling his home to Wade, but did not improperly profit. "Nancy and I have worked hard all our lives to save enough money to purchase a nice home where we could live out our later years," he said. To eliminate any doubt, Cunningham said he had decided to sell his Rancho Santa Fe mansion and donate a portion of the proceeds to charity. When he was finished, Cunningham walked into the university library, ignoring reporters' questions, and exited through a back door into a waiting vehicle. A few days later, Nancy Lifset, the Cunningham staffer who handled all of the congressman's requests on the Defense Appropriations subcommittee, was served with a grand jury subpoena for documents and testimony.

Scott Schramm, who had sold the *Buoy Toy* to Cunningham, testified before the federal grand jury in San Diego on July 19. Schramm did so reluctantly. He considered Cunningham a friend, but he had received a subpoena and had no choice. When he returned to the Capital Yacht Club, he received a letter from Cunningham's attorney, Lee Blalack, who wanted to learn what Schramm had told the grand jury. Schramm simply tore up the letter.

In a sign that the tide had turned, the mantle of the war hero, which had long shielded Cunningham from his critics, was starting to crack. "And am I the only one who's a little put off by his continued reference to his 'service in Vietnam'?" one San Diegan wrote in a letter to *The San Diego Union-Tribune*. "While his service in the military is both noted and honorable (as was the contribution of many vets, including this writer), it does not give him a free pass to cloud the issue of integrity as it concerns his current body of work in the U.S. Congress. He has been in Congress for a much longer period than his service in that faraway place a long time ago."

Cunningham's campaign treasurer sought and received permission from the Federal Election Commission to use the $627,000 balance in the congressman's campaign account to defray the costs of the grand jury investigation. More than seven hundred campaign donors were given the choice of allowing their contributions to be used for legal expenses. Only thirty-three refused and many were supportive. "Thank you for being such a good American congressman for the 40th district. God bless you and your family," wrote one contributor. Cunningham's campaign contributors would ultimately cover the half million dollars in legal bills from O'Melveny & Myers.

Despite the support he was receiving, the congressman began to show signs that the investigation was taking a toll on his health. His conscience, which had slumbered for years while he pocketed cash and demanded bribes to pay off his mansion, suddenly roared to life. His fighter pilot's cool faded and was replaced by severe depression, fear, and anxiety. On August 1, Cunningham called the Maryland antiques store where Wade had bought him $190,000 worth of antiques and tried to convince the owner that she had seen Cunningham give Wade $35,000 cash to pay for the antiques; the dealer said she had seen no such thing. He asked whether the store had any recent "visitors"—FBI agents. Cunningham sounded anxious, and at one point there was a click on the line. What was that? Cunningham asked.

He lost his hearty appetite and tossed and turned at night, unable to sleep and consumed with worry. In a few months, he lost sixty pounds. A physician at the U.S. Capitol identified symptoms of depression, and the congressman told the psychiatrist at the Capitol he was having thoughts of suicide. The psychiatrist was deeply concerned and recommended hospitalization, but Cunningham refused. Cunningham was put on Zoloft for his depression, lorazepam for anxiety, and trazodone and Ambien for insomnia. "I never thought I would take my own life, but I wondered how I could cope with the pain from the moment I woke up in the morning until the evening when I went to sleep," Cunningham said later.

The investigation was also taking a toll on the congressman's wife, who was increasingly being dragged into the case. Federal prosecutors were holding up the sale of the couple's Rancho Santa Fe mansion, which was on the market for $3.5 million. Nancy Cunningham protested that she was innocent, but prosecutors were incredulous and refused to release the proceeds of the sale. In a secret court filing that was made public on August 25, prosecutors revealed that the couple had bought the mansion with proceeds from a bribe that Cunningham had "demanded and received" from Wade. It was clear to Cunningham's attorneys why the government had been keeping the document a secret; Blalack was convinced that Wade was cooperating with the government.

The pain Cunningham had endured and caused others had sapped him of the energy to fight criminal charges that were all but certain. At the end of September, he met with his attorneys at his home in Rancho Santa Fe and instructed them to approach the government and get the case resolved, acknowledging his wrongdoing. "I need to make amends," Cunningham told his attorney. "I need to do the right thing and clear these issues up." He wanted his family protected. His wife, Cunningham said, knew nothing about his dealings with defense contractors. Mark Holscher, Blalack's colleague, picked up the phone and told prosecutors he wanted to talk.

In early October, Blalack met in San Diego with prosecutors and attorneys from the Justice Department's public integrity section in Washington. Many prosecutors allow a defense attorney to make a pre-indictment presentation as to why their client isn't guilty, and the discussions can sometimes lead to a plea bargain. The initial meeting with Blalack, however, proved unproductive.

Neither side made much of a presentation. Blalack asked prosecutors to tell him what crimes they believed Cunningham had committed. Prosecutors gave away nothing. They had expected Blalack to make some kind of presentation of his client's innocence. To them, it seemed that Cunningham hadn't been frank with his attorney, who didn't really know the deal. For his part, Blalack left the meeting having heard no reason why his client should plead guilty. The sale of the house, Blalack believed, was legally defensible.

Sometime after that, the U.S. attorney's office sent Blalack a letter explaining that the congressman faced grave exposure to criminal charges. Written in question form, the letter asked Blalack to explain how it was possible Cunningham could have received some of the illicit payments he had collected from Wade. The letter went beyond the Rancho Santa Fe house, which until that time had been the main focus of Blalack's defense of Cunningham.

The yacht, the mansion, the Rolls-Royce, the antiques—each was evidence that Cunningham had accepted an illegal bribe. Using the proceeds of an illegal bribe to buy a house constituted an even more serious crime—money laundering. His failure to perform the duties of his office honestly constituted a form of "honest services" fraud. Cunningham had compounded his situation with his calls to the antique store, which a prosecutor could argue was witness tampering. Added up, prosecutors warned that Cunningham faced, in a worst-case scenario, thirty years to life in prison. Even if prosecutors were only partially successful, Cunningham still faced fifteen years or more.

Cunningham's attorneys felt that their client would be unlikely to survive a sentence of that length, given his history of prostate cancer. They countered with an offer to plead to one count of conspiracy, which carried a five-year maximum in prison—a sentence, they argued, that would be unprecedented. No other sitting member of Congress had ever immediately resigned and begun serving so long a prison sentence.

Prosecutors, however, continued to seek a plea involving multiple counts and a lengthy prison term of substantially more than ten years in prison. Prosecutors told Blalack he would be lucky to get such a deal, but Cunningham's attorney refused. It meant the sixty-three-year-old Cunningham would be likely to die in prison. He might as well take his chances at trial. Prosecutors never told Blalack that an indictment was imminent, but reporters kept calling to pass along rumors they had heard that charges against Cunningham were forthcoming.

To put this matter to rest, Cunningham would clearly have to spend more than five years in prison. Blalack had another conversation with the congressman, and this time Cunningham was more forthcoming about the scale of his wrongdoing. Coming to terms with what he had done was a slow evolution for Cunningham, but Blalack at least had a more complete picture. Finally, the two sides agreed that the congressman would immediately resign and plead guilty to charges of tax evasion and conspiracy that carried a maximum of ten years in prison "The fact of the matter is Mr. Cunningham went down kicking and screaming," prosecutor Jason Forge said later. "He did not plead guilty until his indictment was imminent and his conviction was inevitable."

As part of his plea deal, Cunningham agreed to be interviewed by federal and state law enforcement agents and tell everything he knew about every person involved directly or indirectly in his criminal acts. He agreed to testify before any grand jury and at trial. If Cunningham provided "substantial" assistance, his sentence could be reduced. If he lied, however, the deal was off.

On November 23, 2005, investigators Jamie Harrison, Sam Medigovich, and Maurice Hattier traveled to Cunningham's home in Rancho Santa Fe. They arrived to find the congressman sitting in a chair on his front porch waiting for them, dressed casually in a golf shirt and blue jeans.

The congressman shook hands and exchanged pleasantries on the doorstep, and then welcomed the three men whose work had so swiftly led to his downfall into his home. Cunningham told them he was moving out, and boxes and stacks of papers were scattered about. Medigovich, an antiques lover himself, complemented Cunningham on one of the armoires he noticed inside the home.

The investigators noticed that Cunningham's clothes were hanging off him. He had lost an enormous amount of weight. He did not seem well. Medigovich was concerned for his well-being.

"Have you got enough food, Duke?" he asked.

Cunningham replied that he not had much of an appetite lately due to the stress of the investigation. The only thing he was consuming was some sort of liquid shake. Cunningham mentioned that Nancy had stopped by recently with some pizza, but there was no sign of her around the house.

The congressman led the men to a breakfast nook. Harrison sat down with him and pulled the thirty-three-page plea agreement from a leather portfolio. Blalack listened in via speakerphone from Washington as Cunningham was instructed to initial each page in the bottom right corner.

It was a bittersweet moment for the agents. This was the kind of case an agent got once in a career, if he or she was lucky—and it was equally rare for agents to be alone with the targets of their investigations without a defense lawyer present. Yet, the feeling was somber, not jubilant. Here was a man who had everything, and he was losing it all with each stroke of the pen. He agreed to forfeit his Rancho Santa Fe mansion, where he now sat scribbling his signature on each page, as well as more than $1.85 million in cash and a long list of antiques— sliver candelabrums, a large wooden serving cabinet, vases, antique oak doors, a sleigh-style bed, Persian carpets, and armoires.

As he signed each page of the agreement, one of the agents noticed a picture of a plane in flight and asked the congressman about it. Cunningham described the tremendous g-forces that affect the body of a jet pilot and remarked that over time in the cockpit, you become quite strong.

The congressman moved quickly through each document, skimming the words on each page, scribbling RHC in the bottom right of each. Within fifteen minutes, he was done. He seemed a little more somber as he led the agents back to the front door and watched them leave with the signed plea agreement in hand.

12

The Most Corrupt

Congressman Randy Cunningham arrived dressed in a blue suit at the San Diego FBI bureau on the morning of Monday, November 28, 2005. He was led into the basement of the building, where he went through booking and had his fingerprints taken. Federal agents then led him into a waiting vehicle. As a courtesy, the government drove him to the federal courthouse downtown and entered the building through the parking garage to avoid any cameras or reporters.

But no mob awaited the congressman when he arrived at the courthouse. The congressman's guilty plea had been kept under wraps. The congressman's staff was not made aware of the plea until that morning, when the chief broke the news in a tearful meeting. The plea had been kept off the public court calendar, but a few reporters who had been tipped to it were in the small courtroom. Only after the hearing was well under way were the rest of the local media made aware of the momentous event that had just taken place.

Appearing somber, Cunningham stood before Judge Larry Burns. "I understand you're a United States congressman and a college graduate, true?" Burns asked him.

"Yes, Your Honor." Cunningham assured the judge that he wasn't taking any medication that would cloud his ability to think or comprehend the events taking place.

Judge Burns went over the charges at great length with the congressman and advised Cunningham of his rights.

"How do you now plead?"

"Guilty," Cunningham said firmly.

A huge bank of cameras had by then assembled in the plaza in front of the San Diego federal courthouse. Cunningham emerged and stood before them and said, "I'm resigning from the House of Representatives because I've compromised the trust of my constituents. When I announced several months ago that I would not seek reelection, I publicly declared my innocence because I was not strong enough to face the truth. So I misled my family, staff, friends, colleagues, the public, and even myself. For all of this, I am deeply sorry. The truth is I broke the law, concealed my conduct, and disgraced my office.

"I know that I will forfeit my freedom, my reputation, my worldly possessions, and most importantly, the trust of my friends and family," Cunningham said, breaking into tears. "In my life, I have had great joy and great sorrow. And now I know great shame. I learned in Vietnam that the true measure of a man is how he responds to adversity. I can't undo what I've done. But I can atone. And now I'm almost sixty-five years old and I enter the twilight of my life. I intend to use the remaining time that God grants me to make amends and I will."

The breadth of Cunningham's wrongdoing as detailed in the thirty-three-page plea agreement was stunning. Page by page revealed that a mansion and a yacht were only part of the congressman's graft, which also included cash, checks, meals, travel, lodging, furnishings, antiques, rugs, yacht club fees, boat repairs, moving expenses, cars, and boats. It was corruption on an awesome scale, which, according to the plea agreement, totaled at least $2.4 million.

That figure, as large as it was, was itself a compromise calculated to avoid a potentially greater penalty under federal sentencing guidelines. The plea agreement did not include the $700,000 that Wade overpaid for Cunningham's house. Nor did it include the true cost of Cunningham's private travel and lodging, which the agreement valued at "more than $10,000," a far too conservative estimate, given that Wade paid $12,975.23 for one charter flight alone. Cunningham's high-class travel and lodging at the Royal Hawaiian in Oahu, Hawaii, the Coeur d'Alene Resort in Idaho, and the Mandarin Oriental in Washington, D.C., makes $2.9 million or perhaps even $3 million a more realistic figure for the full scale of Cunningham's crimes.

There is a rich history of congressional corruption, but never before had a member of Congress been convicted of graft on such a staggering scale. "In the sheer dollar amount, he is the most corrupt," Deputy House Historian Fred W. Beuttler said a few days before the sentencing. "The scale of it is unprecedented." Cunningham's larceny harkened back to the robber barons of the nineteenth century and the Credit Mobilier affair of 1872. Two members of the House were censured for their roles in Credit Mobilier, but unlike the Cunningham scandal, however, no crime was ever alleged.

Members of Congress have been charged with treason, manslaughter, and violating the Sedition Act, but bribery prosecutions are a relatively recent phenomenon. A 1982 review by a Senate select committee found that the first member of Congress indicted for accepting a bribe while in office was Senator John H. Mitchell of Oregon who was accused of receiving $2,000 to influence the issuance of

land patents based on false applications. He died before final disposi-
tion of the case. Representative John W. Langley, a Kentucky Republican, was convicted in 1924 for corruptly using his influence in a
whiskey-selling scheme.

The prosecution of congressional bribery began in earnest in the
1960s. Recognizing that the existing conflict-of-interest laws dating to
Civil War were "inadequate and confused," Congress approved the
passage of the Federal Anti-Bribery Act in 1967, which clamped
down on abuses. By the end of the century, some historians were con-
cluding that outright graft such as that unveiled in Cunningham's plea
agreement was an anachronism.

Corruption scandals of recent years were dwarfed by Cunningham's malfeasance. Dan Rostenkowski, an Illinois Democrat who
once chaired the powerful House Ways and Means Committee, was
accused of graft of more than $500,000. In 1989, House Speaker Jim
Wright, a Texas Democrat, resigned after pocketing $55,000 in royal-
ties on a book of his speeches. In 1980, five Democratic members of
the House and a Republican were videotaped by the FBI pocketing
cash from a phony Arab sheikh in the ABSCAM sting. "Bullshit
walks; money talks," Michael "Ozzie" Myers of Pennsylvania boasted
as he pocketed a $50,000 bribe.

The plea agreement placed Cunningham at the center of what was,
in essence, a money-laundering conspiracy. The congressman sold
property at an above-market cost and bought for far less than what
the market charged, and he collected money for property that he continued to own. He concealed his actions with multilayered transactions involving various corporate entities. Not only did he collect
bribes, he demanded them. He decided how much his friends would
get in return. He twisted arms to help out those who were padding his
wallet. It was a breathtaking betrayal of trust laid out for the American public.

Hoping to head off damage to the Republican Party, which was being rocked by a wave of scandals, President Bush swiftly condemned a man he had once liked to call "the ace." "Any member of Congress, Republican or Democrat, must take their office seriously and the ethics seriously," Bush said while touring the U.S.-Mexico border in El Paso, Texas. "The idea of a congressman taking money is outrageous. And Congressman Cunningham is going to realize that he has broken the law and is going to pay a serious price, which he should."

Cunningham's employees learned of the guilty plea when the chief of staff, Harmony Allen, called everyone into her office and told them the congressman would be pleading guilty and resigning his office. The office was being taken over by the Clerk of the House, and they would have jobs until a successor could be elected. Staffers were instructed not to talk to the media, which would be hounding them.

"Will Duke be going to jail?" someone asked.

Yes, Allen told them, Cunningham will be going to prison.

When she heard about the plea, Dee Dee Castro, a former district staffer, called Cunningham at his home in Rancho Santa Fe. To her surprise, he picked up the phone.

He seemed genuinely glad to hear from her, asking how she was and what she had been doing. Without her asking, Cunningham began to discuss his incredible admissions in court.

"Everything they're saying about me isn't true," Cunningham said. "You'll see."

Castro tried to reassure him. "Duke, I'm not the media. I'm your friend. You don't have to say anything to me."

Cunningham submitted his formal resignation in a letter dated December 1 to Speaker Dennis Hastert and retreated to a ranch east of San Diego owned by his longtime friend Dan McKinnon. Cunningham had first met McKinnon in 1973, and the two had remained friends. Together with Congressman Hunter, McKinnon had been the second of the two main influences who urged Cunningham to run for Congress in 1989. McKinnon and Cunningham, who was dressed in blue jeans and a T-shirt, pulled up at a warehouse December 6, towing a horse trailer loaded with the antiques Wade had purchased for Cunningham, and surrendered them to the government as part of his plea agreement.

Cunningham arrived at McKinnon's ranch emaciated from stress and guilt. He lived in a bunkhouse on the ranch and earned his room and board with manual labor. He chopped wood and dug weeds, fighting off a case of poison oak, and began to regain some of his strength. He spent hours talking with McKinnon, who said he saw Cunningham cry nearly every day.

While Cunningham regained his strength on McKinnon's ranch, his defense attorneys had the difficult task of collecting letters of support for a man now viewed as a pariah. The letters made clear what some of his Navy comrades had known for years—in many ways, Cunningham had stopped maturing as a person following the Vietnam War. The strongest testaments came from Charles Nesby, the black pilot Cunningham had picked as number one in his squadron, along with his backseater, Bill Driscoll, and his wingman Brian Grant. Outside of Cunningham's fellow aviators and his immediate family, the majority of the letters were written by people who barely knew him— his real estate agent, a fellow hospital patient, a handyman, even a complete stranger. One writer, a retired judge and former state assemblyman, called his letter a statement of facts, not a letter of support.

In a bid for leniency, Cunningham's attorneys submitted letters highlighting the former congressman's civic and charitable works. Peter Yarrow, the front man for the 1960s folk trio Peter, Paul, and Mary, had written the judge a letter describing how he and Cunningham, although politically polar opposites, had found common ground.

Cunningham had joined the advisory board of Yarrow's not-for-profit group, Operation Respect, and generated bipartisan support for the group's mission of improving children's welfare, health, and education. Cunningham had presented Yarrow to the Republican Congressional Caucus, and Yarrow described the congressman as "a basically good, decent and caring human being." The heads of several San Diego area charities also wrote the judge.

Prosecutors characterized the letters as a cynical attempt to claim credit for civic and charitable works that were part of his job as a congressman. "It is almost as if Cunningham grew so accustomed to discharging the duties of his office for bribes that he now demands a credit for those instances when he did his job 'merely' for his salary," prosecutors wrote. Cunningham could not support his claim that he had donated significant sums to charities. "To the contrary, the grand total of all the contributions documented in these letters was 100 pounds of beef given to the daycare at Saint Clare's Home."

Almost all his "friends" in Congress had forsaken him. Only one, Congressman Hunter, wrote the judge. As he had so many times over the years, Hunter extolled Cunningham the war hero, quoting from his friend's Navy Cross citation. It was left to Hunter to sum up the legislative accomplishments of his onetime protégé. What Hunter called Cunningham's "capstone bill," which took eight years to pass, exempted police officers from state laws prohibiting concealed weapons.

On February 6, Cunningham traveled to the Beverly Hills office of Dr. Saul Faerstein, a clinical psychiatry professor at the University of California, Los Angeles. Cunningham was only one of the many famous people examined by Faerstein, who has examined troubled celebrities including O. J. Simpson. After speaking with Cunningham over five and a half hours, Faerstein developed an opinion as to why he had gone so far astray. Cunningham's experience as a fighter pilot led to a sense of omnipotence, which grew as his accomplishments did. "If he wasn't killed when pursued by 22 MiGs, was there anything that could bring him down?" Some of this behavior, Faerstein noted, was thrust upon Cunningham by the Navy and society as a whole, which craves heroes.

"With an outsized ego and a mantle of invulnerability," Cunningham was in many ways unprepared for the job of congressman, Faerstein noted. "His capacity to rationalize his conduct was increased by his sense of invulnerability to any harm. The process of rationalizing his behavior blinded him to the corruption it entailed, and led him to behave in ways totally antithetical to his life history, his family background and his moral and religious values." Prosecutors would later take issue with this analysis, noting that the causal connection between Cunningham's military service and his illegal conduct was not only an attempt to avoid personal responsibility, but also a disservice to the veterans whose civilian careers were as distinguished as their wartime service.

In his final weeks at McKinnon's ranch, Cunningham gradually came to realize what he had done. He had arrived somewhat oblivious to how he was being perceived as the poster boy for a corrupt Congress. "Since then it has hit him like a Mike Tyson punch to the head," McKinnon wrote. Cunningham had come to realize his folly. He wrote Judge Larry Burns on February 17 and said he was ready to pay his debt to society. "I am guilty of having accepted money in exchange for giving special attention to certain government contractors. It all started very slowly and innocently," he wrote. "I convinced myself that I wasn't selling my good offices because I have always believed in the value of the programs that I supported. But denying reality does not change what I have done. And the reality is I received money in exchange for giving my friends special attention in Congress. I am so ashamed and deeply sorry for what I have done."

One week later, on February 24, Mitchell Wade entered federal court in Washington, D.C., and pleaded guilty to four felony counts. The forty-two-year-old admitted making more than $1 million in illegal payoffs to Cunningham, corrupting Defense Department officials, and funneling more than $80,000 in illegal campaign contributions to two other members of Congress, Katherine Harris and Virgil Goode. Wearing a dark suit, Wade showed no emotion as he read a statement: "Your Honor, it is with great remorse that I acknowledge the actions in this plea agreement, and I feel deep sorrow for the harm I have caused my family, friends, and former colleagues. I have taken full responsibility for my actions and thus I endorsed early on to assist with all my efforts the U.S. attorneys in both Washington and San Diego. I thank you for accepting my plea."

The stage was now set for Cunningham's sentencing.

At 1 p.m. on Friday, March 3, 2006, Randy Cunningham returned to the San Diego federal courthouse, where he had entered his guilty plea. Police were on hand to hold back the throng of reporters, photographers, television camera crews, and onlookers who crowded at the courthouse entrance. Cunningham arrived in a dark limousine and, unlike his earlier back-door appearance, made his way through the throng while his security guards tried to clear a path. At one point, a television cameraman stumbled and fell in front of Cunningham, who lost his balance and nearly came crashing down as well. By the time he reached the front door of the courthouse, Cunningham appeared pale and shaken, traumatized by the scene he had just passed through. He had lost an enormous amount of weight and seemed frail, a shadow of his former self.

Gregg Parks, Cunningham's former legislative assistant, watched his old boss make his way through the throng. Parks was leaving the world of politics and was in town for a job interview downtown. The courthouse was only a few blocks away, so he walked over and watched his former boss make his way through the media throng, then hung around outside to hear what the sentence would be. Reflecting on his experience, Parks realized that he had lost his passion for politics. "My job was all about writing a speech for Duke or writing a letter for Duke or a bill or getting an appropriations request," he said. "An election is all about getting someone else elected. It's all about someone else. I'm done making a career out of propping somebody else up."

The largest courtroom in San Diego's federal courthouse was packed as Cunningham took his seat. Seated behind Cunningham was his old friend Congressman Hunter, the lone member of the House or Senate at the hearing. Cunningham's now estranged wife was not present. "You need to know, Mr. Cunningham, that we do not have a marriage," Nancy told him as she related it to Kitty Kelley. "We have a business arrangement." The night before sentencing, Cunningham had driven to Nancy's grandmother's house and tossed a duffel bag into the garage stuffed with his personal effects. Along with some of Cunningham's military memorabilia and dirty clothes, the duffel bag held $32,000 in cash. Cunningham had for some time kept a large amount of cash in his home. Blalack says he had let prosecutors know about the cash in a filing, and Nancy's attorneys turned it over to the government.

Cunningham had asked his children, Todd, April, and Carrie, not to attend, but all wrote letters to the court. After his release from prison, Todd, thirty-six, had returned to San Diego and gotten a job as a loan officer for a mortgage company. April, twenty-seven, was a married librarian, and Carrie, twenty-four, was pursuing graduate studies in public health. Cunningham was deeply disturbed by the intrusion into his children's lives due to his own misconduct.

Several Navy pilots who had served with Cunningham in Vietnam also sat behind him. About five or six had been asked to attend as a favor to Congressman Hunter, who wanted to go before the cameras and say that several pilots who flew with Cunningham were in the courtroom that day. Every seat in the courtroom was taken. The jury box was filled with reporters. As big as it was, the courtroom was too small to accommodate everyone, and some reporters were forced to wait outside.

Prosecutors and defense attorneys each had their reasons for allowing Cunningham to be sentenced so soon. Cunningham wanted to get on with his life and get his sentence done with as soon as possible. For the prosecutors, putting a corrupt congressman behind bars was a potent message they were eager to send. Usually cooperating witnesses are not sentenced until they have completed their testimony for the government as a way to ensure their continued cooperation. Cunningham's case, however, was unusual. Prosecutors usually tackle a criminal conspiracy from the outside in, using the testimony of those with lesser roles to implicate the main targets. In this case, the main target—Cunningham—would be the first to go prison. Both sides had held weeks of discussions to see if there was a way Cunningham could begin serving his prison term before sentencing, but in the end decided it wasn't practicable.

Judge Larry Burns called the court to order. Dozens of unsolicited letters had poured into the judge's chambers before sentencing, overwhelmingly urging the maximum possible sentence. "Randy is a full-time continuing disgrace to his past uniforms, oaths of office, service pledges and the national community," one man wrote. "I also urge that at least half his term in prison be served at Guantánamo Bay U.S. prison under the same conditions to which our country is subjecting hundreds of unindicted men from other countries."

Even Cunningham's lawyers agreed that the former congressman would have to serve time in prison. The question before the judge, as defense attorney Lee Blalack put it succinctly, was how much is enough? Judge Burns had mulled the question for many nights as he drifted off to sleep. The longest sentence for a corrupt politician in modern history was the eight-year term imposed in 2002 on flamboyant Ohio Democrat James Traficant, after a federal jury convicted him of taking bribes and kickbacks and ordered him to forfeit $96,000 in ill-gotten gains. But, as Judge Burns acknowledged, Traficant, unlike Cunningham, had said following his conviction that he had been railroaded and had to be expelled from Congress.

Without minimizing his client's egregious crimes, Blalack said the sentence should be six years, more than enough to deter other corrupt members of Congress. "There's nothing about this sentence that can't be accomplished very effectively by locking up a sixty-four-year-old war hero for six years," Blalack said. Cunningham might not survive a longer term, given his history of recurring cancer. Prosecutors asked for ten years. "Anything less will only further undermine the public's trust in our system and respect for our laws," said Assistant U.S. Attorney Jason Forge.

In their sentencing memo, prosecutors excoriated Cunningham for his "unparalleled" corruption. "Cunningham used his status as a war hero to get into Congress, and then he used his congressional office to get rich," prosecutors wrote. "The length, breadth and depth of Cunningham's crimes against the people of the United States are unprecedented for a sitting member of Congress. So, too, should be his sentence." Another document filed by prosecutors scoffed at the former congressman's request for leniency. "As a law maker, Representative Cunningham argued that criminals should be called to account for their misdeeds, calling for increased mandatory-minimum sentences, sponsoring the 'No-Frills Prison Act,' voting for a death penalty for drug kingpins, and opposing 'soft on crime' liberal judges. As a law breaker, defendant Cunningham argues for extraordinary and unwarranted leniency that he consistently opposed for others."

Cunningham, helped by his attorney, rose to the lectern and pulled out a piece of paper. A hush fell over the courtroom as the audience strained to hear. "Your Honor, if you let me go today, which I know you can't, I'd be the best citizen this country has today," he began. "I recently saw a bumper sticker that said, 'You're going the wrong way, but God allows U-turns.' After years of service to my country and going the right way, I made a very wrong turn. I will spend every day for the rest of my life seeking to atone and seek forgiveness for what I have done to my family, my friends, and the people of San Diego.

"Your Honor, I have ripped my life to shreds due to my actions, to my actions that I did myself. Not because someone else did it to me. I did it to myself. I made those decisions. I could have said no, and I didn't. It was me, Duke Cunningham. It was wrong. I need to pick up those pieces of my life, Your Honor, and make every day a constant atonement towards forgiveness and make my life whole. I give you my word I will do that.

"Some people might say that I've lost everything. I've lost my homes. I've lost all my cash. I've lost everything. But, Your Honor, you have no idea what I have gained in this process." The former congressman said his two adult daughters had been taking time to visit with a father whom they saw little of in their youths. "And the knowledge that I have gained about not being vulnerable, about not rationalizing mistakes, I gained that. I think I'll trust people less, Your Honor, so I won't make those same wrong U-turns."

Anticipation mounted in the courtroom as Judge Burns began to address the former congressman in even, measured tones. The judge acknowledged Cunningham's contrition and said he was unable to determine who corrupted whom, whether Wade first approached Cunningham or vice versa. But the judge said he was disturbed by the scope, the duration, and the nature of Cunningham's crimes. "This wasn't a onetime lapse in judgment. It wasn't a single U-turn. You made the U-turn, and you continued in the wrong direction for a period of five years. And I wonder today how much farther you would have gone in that direction but for the intervention of the government agents and the newspapers that tipped them."

Judge Burns told Cunningham he was surprised the former congressman had let himself slide so far. The judge said his court was inundated with drug smugglers, and he often heard defendants say they were driven by desperation to feed their children or pay for an operation. "So I look at you," he told Cunningham, "and I contrast you with other defendants I see. And I think to myself you weren't wet, you weren't cold, you weren't hungry, and yet you did these things."

Cunningham seemed to be in agreement with the judge, nodding several times as he listened. Finally, Judge Burns turned to what he felt was the real harm Cunningham had done. "I think what you have done is you've really undermined the options or the opportunity that honest politicians have to do a good job, to do what they pledge to do when they get elected. You've made it more difficult for them because now they face the cynicism of a very skeptical public, a public that when they talk about politics, they'll talk about Randy Cunningham and how corrupt he was and how he accepted bribes. That's going to be a lasting legacy for some time."

The judge's tone softened as he turned to Cunningham's wartime service, crediting Cunningham for climbing into his jet in 1972 knowing that the people he was defending weren't behind him and didn't appreciate that he was laying his life on the line. At the time, the judge said, he was a high school student who feared getting drafted into an unpopular war. While some, including the prosecutors, believed Cunningham had rested on his laurels for too long, his wartime service resonated with the judge. "You still have some equity left to your service to the country," he said.

"We talk about messages that need to be sent. I agree wholeheartedly that a message needs to be sent to people in politics that we demand their honest services," Judge Burns said. "But another message ought to be sent, and that is you served in the armed forces of the United States with great dignity and great honor, that that will be taken into account at some point, too. Today is that day I take that into account."

Judge Burns pronounced his sentence on Cunningham: eight years and four months in prison and $3.66 million in restitution and civil penalties. Cunningham was ordered to begin serving his sentence right away, denying him one last visit with his ninety-one-year-old mother. With good behavior, Cunningham would shave 15 percent off his sentence, the judge said.

"So effectively, I'm giving you a sentence that's going to let you out before you're seventy-one years old to have a life, if you survive, to do what you aspire to do, which is to atone for what you've done and make peace with your family," Judge Burns said.

"I wish you well, Mr. Cunningham. The court is in recess."

Cunningham seemed slightly confused and unsure whether he would be allowed to remain free. Burly U.S. marshals stood nearby waiting to lead him out of the courtroom as he conferred with his attorney. Finally, it dawned on Cunningham that his last few moments of freedom had just elapsed. As a marshal led him out of the courtroom, past the jury box, and into the holding cell adjoining the courtroom, the former congressman began to weep.

Epilogue

Randy Cunningham is serving his sentence at a minimum-security federal work camp located in the desert outside of Tucson, Arizona. The former congressman is required to work at one of a variety of jobs at the camp, which range from maintenance to landscaping to food service. A typical day at the camp begins at 6 a.m. Inmates work a forty-hour week and earn between 12 cents and 40 cents an hour. In the evenings there is time, if Cunningham chooses, for outdoor recreation. Lights go out at 10 p.m.

The majority of inmates are serving time, like Cunningham, for white-collar crimes or for drug-related offenses, as his son did. All 128 inmates are housed in a giant dormitory, where they sleep in bunk beds. Cunningham is one of the older inmates at the camp and, because of his age, he probably gets a bottom bunk. The food is standard cafeteria fare, comparable to what Cunningham ate in the military, since the kitchen staff uses Army cookbooks to prepare meals. All phone calls, except for conversations with attorneys, are monitored by prison officials. Visitors are allowed only on weekends.

As federal inmate 94405-198, Cunningham will likely serve less time than he would have under "the No-Frills Prison Act," of which he was an early cosponsor in 1995. The bill, which did not pass, would have eliminated the credits Cunningham is earning for good behavior. For each year that he presents no disciplinary problem, Cunningham's sentence is reduced by fifty-two days. As of early 2007, he had a projected release date of June 4, 2013.

Several letters I mailed to Cunningham in prison in the hopes of speaking with him went unanswered. When asked to comment on some aspects of his Navy career, family life, and sexual peccadilloes, Cunningham declined to respond on the advice of his attorney because he remains a cooperating witness in an ongoing criminal matter. For the record, however, his attorney, K. Lee Blalack II, issued a general denial, labeling as "false or at least grossly misleading" nearly all the most damaging allegations I presented in my final letter to the former congressman. "He was a genuine war hero and nothing whispered privately by unnamed sources will ever change that truth," Blalack said.

MZM Inc., the company that Cunningham's bribery helped build, was sold in the fall of 2005 for about $20 million to a private equity firm that specializes in acquiring troubled defense contractors. A new company, Athena Innovative Systems, took over MZM's contracts. Athena operates out of MZM's old address in Dupont Circle. It is run by Jim King, the man Wade once belittled as the "three-star genius." By the time of the company's sale, many of its employees had already moved on. Cindy Bruno, for one, works at her family's real estate development firm in Fresno, California.

Around the same time that he sold off his company's assets, Wade and his family moved into a $1.95 million, 5.8-acre colonial-style house in Great Falls, Virginia, called "Windy Knoll." One evening, I cruised up the long driveway in the hopes of speaking with Wade. As I got out of my rental car, I spotted him through the sidelights of his front door, talking on the phone. I waved and he seemed to acknowledge me. Then he ducked down a hallway, and his wife, Christiane, answered the door and politely thanked me for coming. I have never heard directly from Wade. His attorneys were made aware prior to publication of the allegations raised in this book by Cindy Bruno, Lindsay Peterson, and Randy Cunningham, who claimed in a letter from prison that Wade had brought two women aboard the *Duke-Stir* one night. After objecting to the material, Wade's attorneys were given an opportunity to provide a response for the record, but declined to do so.

Several people whose names surfaced in court documents and news reports in connection with the Cunningham case were never charged with any wrongdoing. Among them was Bob Fromm, the Army program manager who found himself caught between Wilkes and Wade. He was the unnamed Defense Department official in Wade's plea agreement.

The U.S. Attorney's office in Los Angeles reportedly opened an investigation into Congressman Jerry Lewis over his relationship with Bill Lowery, but no charges were brought. Publicity surrounding the probe led to the breakup of Lowery's lobbying firm, Copeland Lowery Jacquez Denton & White. Lowery and Letitia White, the Lewis staffer who had years ago led Tom Casey to the House basement, now work together in a different lobbying firm.

With Cunningham behind bars and Wade awaiting sentencing, prosecutors turned their attention to some of the threads that had spun out of the investigation: Brent Wilkes, Thomas Kontogiannis, and Dusty Foggo, Wilkes's lifelong friend who held the number three job at the CIA.

Foggo had gotten the job of executive director in November 2004 after *The Washington Post* revealed that the man CIA Director Porter Goss had first picked for the post had left the agency years earlier following his arrest for shoplifting a $2.13 package of bacon. Since joining the CIA in 1982, Foggo had worked as a support officer in the directorates of operations, science and technology, and administration, and he had served with the agency in Mexico, Honduras, Austria, Panama, and Germany. Inside the CIA, he had a favorable reputation. In 2002, Foggo received an agency medal for his performance at a logistics facility in Frankfurt, Germany, that provided supplies for operatives at war in Afghanistan. Among the guests at the medal ceremony were Brent Wilkes and Randy Cunningham, whom Wilkes had invited along. In March 2006, the agency confirmed that Foggo's relationship with Wilkes was the subject of an investigation by the CIA Inspector General's office.

According to a former member of Goss's inner circle, tension began to build between Foggo and John Negroponte, the new director of national intelligence. The two butted heads over Negroponte's new role. Foggo, who knew Negroponte from Honduras where they had both served in the 1980s, called him by his first name, which bothered Negroponte. On one occasion, the source said, Negroponte said Foggo needed to be more respectful and call him ambassador or Mr. Negroponte. It wasn't Goss's style to call his people on the carpet, however, and Foggo continued referring to the director of national intelligence by his first name. "You could see that Negroponte didn't like Dusty and Dusty took every opportunity to antagonize Negroponte," said the former member of Goss's inner circle.

On May 5, 2006, Goss was summoned to the White House for an unscheduled meeting. According to the Goss insider, the White House told Goss of their distinct unhappiness with him, of which Foggo may have played a small part. When Goss left the meeting, he was out of a job. The following Monday, Foggo had announced that he would be stepping down. On May 12, Foggo's last day at work, FBI officials stopped him on his way to his seventh-floor office, took away his CIA badge, and searched his home and office at the agency's headquarters.

In October 2006, Nancy Cunningham, the congressman's wife, settled her case with prosecutors in San Diego. She had been under investigation for possible tax violations related to her husband's bribes. At his sentencing, Cunningham had made a last-ditch effort to save his wife, claiming she was in the dark about his bribery. "Nancy knew nothing, absolutely nothing, about this and should not be gone after by the government," he told Judge Burns.

In return for her willingness to accept financial responsibility for unpaid taxes and cooperate with ongoing investigations, prosecutors agreed not to press charges against her. The settlement, however, left Nancy and Randy with a large tax debt to the Internal Revenue Service on the bribes Randy had collected from Wade and, allegedly, Wilkes. While Nancy has consistently maintained she knew nothing about the bribes, she had benefited from them by living in the Rancho Santa Fe mansion, and the government refused to let her claim that she was exempt as an "innocent spouse" for tax purposes. As a result, Nancy and Randy were jointly left with a $920,000 debt for back taxes owed on the bribes. Randy is paying $1,000 a month out of his government pension; her attorney says the Internal Revenue Service may compromise on Nancy's share. Nancy has maintained a low profile and has not spoken publicly except to Kitty Kelley. She works as an administrator in the Encinitas Union School District outside San Diego.

In November 2006, Richard Berglund, a former MZM employee in Martinsville, Virginia, pleaded guilty in Washington, D.C., to one count of unlawfully making campaign contributions in someone else's name. Berglund admitted that he had helped Mitchell Wade make illegal contributions to an unnamed congressman who has been identified as Virgil Goode of Virginia.

The case against Wilkes and Foggo dragged out for months, hampered in part by the CIA's reluctance to provide prosecutors with indictable evidence. In January 2007, Carol Lam, the U.S. Attorney in San Diego, announced her resignation. She reportedly had been asked to step down, for reasons that were unclear, and she refused to comment on speculation that the Cunningham investigation had played a role. On February 13, 2007, two days before Lam was to leave office, a federal grand jury in San Diego indicted Wilkes and Foggo on charges of conspiracy, honest services wire fraud, money laundering, and aiding and abetting. Lam said her departure had nothing to do with the timing of the indictment.

In the indictment prosecutors claimed that Wilkes paid for meals and expensive vacations for Foggo and his family, including a weeklong stay at a castle in Scotland that cost $44,000. In return, prosecutors say, Foggo helped direct a contract worth $1.7 million to a company Wilkes controlled. Separately, Wilkes was named in a second conspiracy charging him with providing more than $700,000 to Cunningham in the form of cash, checks, meals, limo rides, private jet flights, boats, vacations, and prostitution services relating to the 2003 trip to Hawaii. That indictment also named John Michael, the nephew of Thomas Kontogiannis, who was charged with lying to a federal grand jury.

The week before his indictment, I met Wilkes at the Los Angeles office of his attorney, Mark Geragos, who has handled high-profile defendants, including pop icon Michael Jackson. Wilkes was alone in the firm's conference room, surrounded by a laptop, cell phone, and two Blackberry wireless devices, one of which buzzed incessantly. He had lost his business, his wife had filed for divorce, and his nephew,

Joel Combs, was prepared to testify against him. His best friend, a man he said he loved like a brother, had been dragged into the investigation, and Wilkes himself had become a notorious figure in his hometown. Despite all this, Wilkes was quite gracious, and seemed in good spirits as, over the course of six hours, he calmly answered questions on one sordid allegation after another. "I'll give you a second to figure out what other despicable things I've done," he joked as he turned to his buzzing cell phone.

Wilkes was trying to make the best of the mess his life had become over the past eighteen months. Always looking for an opportunity, Wilkes said he had been working to develop a TV series for HBO or Showtime titled *Bottom Feeders* about his experiences in Washington. And that was just one of the projects he was working on at the time. He was also preparing for an indictment he had known would be coming for more than a year. He had never bribed Cunningham, Wilkes told me, and he was committed to proving that in court. "I'm burdened by the truth," he told me more than once.

After entering a plea of not guilty, Wilkes released a statement that he welcomed the opportunity to fight the charges in court. The past eighteen months, Wilkes said, had become a "living hell" thanks to the government's "vendetta" against him. The "tawdry" nature of the investigation was revealed in the indictments—"partly phony tabloid journalism, partly the handiwork of prosecutors more interested in forcing me to plead guilty to something I did not do than in learning the truth." Now that the case had moved into court, Wilkes predicted that the truth would finally emerge.

"I guarantee you, I will be vindicated," he concluded confidently.

The unanswered question of the Cunningham scandal is: who else? Had Cunningham secured hundreds of millions of dollars of earmarks over the years by himself? Some members of Congress wondered the same thing. "How did one member of the Congress sneak millions of dollars into a series of bills to favor a constituent or client that was, in fact, as we now know, bribing him?" asked Representative John Shadegg, Republican, of Arizona. While the fruits of the Cunningham conspiracy—the millions of dollars in gifts, personal property, and services—are all laid out in court papers, exactly how one congressman used his office to win earmarks remains very much a mystery. The answer to the question how Cunningham did it is: no one knows. Or if they do, they aren't saying.

The House Appropriations Committee conducted an informal review of Cunningham's earmarks, and the chairman, Congressman Jerry Lewis, said he was satisfied that they were all legitimate. Rumors of prostitutes being provided to Cunningham and possibly other members of Congress finally roused the House Ethics Committee from its slumber and prompted an informal inquiry from which no findings have ever been made public.

Congressman Hunter, the chairman of the House Armed Services Committee, directed to his staff to review the earmark requests submitted by his old friend. The review found nothing to indicate that committee staff or other members of the Armed Services Committee had done anything improper. Hunter, meanwhile, had other priorities; he was in the early stages of preparing a long-shot bid for the presidency of the United States.

Only the House Intelligence Committee produced findings of any significance. A five-page executive summary released by Democrat Jane Harman of California in October 2006 revealed that House intelligence committee staff ignored numerous "red flags," including questions about Wade's ethics and integrity, and the corrupt conspiracy between Cunningham and Wade "seriously impeded" the intelligence committee's ability to oversee the Counterintelligence Field Activity. Harman's decision to release those findings outraged Republicans, who retaliated by suspending the security clearance of a Democratic committee staff member.

Congress' inability to investigate itself, so well demonstrated by the Cunningham scandal, is a dangerous sign. There will always be a contractor looking for an edge over his or her competitors, and as the government continues to grow and issue more regulations, the rewards of bribery and the temptation for corruption are only likely to increase as well. It's often noted that the value of earmarks in the annual Defense bill rose from $4.23 billion in fiscal 1994, shortly before the Republicans took power, to $9.43 billion in fiscal 2006. Few bother to note that the growth in earmarks have kept pace with a similar rise in defense spending.

If lawmakers are serious about ending corruption, they should create a bipartisan, independent panel to investigate ethical violations and endow it with subpoena power. Outsiders, too, should be allowed to file ethics complaints. Similarly, an independent special counsel should be appointed to investigate the appropriations process. Federal investigators and prosecutors did an admirable job in the Cunningham case, but there are limits to how far such probes can go. Any inquiry that led deep into the appropriations process would put federal agents and prosecutors in the difficult position of investigating the very people who ensure they get paid.

In the end, there was a political price to be paid for Cunningham's corruption. Democrats regained control of both houses of Congress for the first time in twelve years in the midterm election of 2006. Exit polls showed that corruption in Congress was a top concern for voters, to the surprise of the Washington punditry. One notable exception to the election results was in Cunningham's former San Diego County district, which remained in Republican hands.

The first Senate bill introduced in the Democratically controlled 110th Congress was an effort to clamp down on a host of abuses. The bill, which passed overwhelmingly in February, attempted to make the legislative process more transparent by, among other things, revealing the sponsors of earmarks, disclosing whose private planes members of Congress were flying on, banning gifts from lobbyists, and restricting lobbyist-paid junkets. Another section of the bill eliminated congressional pensions for members convicted of bribery, conspiracy, or serious ethics offenses. Senators John Kerry and Ken Salazar, who introduced the provision, dubbed it "the Duke Cunningham Act" and displayed the "bribe menu" from Cunningham's sentencing memo.

While in prison, Cunningham continues to collect his pension, since only members of Congress convicted of a crime against the United States, such as treason or espionage, lose their pensions under the rules. (The value of Cunningham's pension is not public.) Cunningham also collects slightly more than half his military salary at the date of his retirement. Basic pay for a Navy commander in 1987 was about $43,000 a year, but Cunningham's salary was likely higher to reflect his years of aviation service.

The Democratically controlled House introduced a series of rule changes that covered much the same ground as the Senate bill, but it took only about a month for lobbyists and members of Congress to figure out ways around them. *The New York Times* reported that lobbyists were invited to pay for birthday parties, a Bob Seger rock concert, Broadway shows, and a California wine-tasting tour.

This has been the history of ethics reform in Congress. Lawmakers pass new laws and rules and praise themselves for eliminating abuses, only to see them swiftly undermined. During the debate on the Senate ethics reform bill, Bob Bennett, a Utah Republican, noted that reform attempts can only go so far. "The fundamental fact remains that you cannot corrupt a senator or a congressman unless that senator or congressman is himself or herself basically corrupt," Bennett said. "We can write all of the rules we want, but if a member of this body has the instincts of corruption in his soul, he will find a way around the rules."

Randy Cunningham had the instincts of corruption in his soul. Beneath the uniform of the decorated war hero was an insecure and immature man. There were hard lessons he could have learned along the way that might have forced him to grow up, but too many times his shortcomings were covered up. As a result, his ego grew incommensurately with his accomplishments, and he came to view his life as an extended coronation. The Medal of Honor, the positions of power, wealth, and a life of luxury he saw as his due.

Becoming a Navy ace made possible everything that followed in Cunningham's life, and, at the same time, it slowly destroyed him. His wartime heroism won him an office for which he was spectacularly unqualified. Even before he had arrived in Congress, he had already come to believe that the rules did not apply to him, and Washington was not about to disabuse him of that notion. His utter lack of humility made him highly susceptible to flattery, and it did not take long for kindred spirits to recognize elements of their own venality in Cunningham. He allowed himself to become so corrupted, so consumed with feasting on the spoils, that all that remained was an empty shell of a man.

The tipping point seems to have been Cunningham's battle with cancer. It is almost as if the cancer ate away whatever moral fortitude was left in him. It began with small gestures, such as a meal at The Capital Grille, but the gifts grew swiftly and steadily and Cunningham soon abandoned himself to everything that had been denied to him as a five-and-dime store owner's son living on a congressman's salary.

It is no coincidence, too, that the scale of his corruption mushroomed after the September 11 attacks. Washington became a city awash in money. Defense contractors were making fortunes and former representatives were making millions as their lobbyists. It must have grated on him that he, a man who had sacrificed so much for his country, was surrounded by young, former Hill staffers earning millions as lobbyists. Had he been willing to leave office, he, too, could have afforded his own mansion and yacht.

Randy Cunningham is an extreme case, but he is a creature of Congress. There are few other ways that a man such as Cunningham, limited in both his means and his character, can in a few short years attain such power. Voters weren't willing to hold him accountable, and Congress wasn't about to do it for them. Nor did Congress provide any guidance in the wise use of money; the appropriations process is rife with hidden abuses, while campaign coffers have become virtual slush funds with contributors unwittingly paying for travel on private jets and expensive meals, among other perks.

"The system invites abuse. It invites the use of power," said Ron Packard, a former San Diego area representative with a clean ethical record who called himself Cunningham's one-time mentor in Congress. "It almost rewards wrongdoing because you reach the point in Congress where you feel that you can get away with anything.

"Every time you break the rules, you have a decision to make," Packard continued. "Your decision is: Do you stop it right there or do you just kind of rationalize and say this is not going to matter that much? The next time, it's a little bigger. You have the same decision to make. Your tendency is to make the decision the way you did that first time. It grows and grows until the representative decides 'I'm not going to go any further.'

"There's never a time when this is the last and only temptation to break the rules," Packard said. "There's always another time. And if you're willing to rationalize and break the rules and say, 'It's OK,' the next time is a little bigger, a little more of a problem for you, but you'll find a way to make the same kind of decision.

"Eventually, those decisions lead you into prison."

Acknowledgments

I never expected to meet such extraordinary people while writing a book about political corruption. Randy Cunningham could have learned a thing or two from a man like Jack Ensch and some of the other Navy officers in this book who have led such exemplary lives. Some readers will no doubt view Cunningham's former Navy comrades as heaping even more humiliation upon him. In my view, his comrades spoke out because they viewed Cunningham's acts as a betrayal. The military, unlike Congress, sees lessons that can be learned from failures as well as successes.

Similarly, it took guts for MZM's former employees to discuss their experiences, including some identified for the first time publicly in this book. Mitch Wade is a secretive man whose portrait could not have been drawn without the help of Cindy Bruno, Lindsay Peterson, Scott

Rubin, and more than a dozen other former MZM employees. It's worth noting that the MZM employees I came to know were decent, highly ethical people who are embarrassed that their names have been linked to such a scandal. I hope the book removes a little of the stain that Wade's admitted corruption may have left on them.

Nearly everyone whose name appears in this book was asked for comment, and I interviewed nearly two hundred people from July 2005 through February 2007. There are many, many people whom I cannot thank publicly because they have asked me not to identify them. They should know that their insights were invaluable.

I could hardly have asked for a more considerate and understanding boss than Anthony Marquez, who runs the Associated Press's news operations in California. He granted me leave to write this book and graciously agreed to keep my job open until my return. Elliot Spagat ably shouldered a workload made even heavier by my absence.

My agent, Alice Martell, immediately recognized the importance of this story and guided a first-time author through the shoals of publishing. I am lucky to have found her.

At St. Martin's Press, Charles Spicer has been a tremendous editor throughout the project, and Yaniv Soha has been nothing short of amazing. Henry Kaufman provided excellent counsel and advice, and Michael Denneny brought his incredible experience to bear in the editing this manuscript.

I owe a debt of gratitude to the always gracious Marcus Stern without whom there would be no story to tell. As I've told him, I am only picking up the crumbs he left behind. Many others deserve special thanks: Alex Roth, Ken Silverstein, Jane Mayer, Allison Hoffman, Chitra Ragavan, Gerry Braun, and Jan Caldwell. It was Sasha Abramsky who showed me it could be done. David Sciarretta, Donna Marganella, and everyone else in Amy Wallen's writing group helped greatly with early drafts, and more important, convinced me I was on the right track. In addition to being an excellent neighbor, Fabio Rigo de Righi taught me how to pace myself. Michael Rubottom generously contributed the author photo, and I'm thankful for our friendship.

Writing a book takes a toll on those closest to you. My son, Ryan, who learned to crawl, walk, and talk while this book was being reported and written, couldn't understand why his father couldn't always play with him. Above all, I am grateful to my wife, Anita. This book is dedicated to her and could not have been written without her reassurance, understanding, and support. *Feasting on the Spoils* emerged out of a difficult period following Ryan's birth and it was my hope that I could turn that dark time into something uplifting. That's what her love does for me.

Index